2495

תורפיה

Torah Therapy

A Guide to Therapy
in the Spirit of Torah

Rabbi Elimelech Lamdan

FELDHEIM PUBLISHERS
JERUSALEM   NEW YORK

First published in Hebrew as *Torapia* (Feldheim Publishers, 2002)

ISBN 1-58330-836-9

First published 2006

FELDHEIM PUBLISHERS
POB 43163 / Jerusalem, Israel

208 Airport Executive Park
Nanuet, NY 10954

www.feldheim.com

10 9 8 7 6 5 4 3 2 1

Printed in Israel

Education Center
YESHIVAT HANEGEV - CHANOCH LANOAR
In memory of the late Mr. Jacob Rosenberg z"l
P.O.B 49 NETIVOT 87256
Telephone (07)-9941216, 9942488
Fax (07)-9944164

קרית חנוך
ישיבת הנגב - חנוך לנער
לזכרו של ר' יעקב רוזנברג ז"ל
ת.ד. 49 נתיבות 87256
טלפון 9941216, 9942488-07. פקס 07-9944164
חשבון בבנק המזרחי 405471 סניף 428
אנשור מוסד' צבור' לצורך מס הכנסה 550061857
עמותה מס' 1-185-006-58

Rosh Yeshiva: Rabbi I. S. Meyer - ראש הישיבה: הרב יששכר מאיר

המשרד בירושלים:
טל' 02-6422651

Jerusalem Office
Tel 02-6422651

Greetings to my dear friend and student,
Rav Elimelech Lamdan,

I have seen some of the proofs of your book [*Torapia*], and it seems to me that there is a great need today for just such advice and guidance based upon the wisdom of the Torah among many couples, including the Torah-observant community. Therefore, may it be God's will that you speedily complete this project and publish the book that you have written on these matters, continuing in the spirit of what I have already seen, and may you have much Divine inspiration in doing so.

Your friend,
Yissachar Meir

הרב שמחה כהן
רחוב סעדיה גאון 19
בני ברק
מחבר ספר הבית היהודי

Anyone involved in the world of Torah and interested in developing his *yiras Shamayim* knows that advancement in these areas is dependent upon improving one's *middos* and character. Improvement, however, is possible only if one is able to understand his own makeup — his personality traits and motivations.

In-depth analyses of the human personality is not something new to the Jewish people. Anyone who has carefully studied the descriptions of all the people discussed in the Torah along with the Rabbinic commentaries on their personalities and behavior will learn the deep motivations behind their actions, especially those that at first may not seem proper.

Rav Leib Chasman, of blessed memory, used to say, "When the Torah tells us about Avraham, Yitzchak, Yaakov, Moshe, Aharon, and all our other ancestors, and — in contrast — when it tells us about Esav, Potiphar, Pharaoh, Bilam, Balak, etc., it is not just giving us a historical description about figures who lived a long time ago, but rather it is trying to teach that each of us has in his personality bits and pieces of Avraham, Yitzchak, etc. — and also bits and pieces of Esav, Bilam, etc. By studying these figures and what the Torah writes about them, we are supposed to try to increase those aspects of Avraham that are within us and those aspects of Yitzchak that are within us, while at the same time we are supposed to try to minimize those aspects of Esav that are within us, and those aspects of Bilam, etc. that are within our personalities."

Throughout *Tanach*, the Prophets have called upon each and every one in the Jewish nation to analyze his *middos* — to really get to know them. After the era of the Prophets, the *gedolim* took their place and assumed this role. Over the last few hundred years, this trend towards self-analysis and studying one's *middos* has accelerated, and with the development of yeshivos as we know them today, it has become standard to appoint a *mashgiach* to stand alongside the *rosh yeshiva* at the helm of the yeshiva. His job is to motivate the students to work on their *middos* and improve their characters. Many works have been written on this topic, some as early as a thousand years ago. For example, one of the first was *Chovos HaLevavos*, by Rabbeinu Bahya ibn Pekuda. Among the more famous of the classical *sefarim* in this genre are *Shaarei Teshuvah*, *Orchos Tzaddikim*, and *Mesillas Yesharim*. In the last few generations, many many books have been written in this area — the more famous among them being *Michtav Me'Eliyahu*, *Ohr Yechezkel*, and *Aley Shor*.

Rav Elimelech Lamdan, in his *sefer Torah Therapy*, deals in an in-depth manner with the personality of man, something specifically appropriate to those who are seeking to improve themselves. He has presented revolutionary new methods and techniques that are drawn from our traditional Torah sources. He teaches us how to recognize and understand our own character traits, and his language and methods are especially suited to our generation. He brings together in his book the results of his own efforts at self-development, his years as a teacher of Torah, his experience working with Jews returning to their heritage, the wisdom from his lectures, and the practical experience gained leading self-help groups and counseling individuals and couples.

The serious reader who carefully studies the theoretical underpinnings of Rav Lamdan's methodology described in the first section of the book, and who then applies the practical suggestions found in the second section of the book, will surely profit from the experience, and without a shadow of a doubt will ascend in his level of *avodas Hashem*.

Rav Simcha Cohen
Author of *The Jewish Home*

Contents

Acknowledgments

I AM INDEBTED TO Hashem for enabling me to write and publish this book, just one of the infinite gifts that He has bestowed upon me. I would also like to thank all the many people who assisted in this project. First and foremost among them is my wife, Ziva, without whom I would not have learned half of what is written in these pages.

Torah Therapy was first written and published in Hebrew as *"Torapia"*. I subsequently learned from some of the readers' feedback that the Hebrew edition was too succinct. Although I made small changes in the second and third editions, it is only in the present English edition that I have supplied more examples and clarified the more complex ideas. Since this is by its nature always "a work in progress," I believe that there is still much more that could be done to convey my message in a better way. Therefore I gratefully welcome all comments and criticisms from the readers to this end.

Rabbi Elimelech Lamdan

How to Read This Book

I WOULD LIKE to make the following suggestion to the reader:

1. Read the Foreword.
2. Read the Introduction to Part I — "Torah Therapy and Diagnosis."
3. Read the Introduction to Part II — "Torah Therapy."
4. Read the last chapter, chapter 14 — "Stages of Therapy."

Then if you are really interested in learning the material, start from the beginning and slowly digest it all in sequential order.

The reason I recommend doing it this way is that many readers are interested in the application of Torah Therapy, but do not have the patience to read through its theoretical foundation that is presented in the first half of the book. This way, the reader can get a feeling of the general ideas along with the therapy in action.

On the other hand, I believe that Torah Therapy must be demonstrated first as a natural consequence of Torah and not just as another approach to psychotherapy. Thus it will be of great benefit to read the book in its logical sequence.

Pleasant reading!

Foreword

"OH, CHAIM, you forgot! Again! And you're not listening to me, as usual! I'm getting fed up!" Sara's face reflects her frustration and hints at a greater tumult within.

Chaim's face is impassive, as if chiseled from stone. But his heart is being squeezed and twisted from pain and frustration. This is Chaim's standard reaction to the angry words and accusations that are periodically tossed at him by his usually loving and gentle wife. A glimpse into Chaim's thoughts during these dark moments would reveal shocking images of violence, self-mutilation and even suicide. This is how a couple that appears "normal" is actually separated by a vast emotional chasm.

This sad state of affairs is more common than is generally admitted. In times of acute emotional stress, many people find themselves frustratingly unable to communicate their feelings and thoughts. They feel as if stuck in a blind alley, unable to relate intimately to those who figure prominently in their lives. When they try to rebuild these relationships by understanding what the problem was, they often feel confused and at a loss. They cannot explain what happened. Perhaps they momentarily lost their sanity. Reason, order and stability disappeared and were replaced by tumultuous emotional storms and irrational conduct.

Spiritual healing is required in such cases. The roots from which stemmed these moments of irrational behavior and the consequent damage to intimacy must be explored. Often these roots turn out to be deeply ingrained memories from one's childhood. They include negative emotional experiences, often of a traumatic nature. The memories, more often than not, are unconsciously repressed, as described by Rabbi Yisrael Salanter, the father of the *Mussar* movement.[1] He refers to these fierce emotional memories that serve as a basis for irrational behavior as the "dark forces." They are the real source of the person's internal and external "hell." They reveal themselves when the person suddenly erupts from stress.

This behavior, which seems to border on the insane (because the person loses control), is — as previously said — not exceptional or uncommon. It happens even in the homes of observant Jews. Although the observance of Torah and adherence to its precepts are supposed to protect us somewhat from the turmoil and vicissitudes of everyday life and make us more sensitive to other people's feelings, nevertheless, senseless behavior and confused emotions can be found here as well. Perhaps their presence is even more disturbing in these homes because "as great as a man is, even greater is his *yetzer*."

Much to our surprise and consternation, the *yetzer ha-ra* is constantly present, lying in wait — patient and unobtrusive — for the right moment to attack. It might have been there, biding its time, for a day, a month, a year, five years or twenty. Then, when the time is ripe, its ambush is shocking. It is all the more upsetting because we — the ones who let our feelings overwhelm us — are *bnei Torah*, upstanding and decent servants of Hashem. How is it possible that so many years invested in learning Torah and observing its commandments, attending

---

1. Rabbi Yisrael of Salant, *Or Yisrael*, letter #6.

shiurim, working on our *middos* and investing so much time and effort to do God's will — all this is powerless against the sudden onslaught of the *yetzer ha-ra*?

The first half of the book deals with this question and others stemming therefrom. The second half describes techniques for treating this "sickness of the soul."

Torah Therapy offers treatment in the spirit of the Torah, within the context of one's personal spiritual evolvement as an *oved Hashem*. Its unique techniques, which are rooted in the Torah itself, are described in the last chapter. This book was written in the spirit of: "Man shall aid his friend and say unto his brother, be strong."[2] However, because I tried to firmly base this therapy on Jewish principles, it is no easy "layman's manual." It should be read slowly and carefully, some sections perhaps more than once, in order to do justice to its contents.

The point should be made that Torah Therapy is merely one of several existing methods that apply Torah to our everyday challenges. It is tailored specifically to the therapeutic framework, even though it has uses for all. However, it is far from perfect. There is one — and only one — perfect cure for all our maladies, and that is Torah! Accepting this, the reader is invited to turn these pages and benefit, each in accordance with his will and comprehension.

May the following pages contribute to strengthening Torah and its adherence, and thereby increase Hashem's glory, bringing us closer to the coming of our *Mashiach*, may it be speedily in our days, Amen!

---

2. *Yeshayahu* 41:6.

Part One

Torah Therapy and Diagnosis

He who has no self-awareness most certainly will not find peace with himself...and the knowledge of his inner world must he find by himself, with almost no help from others.

(Alei Shur, part 1, p. 131)

Introduction to Part One

THE WORLD IN WHICH we live, constantly created by God's holy Word, is somewhat of a Divine dream. Similarly, our inner world is essentially our personal creation, the fruit of our imagination and our thoughts. We build our world and destroy it, only to rebuild it once again, while adding to it and changing it in endless repetitious patterns, from the day we are born until the day we die. As such, we serve as "partners" with God in this Divine creation, for better or for worse.[3]

This means that, for all practical purposes, we are in charge of helping ourselves, with God's endlessly benevolent assistance. Just as we were involved in creating our inner world, including its problems and difficulties, so can we solve problems and difficulties with our fellow man by using these same forces of thought, imagination and faith. The key to doing this is exerting control over our imagination and thought processes.

---

3. Rabbi Moshe Chaim Luzatto, in his classic work *Mesillas Yesharim*, chapter 1, explains man's purpose in this world. He demonstrates man's potential to actually change the physical world by bringing the *midrash* concerning our forefather Yaakov, who merited that the many stones under his head would coalesce miraculously into one big stone. The *midrash* continues to say: "See to it that you do not spoil and destroy my world." This negative "partnership" with our Creator is — sadly — abused in our present day and age.

3

The words Torah Therapy suggest that the true and successful therapeutic techniques, reputed to "solve all your problems," have our holy Torah for their source. Truly effective therapy is that which our Creator presents us through His teachings in the Torah. The divinely revealed cure for all that ails us has been available for ages and for everyone. All we have to do is learn and practice its precepts. Torah Therapy does not deny whatever wisdom or benefits are available in *toras ha-goyim* (non-Jewish schools of thought). It includes them within its Jewish framework.

Is it coincidence that the Hebrew word *terapia* (therapy) is written with the same letters as the Hebrew word *terufah* (medicine)? Most likely not, especially since the discovery that many words from varied cultures with seemingly no common linguistic roots are nevertheless derived from the one ancient "language of languages," *lashon ha-kodesh*, the ancient Hebrew language with which the world was created. This connection symbolizes the derivative relationship between modern therapy and its Divine origin — the Torah.

The idea that therapy is rooted in Torah is strongly hinted at in the Talmud Yerushalmi.[4] The Talmud quotes Rabbi Yochanan, who explains a passage in *Yechezkel* concerning the glorious future after the coming of *Mashiach*. He describes how a stream of fresh water will miraculously spring forth from the earth in front of the Third Temple, the *Beis HaMikdash*, and will bring life to all who drink from it. On the bank of this stream will stand trees whose fruits will be eaten and whose leaves will serve as medicine. Rabbi Yochanan comments on this: "*tarpei meitzitz aleiha*," meaning that eating its fruits would cure illnesses. The Talmud asks: How is this possible, and answers as follows: Rav and Shmuel each answered a different answer.

---

4. *Shekalim*, chapter 6, *halacha* 2.

One said *"lehatir peh elyon"* (to untie the upper mouth), and the other said *"lehatir peh tachton"* (to untie the lower mouth).

These words obviously need explanation. The passage may be understood as referring to the "waters of Torah," that will flow out from the *Beis HaMikdash* and enter our thirsty souls, bringing forth the fruits of life. While satiating us physically and spiritually, they will also cure our interpersonal maladies, untying emotional "knots" that, until then, had bound up our mouths, cutting off communication with our loved ones.

This work is a modest attempt at presenting a singular Jewish approach toward treating emotional problems. These problems range from the normal, everyday pressures of modern life to the deeper neurotic and, perhaps, even psychotic disturbances. It is based solely on traditional Jewish sources, from the *Chumash* to recently published Jewish books. The language has been simplified somewhat in order to make it easy to understand. Moreover, there is nothing really novel in the book, for everything has already been written. What remains to be done is to sort, explain, demonstrate, emphasize and edit the tremendous amount of wisdom that is our heritage. Perhaps this function was not necessary in previous generations. Today, however, there seems to be a substantial need for simpler and more detailed descriptions of the Jewish approach to healing emotional disturbances. This is the goal of the book, even though achieving it completely is quite impossible.

For example, Rambam, in his *Mishneh Torah*,[5] presents his now famous "middle-of-the-road" method for achieving righteousness, the golden rule for correct conduct. He explains the theoretical basis and offers a few examples, and that is all. This succinct teaching might have sufficed for previous generations.

---

5. *Hilchos De'os*, chapter 1.

Nowadays, however, there are only a very few *bnei aliyah*[6] (those who strive to ascend the path of Torah) who can actually practice this method. Most people seeking self-improvement need a simpler step-by-step version of this process, labeled "the middle path" (*ha-derech ha-beinonis*).

Alas, how true it is that a tremendous vacuum is to be found today in the sphere of *practical* Jewish wisdom, especially concerning interpersonal relationships (*bein adam le'chaveiro*). This vacuum begs to be filled, at least partially, for the sad fact that the mitzvos dealing with man's behavior towards his fellow man are often neglected, if not trampled upon. Too often we are reminded of the famous saying, "Jealousy, material desire, and [the need for] respect push a man outside of the world."[7] This state of affairs is so common that many people accept it as natural or disregard it completely. Of course, many excuses are offered to legitimize this behavior, passing it off as normal.

Yet there are many good and brave souls who try to fill this moral vacuum by drawing upon non-Jewish sources, spiritual wells whose waters were filled by the wise and not-so-wise men of the world at large. Therefore, even when these waters quench their thirst, their Jewish souls can be only partially satiated, for a short time only. The Jewish soul is satisfied only by drinking the waters of the Divine Torah. These same waters were drunk by our forefathers long ago, when other nations lacked the basic knowledge of writing and reading.

Still, the holy waters of Torah must be drunk by us actively, and not simply appreciated from afar. This is contingent upon

---

6. *Bnei Aliyah* was coined by Rabbi Shimon bar Yochai (*Sukkah* 45:2) as a description of true servants of Hashem, who constantly strive to ascend the ladder of Torah and its observance.
7. *Pirkei Avos* 4:21.

our choice and our freedom of will. Whoever desires may come and drink. He who is needy may enter and eat — *"kol man ditzrich leisei ve'leichol."*[8] Or, as King David wrote, "Savor and see how good is God. Happy is the man who finds shelter in Him."[9]

---

8. *Ta'anis* 20b.
9. *Tehillim* 34:9.

Chapter 1
Who Am I?

What Is Man?

We are called "sons of man." We are the progeny of *Adam HaRishon*, who was created by God. The word *adam*, man, has the same root letters as *dimyon*, imagination. Thus, we can conclude, they must be connected in some way. Man is the only being that has free will. The ultimate employment of this is in the way he chooses to view himself and other people. He may choose to identify himself with *adamah*, the earth, from which his body was created,[10] and which also has the same root as *adam*. Or he may choose to identify himself with his spiritual source.

In this case the words of the prophet, *"Adameh le'elyon"* (I will resemble the higher [beings]) will apply.[11] What is it that chooses the direction that his imagination shall take? The answer is — that Divine source within man, his innate bond with his Creator.[12] In summary, that which is called "man" is the imagination, and that which operates the imagination is the Di-

---

10. "And the Lord created man, earth from the ground..." (*Bereishis* 2:6).

11. For a fuller explanation, read Rabbi Shlomo Wolbe's *Alei Shur*, volume 2, chapters 1–2, in which the definition of man is beautifully elucidated from our holy sources.

12. The ability to choose must stem from outside the sphere of nature

vine source within.

"Man is free in his imagination," writes Rabbi Yisrael Salanter in his *Igeres HaMussar*. However, if he is unaware of his potential to control his imagination, then he is lacking in his *adam*. One may conclude, therefore, that fulfilling one's inherent being is achieved by controlling one's imagination, and directing it correctly.

God, the Soul, and the World

Am I a soul? And if so, why do I not recognize it? Furthermore, how did I get here? For what purpose, if at all? These are key questions that every thinking individual must come to ask himself over the course of his lifetime, and even attempt to answer. Whoever disputes the need for this line of thought and the significance of these questions contradicts thereby the essence of his personal *avodas Hashem*, the service of God.[13]

Let us try to answer several of these questions succinctly. Our Sages tell us that man's creation by God was a form of separation (from our point of view) from His infinite Self. Thus was man's soul brought into existence. This soul can recognize itself as a separate entity only vis-!-vis the external world which God created for him. The reality of this world is the combination of God's Divine will and man's imagination, with which he views his world.[14]

In describing this subjective aspect of man's world, a wise man once commented: "I am not who I think I am. I am not what you think I am. I am that which **I** think that **you** think

---

(which is defined as a predetermined and constant set of laws). Therefore, this freedom originates in the Creator and is transferred to man through his soul, which is that part of his spirituality closest to God.

13. See Rabbi Shlomo Wolbe, *Alei Shur*, volume1, p. 141.

14. See Rabbi Eliyahu Dessler, *Michtav Me'Eliyahu*, volume 1, on "Being and Achieving" (*Havaya Ve-hassaga*).

that I am."[15]

In other words, even though the world was created for us, we are not initially aware of who we are. We lack self-consciousness. We therefore define ourselves according to the reactions we solicit from those surrounding us, accompanied by our personal interpretation of these reactions. Obviously this interpretation is grossly imprecise, if not wholly mistaken. Only our Creator can reveal to us, by means of the Torah, who we really are.

The Self-Image

For example, when a baby sees his parents' anger, he assumes egocentrically that he is the cause. When this interpretation of their reactions repeats itself often enough, he mistakenly concludes that he is unloved and undeserving of anyone's love. This feeling is enhanced and reinforced by registering those external events that prove it to be true. Thus, over a period of months and years, a negative self-image gradually arises. If, on the other hand, this child were to receive warmth and loving support from his parents, his self-image would accordingly become positive.

A person behaves in line with his self-created image throughout his life, for better or for worse. He views the world and the people who surround him through his subjective eyes and self-imposed feelings of his worth. It may seem like a beautiful world...or a very ugly one. Of course, this evaluation can be changed by changing his self-image. This, however, is a long and arduous process, which shall be discussed later within the context of *avodas Hashem*.

How does one **react** to external events in accordance with

---

15. This is quoted in the book of Rabbi Avraham Baharan, *HaChevrah V'Hashpa'atah* (*Society and Its Influence*).

his self-image? Let us take an example of a child who is accustomed to continuous criticism and a lack of compliments or encouragement. As he matures, he naturally expects similar treatment from his peers, in line with his self-image. Therefore, upon receiving a compliment from someone, his reaction would be a feeling of disbelief. Instead of smiling or thanking the person, he would remain silent and stony-faced, if not overtly hostile. This negative reaction stems from the strong suspicion that the compliment was a self-serving lie or a cruel taunt clad in false virtuousness. The surprised friend, in turn, feels rejected and hurt that his compliment elicited such a negative reaction, and feels that his favor was returned unfavorably, "ra'ah tachas tovah" (bad in lieu of good). This is just one of many experiences that occur daily, without our even realizing it, wherein one's self-image directs his interpretation of external events and subsequent reaction.

Unthankfulness — K'fius Tovah

The first negative attribute — middah ra'ah — that man displayed was the k'fius tovah that Adam HaRishon expressed after eating the forbidden fruit of the Tree of Knowledge, the etz ha-daas. He blamed his wife for his sin, and this, Rashi explains, is k'fius tovah.[16] Instead of thanking God for this gift of partnership and support, he did exactly the opposite. What is the connection between his sin and this bad attribute? Sin may be considered the fruit of man's power of imagination. In accordance with his imagination, his self-image and his connection to God, man proceeds to act. His imagined self-image is necessarily lacking, and therefrom stems the sinful act, which is intended

---

16. "The woman which You had given unto me, she offered me from the tree and I ate" (Bereishis, 3:12). Rashi comments: "Here is where he denied the goodness [of God]."

to fill that vacuum. The disappointing result, in turn, reinforces the feeling that one is lacking, and one is inclined to repeat the sin with greater ease. This feeling seems to be the root of *k'fius tovah*.

A person who is lacking in thankfulness is constantly, if dimly, aware of this internal vacuum. He is driven consciously and unconsciously to fill it up through his connections with the external world and, ultimately, with his Creator. This is a life-long process which begins in childhood, when the love and security that are endlessly sought after are necessarily "short-changed" by well-meaning but limited parents. This overall feeling of unhappiness underlies the negative behavior of *k'fius tovah*.

Thus we have a short (if somewhat oversimplified) description of the *yetzer ha-ra* — the evil inclination, which is the cause of sin. How and when did it come into existence? How did this force come to overpower man's pure soul? As always, the answers are to be found in our holy Torah.

Chapter 2
The Yetzer Ha-Ra

The Yetzer Ha-Ra as Described in the Torah

The Torah tells us in *Bereishis*[17]: "And God formed (וייצר) man." The word for "formed," *yitzeir*, is written with an extra *yud*. Rav Nachman bar Rav Chisda explains[18] the seemingly redundant letter as referring to the *yetzer ha-ra* (the bad inclination), which was created along with the *yetzer ha-tov* (the good inclination).

Rabbi Shimon ben Pazi, however, maintains that there are not two different inclinations. Rather there is one *yetzer* that is involved in a struggle between two opposing poles: "*oy li mi-yotzri, oy li mi-yitzri.*" On the one hand I want to fulfill the will of my Creator, and on the other hand I want to fulfill the will of my *yetzer*. Rabbi Yirmiyah ben Eliezer explains the double letters by referring to the *pasuk* in *Tehillim*[19]: "*Achor v'kedem tzartani*" (You created me front and back). In other words, there is one creation with two opposing characteristics which are called "front" and "back." These two opinions, unlike that of Rav Nachman, are not refuted.

We may conclude therefore that the *yetzer ha-ra* is no more than a negative aspect of man's nature, standing in stark con-

---

17. *Bereishis* 2:7.
18. *Berachos* 61a.
19. *Tehillim* 139:5.

trast to his inherently positive nature. These two opposing characteristics of man's nature are further explained in two more passages which seemingly contradict each other:

1. "And God created man in His image, in the image of God he was created."[20]
2. "The inclination of man's heart is evil from his youth."[21]

By understanding each sentence individually, the apparent contradiction is dispelled. Thus the meaning of this "double creation" can be applied to our knowledge of the dynamics of the self-image, which were sketched in the previous chapter.

Two Creations: Briah and Yetzirah

The Torah uses two words to denote creation: *briah* and *yetzirah*. Our Sages refer to *briah* as *yesh me-ayin*.[22] This concept of ex nihilo cannot be truly grasped by the human mind. Nevertheless, we may approximate its meaning by comparing it to the second concept of *yetzirah*. This word is explained by our Sages as *yesh mi-yesh*, meaning "something out of something." This idea is simple to grasp, because we are always involved in "creating" some "thing" out of the raw materials that we find in our world. The creation of these raw materials, however, *yesh me-ayin*, is accomplished by God alone, the Creator of all things. Thus we vaguely approach the understanding of creation ex nihilo by defining the borders of our concept of human creation, *yesh mi-yesh*.

Man, the Creator "Yesh Me-Ayin"

Still, we find that despite his limitations, man can create ex

---

20. *Bereishis* 1:27.
21. *Bereishis* 8:21.
22. *Bereishis* 2:7. Note the Malbim's explanation.

nihilo, so to speak, **within his mind**. In addition to the physical manipulation of the world around him, which, as discussed, is *yesh mi-yesh* creation, he creates a whole world within himself, by the fertile and seemingly unlimited use of that powerful human tool: his imagination. In this sense, he becomes a "creator" in his own right. Moreover, our Sages teach us that this subjective world is not unreal, for all its tenuous and unstable appearance. It is a **real** creation, as depicted by its ongoing and powerful influence on man's behavior. Even the external world surrounding him is actually grasped only through the medium of his subjective "inner" reality, which is the product of his personal creation.[23] In this sense we may understand the Torah's description of man as a *tzelem Elokim*, created in the likeness of God. Thus we can understand the description of man as a "partner" of his Creator. His private internal world is accordingly termed "the small **world**."[24]

Man, the Creator Yesh Mi-Yesh

If we look deeply into our minds, we can detect two different levels of mental activity. These two levels — when compared one to the other — may be associated with the two forms of creation, *yesh me-ayin* and *yesh mi-yesh*.

Man's inner world begins its creative evolvement from the moment of birth. Mental production is derived primarily from the external "raw materials" that the baby senses and absorbs, at the same time modifying these stimuli in accordance with his inherited mental and emotional attributes. This personal creation may be termed *yesh mi-yesh*. The child internalizes his im-

---

23. See footnote no. 3 in the introduction to Torah Therapy and Diagnosis.

24. The concept that man takes an active part in *tikun ha-olam* is a basic principle of Judaism. This eternal "partnership" endows man with significance much greater than his personal and private life.

pressions of daily experiences. He begins with his basic physical and emotional needs and their satisfaction, usually offered by his mother. This personal world is initially the sum total of the child's relationship with his environment.

As time goes by, the second aspect of mental creation gradually comes into play. In contrast to the externally stimulated mental creation, this creation is internally motivated, by gradual awareness of the soul's connection to God. This is a higher, more abstract, aspect of one's world, and in that sense can be termed *yesh me-ayin*. This "small world" is created as a person matures spiritually. It takes a lifetime, and it is eternally evolving.

Why Is the Yetzer Evil?

Now we may begin to understand why "the imagination of man's heart is evil from his youth." As we saw, the Talmud teaches that the good and evil inclinations are not two distinct and separate entities. Rather, they are two opposing inclinations of the "imagination of one's heart," positive versus negative, good versus evil. In this light we may better understand Rashi's explanation of the word *mi-n'urav* (from his youth): "*mi-sheninar...mi-me'ei imo*,"[25] when he is shaken out of his mother's womb.

The moment of birth is the very moment in which the evil inclination comes into being. The baby's sensory perceptions of the new external world into which it is born, and the emotions — both good and bad — accompanying these experiences form the sum total of his knowledge at that point. **Lacking a developed mind, the baby accepts these experiences as they are, and uncritically integrates them within his consciousness.**

What is so evil about this natural process? After all, the baby

---

25. Rashi, *Bereishis* 8:21.

has no choice in the matter. Why is it sinful to accept without question the judgements of parents, friends and society? The answer, says the Maharal of Prague, in his *Drush Al HaTorah*, is that evil is not necessarily connected to negative **choice**. Evil is that which is untrue. Evil purports to see as real and existing that which is unreal and nonexistent. The opposite is the case with goodness. When God created the world, He "saw that it was **good**," meaning real and true, and therefore beneficial. That which is unreal and untrue, evil, is destructive.

Therefore the imagination of a baby reacts to the external world by building a **false** world. This natural inclination is necessarily evil, as defined above, even though no baby has a choice in the matter. In the greater context of God's intent and man's purpose in *avodas Hashem*, this evil serves a higher purpose, because man's quest for truth must begin with falseness. Otherwise there is no reward, for without effort there is no pleasure.

What Is "True Reality"?

"You have been shown that the Lord is our God, there is no other."[26]

This is **the** absolute truth. We are required to know this truth in our minds and let it pervade our hearts.[27] It means that there is no true existence other than that of God. Even though our perceptions testify to a concrete reality, it is nevertheless a subjective one. Therefore our everyday existence is termed *alma d'shikra*, the world of falsity. This false world of our imagination, which we have created in partnership with the Creator, as

---

26. *Devarim* 4:35.

27. *Devarim* 4:39. To know in one's mind is "today," but to internalize it in one's heart is a lifelong task. Therefore, "And you shall know today, and you shall bring into your heart that God is the Lord."

explained previously, is entered into at birth. That is the meaning of the statement: *"ki yetzer lev ha-adam ra mi-n'urav"* — for man's inclination is evil from his youth.

The Lost "Gan Eden"

Is human consciousness of God's infinite omnipresence merely a philosophical idea misinterpreted by wishful thinking, or do we in truth grasp something in the reality of *"ein od milvado"*[28] (there is nothing besides Him)? The answer to this question is to be found in the book of Iyov. Iyov says: "Who shall give me the early months, as [these were] days when the Lord watched over me."[29]

The Talmud[30] explains that these months refer to that period of fetal development up until birth. This is a most joyous time for the yet unborn child, more so than any time after its birth. The Talmud reveals that the child — while still in its mother's womb — is taught all of Torah and is given to see the the world "from its beginning to its end." A candle burns above its head (in a spiritual sense). In essence, the unborn child is consciously connected with God.

The Talmud continues: "As soon as he exits into the outside world, an angel comes and taps him on his mouth, thereby causing him to forget all his Torah, as it is written — 'Sin awaits at the exit.'"[31]

Every person, therefore, contains within his psyche the first-hand experience of being at one with his Creator. Having experienced this transcendent mystical union, he constantly

---

28. *Devarim* 4:35: "You have been shown to know...there is nothing besides Him."
29. *Iyov* 29:2.
30. *Niddah* 30b.
31. *Bereishis* 4:7.

seeks, throughout his life, to experience it once more. Even though it is forgotten from his consciousness, its impression remains intact within his deepest memories, or — if you will — his subconscious. This is the primary force that drives man to achieve. **It is his basic motive for living and for seeking pleasure.**

Trauma of Birth

In light of this prenatal oneness with existence, we may better understand the spiritual trauma that accompanies birth. As the child issues forth from the sheltering womb into the strange and cold light of day, the exquisite pleasure of unity with God is suddenly and roughly terminated. This man/child is physically and spiritually thrown out of his personal "Gan Eden," and abruptly thrust into the barren strangeness of a totally new world. Even in its blaring artificial light, he is alone in a dark spiritual void. At this terrible moment his previous emotions of joy, security and calm give way to strange new feelings of fear, of strangeness and solitude, of stressful anxiety that threatens his very existence. This is the terror of the unknown that every human being undergoes at birth.

If, as explained above, man's *yetzer* originates at birth, small wonder that it is tainted with a very negative impression of its existence in this new world. The *yetzer* is *ra* (bad) because it is forced to experience trauma. This painful initiation leaves its mark upon all of mankind.

The Life Instinct

The trauma of birth creates a lifelong impression upon man's mind and heart. He will forever strive if unconsciously to reaffirm his inner connection with his Maker, and thus experience once again the joy of oneness with Him. This instinct is the basic momentum that energizes man throughout his life. It may become a conscious drive in later years, but initially it causes the child to seek his lost "Gan Eden" at his mother's breast, his father's lap, his family, his acquaintances, his fellow members of a lodge or a political group, etc.

Although different psychological schools of thought view various instincts as the primary force in life, be it the life instinct, the social instinct, or any other, the Torah says otherwise. These are all secondary to the basic human instinct inherent in all of mankind, to reunite with our common Creator. This instinct does not become conscious — if at all — until years later, when emotional and mental maturity is gradually reached. Whether conscious or unconscious, the presence of this instinct was overtly demonstrated countless times in Jewish history, when young and old sacrificed their lives by remaining loyal to God.

The urge to reestablish the lost connection to the Divine is, as we saw above, natural and healthy. However, the **direction** normally taken in seeking this connection is "bad," as stated in the Torah: "...for the inclination of man's heart is evil from his youth." This is so because the search is externally oriented (as previously explained) and therefore preordained to fail dismally. Not only does this direction lead to disappointment, but it also serves to perpetuate itself in an ever more desperate cycle of reaching "out" for an elusive nothingness. This is "bad" because it contradicts man's natural and basic need to find unity with his Divine core. Despite this false inclination to find unity on the "outside," it is overwhelmingly strong. This belief reinforces itself by means of habit (which will be discussed later.) As time goes by and this cycle becomes second nature, we become ever more certain that our satisfaction is to be found somewhere "outside," perhaps over the rainbow. This process is mostly unconscious.

The Good Inclination — Yetzer Tov

We may now better understand that the inherent drive that seeks to quench man's innate thirst for unity is termed "good" (*tov*) when the direction of seeking is reversed. Rather than an external orientation, which is endlessly disappointing, we seek **and find** this unity within our own selves. When the orientation is internal, the inclination is good, for it is beneficial and ultimately satisfying. It is there, in the depths of our consciousness, that we find that missing link with our Creator, the link that was sundered at birth. There, however vaguely at first, we rediscover our personal souls. This innermost part of the human spirit is, by definition, forever connected to God. Through this personal "holy of holies," we may gradually, and over many years, reconnect not only with God, but with the world around us. By use of this good internal orientation, the world is no longer an alien conglomerate of separate details, but a unified fabric of endless dimensions in which these myriad details are interwoven to create one unified whole, the creation of God.

Change of Direction

If man is naturally inclined to seek satisfaction from the outside world, and this external orientation reinforces itself over the years, how is it possible for him to change direction and focus internally? How can this switch occur when one is constantly searching for the end of the rainbow, "out there somewhere"? What he must learn to do is employ his *daas*, his knowledge and depth of understanding.

This knowledge was present in the unborn child during his *yarchei kedem*, the months he spent within his mother's womb. It is gradually reacquired (to a minimal stage) by the time he reaches the age of *daas*, thirteen for the male and twelve for the female. This quality, together with Torah education and fulfillment of *mitzvos,* enables us to change our orientation. Even without education and/or *mitzvos,* one is pushed into rediscovering his *daas* by the ever-increasing disappointments suffered by searching externally for fulfillment. Eventually, when these frustrations cannot be endured any more, most people come to realize that the search must end where it began: internally. It is at that point that the spiritual, rather than the physical, becomes the focal point of one's life.

The obvious question is: Why? Why did God see fit to create man with *daas* that disappears upon birth? The *yetzer ha-ra* thus takes control, and it is that much harder to apply our newly-acquired *daas.* Why is it necessary for man to grow accustomed to searching externally for fulfillment, only to realize after many heartaches and headaches that he had been barking up the wrong tree for so long?

To answer this we need to understand the purpose of creation as a whole. Although this vast subject is outside the sphere of this book, nevertheless it behooves us to answer the above question by shortly digressing. Upon understanding the general purpose of creation, we can more readily proceed to comprehend man's role as an *oved Hashem,* God's servant.

The Purpose of Creation

Rabbi Moshe Chaim Luzzato, the famous Kabbalist of the 17th century, says in *Derech Hashem* that it is illogical to attribute to God a causal framework of thought. After all, He **created** this process of cause and effect, so He must be **outside** of its limitations. We humans, however, must of necessity think in terms of cause and effect because we were created within this framework and are limited by its principles. Therefore, while keeping in mind our human limitations, we may nevertheless attempt to approach some understanding, albeit in human logical terms, of the purpose of creation.

The gist of the Ramchal's answer is as follows. It is the nature of the Creator, who is all goodness, to offer goodness to others. The maximum goodness is to allow man the pleasure of enjoying the products of his own efforts. When he reaps what he has sown, his pleasure is infinitely greater than when he receives the fruits of others. (These free gifts are called *lechem chesed* by our Sages, or *nahama d'kisufa* — bread of embarrassment by the Zohar.) Since the greatest pleasure is to be consciously connected to God, it follows that there is no greater goodness than to allow man to reach this goal as much as possible **through his own efforts.**

To this end, God created a world of nature that effectively conceals His presence. This forces man to exert all his effort to discover God. It is the universal "game" of hide-and-seek. Man's free will is constantly challenged on this long road of revelation, and is experienced as a vicious battle between his good and evil inclinations. These two opposing forces, as previously described, are quite evenly matched, and the battle therefore is very difficult. However, the greater the effort, the greater is the pleasure in the rewards. Thus we may understand the words "And God created man" (*vayitzer* — with two *yudim*, referring to the two opposing inclinations) as referring to this bipolarity within human nature. This is the product of His ultimate goodness.

In this light we may more easily accept the concept of a natural world which is seemingly devoid of Divine intervention. What was, will be. Nature seems to take its course according to eternal laws without regard to man's existential and teleological theories. This concealment of Divine presence is necessary in order that man may use his own free will and effort to rediscover the truth underlying this "natural" world. Therefore, our Sages refer to this world to as a *prozdor*, a corridor, for it is no more than a temporary passage to the blissful state of eternal connection with God.

Balancing the Two Inclinations

Rabbeinu Bachye, in his famous *Chovos Halevavos*,[32] describes the means by which the two opposing forces are matched evenly so as to allow man's free will to be the deciding factor in this constant war. Man's *daas* — knowledge and understanding — must be neutralized from birth for twelve or thirteen years. During this period of childhood, the evil inclination is built in strength, as man seeks satisfaction from the external world. Thus, by the time that the *daas* gains foothold and establishes itself as a driving force, the true battle of matched powers ensues. The habit of the external orientation is counterbalanced by the good inclination to seek satisfaction from within. At this crucial point man's will is free to sway towards one side or the other. Without this freedom of choice, he would not be able to enjoy the fruits that await him in the world to come.

Sins and Commandments

In this light we may find a deeper understanding of the concepts of sin and commandments. Those actions that serve to reinforce the evil inclination of external orientation are sins. Those actions that reinforce the good inclination of internal orientation are *mitzvos*, God's commandments. The consequence of obeying God's will, observing His commandments, is the gradual reawakening of our consciousness to the inner connection with Him. Likewise, when transgressing His will, we gradually feel more isolated and distant from His Divine presence.

---

32. *Shaar Avodas Elokim*, chap. 2.

Torah as Medicine

In similar fashion we can understand the words of the wisest of men, King Shlomo: "[Torah] is medicine for your body and an elixir for your bones."[33] This, says the Vilna Gaon, refers to the observance of 248 positive commandments and 365 prohibitions. The source that connects Torah observance and consequent good health is obvious: *"If you shall listen to the voice of God, your Lord…and observe all His commands, all maladies that I applied to Egypt I shall deny you, for I am God who cures you."*[34] Rashi comments: "…This simply means that I cure you by teaching you Torah and *mitzvos* so that you shall escape them [these sicknesses], as a doctor who prescribes to a [sick] man: 'Don't eat those foods that bring sickness unto you.' And this is the balance [achieved] by *mitzvos*, as it is said: '…it is medicine for your body.'"

We learn two new things from the above. First, we are reminded of that famous principle offered by Rambam: "A healthy *nefesh* (spirit) within a healthy body." In this light, the Ran explains in his *Drashos HaRan* that the source of all physical sicknesses is a sickness of the spirit, because there are 248 limbs and 365 vessels of the spirit, which parallel their physical counterparts.[35] The Torah does not differentiate between physical and spiritual (mental) sicknesses, as both are dependent on observance of Torah and *mitzvos*.

Another commentator, the Alsheich *HaKadosh*, explains in *parashas Tazria* (chap. 13:2) how leprosy evolves. It originates in the sin of *lashon ha-ra* (speaking evil of others), and the conse-

---

33. *Mishlei* 3:8.

34. *Bereishis* 15:26.

35. The sixth *drush*, and we quote: "I have no doubt that mental illness is the cause of physical illness, and that the body cannot be healed without healing the *nefesh* as well."

quent impurity taints the spirit to such a degree that (in Biblical times) it was insufferable. As a result, this impurity is "pushed outside" of the spirit, to the body, resulting in leprosy. The pure soul was unable to cope with the spiritual impurities of *lashon ha-ra* and therefore had to let the physical body cope with it, as described in detail in the Torah. Here is another very clear description of the deep connection between the spirit and the body. We also learn that the physical reveals the spiritual when the pain of the spiritual is unbearable.

The second idea learned from the Rashi above is that of balance. Sickness in whatever form, whether physical or spiritual, is a property of imbalance between all those forces that are involved in the human makeup. He who created this miraculous conglomeration of energies, the total of which is man, prescribed the formula for the continuous maintenance of man, in such a way that these forces balance each other and support and reinforce this extremely complex system. That formula is Torah and its observance. If this prescription is not adhered to fully, the result is the imbalance of forces and energies that are known as sicknesses. The unbalanced, or sick, person deteriorates very gradually, first spiritually and then physically. As a result, there is no apparent and obvious connection between the symptoms and their original cause. (This "natural" blindness is also the will of God, as explained above.)

The Definition of "Sickness"

It is clear that the body's health is dependent on the spirit's health and vice versa. The source of health in both cases is one and the same: the fulfillment of God's Divine "prescription" by full observance of His commandments. We must conclude therefore that man is to be considered sick from the very moment that he is born. Despite the appearance of health, from the holistic point of view the newborn child must be sick, for he is unable to fulfill God's commandments. Eventually, as the years pass, this initial state of imbalance is reinforced by the evil inclination, the *yetzer ha-ra*, and the child/man becomes even further removed from his Creator (from his personal point of view.)

This gradual shift towards greater imbalance can only be corrected by the knowledge — *daas* — that enables man to observe the *mitzvos*, those seven commandments that apply to the sons of Noah (all non-Jews), and the 613 commandments that apply to all Jews. Thus new balance is eventually achieved and human sickness slowly disappears. It is obvious that man's health is directly proportional to his knowledge about himself, his Creator, the world within which he lives, and his fellowman. In short, his *daas*. Our Sages tell us: "Man does not commit a sin unless the spirit of *shtus* has entered him."[36] *Shoteh* (the root of *shtus*) means digression. The spirit of *shtus* is the human weakness that causes him to digress from the way of Torah and *mitzvos*, thus bringing upon himself spiritual and then physical sickness.

What is the primal cause within man that results in his health or his sickness? The answer, of course, is his free will, that part of him which makes him a "partner," to a small extent, with his Creator. The means by which the free will is employed is the imagination. The expression of the imagination is the raw material of what we term *middos*. What are *middos*? This must be explained in the following chapter.

---

36. *Sotah* 3a.

Chapter 3
Middos

What Are Middos?

Middos can be superficially translated as human attributes. Rambam called them *dei'os*, from the root *daas*, knowledge. He maintained that one's *daas* is the basis for all his attributes. *Middos* are the natural expression of *daas*. Therefore, we can conclude, bad *middos* are caused by the lack of *daas*, and good *middos* are caused by the acquisition of *daas*. But what exactly is *daas*?

In the previous chapter we saw that *daas* enters the child's being quite gradually, and only upon reaching the age of twelve (for girls) or thirteen (for boys) is a person considered a *bar daas*. He is called "*bar mitzvah*" because he now has sufficient *daas* to take responsibility for observing *mitzvos*. Now, however, we must define *daas* in more detail in order to fully comprehend its myriad expressions: *middos*.

חב״ד — Chochmah, Binah, and Da'as

Daas is defined by our Sages as the synthesis of two attributes: *chochmah* (wisdom) and *binah* (comprehension). In our daily prayers we ask Hashem to "bestow unto us *chochmah, binah, v'daas*. What are we praying for? Let us begin with *chochmah*, wisdom.

Our Sages said: "Who is wise?...He who sees that which will

be born."[37] True wisdom is the ability to foresee end results based only on initial thoughts. In other words, the attribute of wisdom, which is deep thought, allows man to understand the goal and purpose (the actual "deed") that is desirable.

A fitting analogy would be the process of building a house. At first one requires the ability to imagine the finished house: its layout, its exterior form, its interior possibilities, etc. The architect possesses the wisdom required to "view" this house, in accordance with the specifications of the client, and portray it on paper or using a three-dimensional model. The initial thought or imagination became an existing reality...in miniature.

However, this model would be inefficient if it did not take into account all the requirements of the owner. These must include directions for air and light, limitations such as staircases, proximity to neighbors, and financial status. These and many other considerations are weighed and decided by the attribute of *binah*, comprehension.

The root of *binah* is also that of *bin* (meaning "between"); and therefore it deals with the numerous details that come "between" the major concepts of the "master plan" drawn by wisdom, *chochmah*. By comprehending the "depth" of the whole, *binah* is employed to analyze it into its components, assign specific requirements to whichever part of the whole they fit, and synthesize all the fragments into a reconstructed unity.

This is the job of the building engineer. He must make use of his *binah* in order to translate the overall picture of the house, drawn by the architect, into the detailed schematic building plan, without which no house can be built. All these details are necessarily linked to each other. Moreover, they are interdependent to the extent that the minutest change in one must

---

37. *Tamid* 32a.

perforce influence all the others. For example, if one room must hold heavy furniture, such as a large safe, the floor must be made thicker, or of stronger material. This, in turn, requires greater support under the floor, which, once again, necessitates deeper ground support. Details such as length and width of each component must be figured out and then sketched exactly in place.

Still, the whole concept is theoretical. It is only a sketch on paper. In order to realize the dream it must be actualized. That is the foreman's job. And that requires the attribute of *daas*. This *middah*, or attribute, combines the **overall** picture which is the goal, with the detailed plan (*chochmah*, wisdom, with *binah*, comprehension), and translates the result into the actual building. To be more precise, the foreman uses his *daas* to oversee the construction which is carried out by his employees. He does not have to lift a finger, but merely conveys the commands which originated with the architect and the building engineer. The foreman's knowledge may be termed *daas elyon*, the higher knowledge, and the employees who actually do the work may be said to symbolize *daas tachton*, lower knowledge.

Daas Elyon and Daas Tachton

Daas is often called *ratzon ha-lev*, the will of the heart. By means of the heart's will, man actualizes his thoughts, thus giving physical form to what existed only in potential. The will itself can be subdivided into the general intention (the "foreman"), and the specific desire that is acted upon (the "employees"). It is obvious that just as the employees should obey the foreman, so should the lower *daas* express the intentions of the upper *daas*. But that is not necessarily the case. More often than is supposed, the two parts of the will are in conflict. The result is chaos. Just as the building's construction is delayed, if not harmed, by rebellious workers, so does man's spiritual being and development suffer loss or even breakdown when his *daas* is in conflict with itself.

Because of habit (which will be elaborated upon further on), one may find himself being drawn to an action which is exactly opposite to the direction which he wishes to take. His *daas tachton* has taken over like some giant robot, after years of repetitive action, even as his *daas elyon* is screaming to stop. This is man's personal war, for and against himself. It would seem correct to place the battlefront between the good and the evil inclinations along the dividing line between the *daas elyon* and the *daas tachton*. Between these two powerful forces man stands alone, wielding the sword of **free will**, and deciding the outcome of the battle by joining one side or the other...every day anew...every hour...every minute. This then is our mission: whenever the habits acquired over the years are in opposition to their commander, the higher *daas*, we must coerce them to obey.

Daas, the Great Unifier

The attribute of *daas* is the source of those *middos* (attributes) that find external emotional expression, such as anger, love, sadness, joy, etc., and behavioral expression, such as laziness, aggressiveness, introversion, extroversion, etc. As such, *daas* can be called a unifying link (*kesher/gesher*[38]) between man's inner world and the external world surrounding him. This is the deeper meaning alluded to by the Torah in describing man's relationship to his wife as symbolized by Adam and Chava:

---

38. Rabbi Yitzchak Hutner, *z"l*, in his *sefer Pachad Yitzchak*, often mentions the concept of the connection/bridge (*kesher/gesher*) when describing the miracle of the spoken word. It is a connecting bridge between the internal world of spirit and the external world of matter, which are otherwise completely separate and distinct.

*"V'ha-adam **yada** es chava ishto"*[39] (And Adam knew Eve, his wife).

The linkage of *daas* is the result of numerous attributes that include infinite combinations of rational and emotional beliefs and attitudes, in constant flux and dynamic change. The sum total makes for man's attitude and connection, for better or for worse, with the world outside him and with the people surrounding him. In short, man's capacity for communication is in direct proportion to his *daas*. The greater (and deeper) the *daas*, the greater is the connection between the "inside" and the "outside."

Daas and the Child

As mentioned above, *daas* does not appear to function fully until the age of *bar daas*, twelve for girls and thirteen for boys. Therefore there is no real communication (of the sort to be found between adults) with children. Because their *daas* is insufficiently developed, they are incapable of fully expressing their childish desires and feelings, especially in regards to their parents, brothers and sisters. This incapacity is not merely a technical difficulty. It stems from the lack of *daas*, which is, in turn, a lack of **free will.** If a child cannot express **to himself** his desires, feelings and thoughts, then he cannot grasp or weigh the possible directions that may be chosen from one moment to the next. Since he has no free will, he is not held responsible for observing *mitzvos*.

This does not mean that the child is enclosed in an impenetrable world of his own. It simply means that his contact with others is limited to those selective attributes with which he was born and/or developed, that enabled him to satisfy his innate need for satisfaction. This contact with others is one-sided in

---

39. *Bereishis* 4:1.

that its basic drive is dependency on others for self-gratification. He has no ability to choose, through free will, to give for the sake of giving. A child's sole drive, unconscious though it may be, is to restore to himself the tranquil joy of being connected with God.

This is an egocentric attitude. As such, it does not allow for true mutual contact in depth. Nevertheless, it is logical and justifiable, as previously explained. It would therefore be unreasonable to expect a child to be altruistic. Nor should we be disappointed when he expresses his egocentrism. Such is not the case when we encounter an adult who is egocentric.

The "Autistic" Adult

The child's dependency does not bother him, for he lacks the *daas* that would enable him to be aware of his status, thereby allowing him to change it. Only when allowed free will can he feel that his life is "in his own hands" in the sense that he may choose other paths for self-gratification. Even though *daas* enters his being gradually and continuously from the day of birth, its presence is not really felt until the beginning of "the age of maturation." From that point on, one becomes more and more conscious of the inborn instinct to give and take equally, to satisfy the needs of others as well as his own. The result is a deeply satisfying relationship, which is a mutual two-sided exchange that was totally lacking in childhood. This "adult" relationship of equality is made posssible by the development of the *daas*. This, in turn, allows man to realize that independence is the redirection of his dependence on God and his own free will.

If the maturing child persists in maintaining his dependencies by disregarding the powers of his newly developed *daas*, he therefore remains egocentric even as he grows older. However, he can not "turn off" this powerful attribute of self-knowledge (even in its limited form) to the extent that he is unmindful of his existential status. He is alone. His egocentricity confines him to painful solitude even as he is surrounded by many, including those who love him. Gradually this feeling of separation increases until he feels he is a stranger to others, to God, and, most painful of all, to himself. As this spiritual solitude begins to close upon him and suffocate him, he is more and more pressured to find release from what is, in essence, his private hell. His panic increases, and he is ever more confused and at a loss to find the internal "key" to his freedom, the *daas* that enables his free will. The habit of depending on the strengths and decisions of others and the neglect of his own newly developed *daas*, causes man's freedom of will to atrophy.

Avodas Hashem, the service of God, is the cure for this malady. By observing His commands one brings his *daas* back to life, while proportionately lessening his dependence on the will of others. By freely choosing to rely on His will and His alone, one is strengthened to stand up for his beliefs, even when they are in opposition to the will of others. This is easier said than done. The deeply ingrained habit of dependence on others can be uprooted only gradually. The habit of satisfying one's needs, both physical and spiritual, through the external world and by means of others, is difficult to break. Without the seemingly miraculous revitalization offered by Torah and its observance, man would remain despairingly alone and disconnected from his higher will.

This tremendous effort of reasserting one's individuality is considered the "battle of *middos*." In other words, our better half — the *yetzer ha-tov* — which is rooted in our higher will (*ratzon ha-elyon*), must fight our egocentric side, the *yetzer ha-ra*, which is rooted in our lower will (*ratzon ha-tachton*). The battle is staged in the area of our non-physical being that is called *middos*. This "front" is quite foggy and undefined, thus increasing the confusion and the difficulties facing us in this mysterious internal war.

Let us attempt to define more clearly what we mean by the term *middos*. After all, this is the "battle of *middos*," and winning a battle is always dependent on knowing one's enemy.

The word *middah* stems from the root *madad*, measurement. Every act of measuring involves two basic components. One is the background scale, depicting the units of measure, such as pounds, or inches, or degrees of heat (C° or F°). The other component is dynamic, the part of the measuring device that is sensitive to the object being measured. For example, the mercury within the thermometer is sensitive to the heat being measured, and reacts accordingly by moving up or down the static scale printed on the back of the thermometer.

Both these components are to be found within man's spirituality. The constant and unchanging "background" is the soul, the *neshamah*. It is described in the Talmud as "the invisible viewer who looks out from within the innermost room" (*ha-roah v'einah nireis me-chadrei chadarim*[40]). The other component is the totality of man's attributes, his *middos*, which are in constant flux vis-!-vis the static soul. These two concepts are discussed by Rabbi Eliyahu Dessler, z"l. He calls them *havayah* — being — (referring to the soul) and *hasagah* — achieving — (referring to the *middos*).[41]

Being and Achieving (Havayah and Hasagah)

Rav Dessler explains that being, *havayah*, is the consciousness of our own reality, our "ego-ness." "I exist" is the indisputable axiom of every living man, regardless of his faith. This is the constant and unwavering expression of the soul. Against this silent

---

40. *Berachos* 10a.
41. *Michtav MeEliyahu*, vol. 1, p. 284.

but ever-present "backdrop," man experiences his *hasagos*, achievements or attainments, which are synonymous with *middos*.

These *hasagos* are defined as "the awareness of one's relationships with the external world." This, in turn, is composed of three stages or types of awareness:

1. Awareness of some "thing" which is lacking (spiritual or physical)
2. Awareness of the desire to fill this need
3. Awareness of pleasure in satisfying this need

Our *middos* are expressions of these three basic components termed *hasagos*. They are constantly changing at variable speeds, differing from subject to subject and from one person to another. These three elements, pertaining to awareness of need, the desire to fill it, and the pleasure derived therefrom, are grasped by the ever-present and passive "observer" — the *havayah*, our being, the unequivocal expression of our soul. These *middos* are the active component of our internal measuring scale. Our soul is the passive "background" component, the fixed scale, relative to which we may judge our progress from one moment to the next.

The Three Sources of Middos

According to Rambam,[42] our *middos* arise from three sources:

Some *middos* are inherited among the millions of genetic traits passed down from one generation to the next.

Some *middos* develop as the result of a **disposition** towards that trait, also naturally inherited.

Some *middos* arise due to the influence of the external

---

42. *Mishneh Torah, Hilchos De'os*, chap. 1, *halachah* 2.

world, especially of people, and the decisions made as a result.

Where Are Middos Located?

After dealing with the **source** of *middos*, we are now prepared to deal directly with *middos* themselves. At this point, there seems to be some confusion. It seems that defining *middos* themselves, or — if you will — finding their location within our human structure, is no simple matter. We all know, more or less, what we refer to when we mention our attributes, *middos*, but we can't seem to pinpoint their "location."

There is one thing we do know. Their origin is within man's *daas*, which is in turn divided into upper and lower sections. What we actually observe is the **expression** of *middos* in action, emotion, and thought. Because they can be seen, felt or thought, there often seems to be a contradiction in their expression. This, as we have seen, originates in the dichotomy of the *daas*. It is the apparent contradictions between the three levels in which *middos* are expressed that causes confusion. When we try to clearly define our *middos*, we often give up in frustration.

To further clarify, we may compare the three levels of the expression of *middos* to a buggy ride in the countryside. The active level of the body and its appendages is analogous to the horse pulling the buggy. The emotional level of expression is analogous to the man driving the buggy by holding the reins controlling the horse. Finally, the thought level of expression is analogous to the purpose and destination of the ride as a whole, which gives it its meaning. (For example, the purpose may be an hour of leisure meant to ease the strains of tedious work, or a business trip, and so on.)

These three levels, as seen by the above analogy, do not necessarily operate in harmony with each other. The driver may be dozing, the horse may be stubbornly resistant to its reins, and the buggy might have a broken wheel. The spiritual "compartments" which deal with these three levels of *middos* are the *nefesh,* which controls the body, the *ruach,* which controls emotions, and the *neshamah,* which controls thought. These three concepts are discussed in the next chapter.

Chapter 4
Nefesh-Ruach-Neshamah

Am I One or Many?

Is man comprised of several components that are not necessarily synchronized? Perhaps these seeming inner contradictions are purely subjective and don't actually exist. This is an important question, not just in theory, but also in our everyday lives. We often feel confused when our thoughts contradict our actions, or when both are contradicted by our emotions, or any other similar combination. We may even feel that we have a split personality, that we are two or even three different persons.

Our only recourse is to turn to Torah and let our Creator show us how to solve this seeming contradiction. To turn to Him for help is both natural and logical. Only God, through Torah, can reveal the unifying internal source of the external differences. After all, He purposefully created us like this — externally fragmentized, but internally unified.

The solution that Torah offers us is to be found in comprehending the three major spiritual forces within us. These are the *nefesh* (ego), the *ruach* (spirit), and the *neshamah* (soul). These are personal life-energies operating simultaneously and analogously on three different levels. Nevertheless, they are one, a unified, distinctly personal life force. How is that possible?

The "Oneness" of Man

Rabbi Chaim of Volozhin in his book *Nefesh HaChaim*[43] offers an analogy to explain these forces. He compares them to the process of glass-blowing. In order to make a glass object, the glass-blower first loads a small mass of molten glass onto the end of a long metal tube. He then blows air into the tube from the other end. The blown air travels through the tube and penetrates the center of the molten glass. As a result, it starts expanding like a balloon. The glass-blower simultaneously blows and twirls the growing glass bubble so as to fashion it into whatever shape he desires. The process can be very artistic, and the result is quite remarkable.

This analogy demonstrates, to a certain extent, the way that God created man. The Torah states: *"Va-yipach be-apav nishmas chaim"* (And He blew the spirit of life into him).[44] The "breath" that issued from God (so to speak) is the *neshamah*, man's soul. As it "travels" the length between Him and man's body, it is termed *ruach*, man's spirit. And when it enters man and gives his body shape and life, it is called *nefesh*, or ego. This transformation from the invisible and transcendent oneness into the physical and multifaceted living body of man is truly an artistic and miraculous creation.

How Are We Aware of Nefesh-Ruach-Neshamah?

As previously stated, we operate simultaneously on these three levels of our everyday existence. We use them and feel them throughout the day, even though we are unaware of the processes we employ to integrate them. Our Sages[45] refer to this as the familiar three-level experience commonly called "thought,

---

43. *Nefesh HaChaim, shaar* 3.
44. *Bereishis* 2:7.
45. See Rabbi Yehuda Halevi, *The Kuzari*, treatise 3:5.

emotion and action." Each of these is directed by a distinct life force. The *neshamah* activates thought processes. The *ruach* activates emotions and "imaginations of the heart." And the *nefesh* activates the blood (*"ki nefesh ha-basar ba-dam hee"* —for the *nefesh* of the living being is in its blood[46]), thereby supervising the bodily functions.

Each of these three functions resides in a specific and central place, from where it supervises and coordinates its unique processes. The *neshamah* supervises from within the brain (*mo'ach*). The *ruach* supervises from within the heart (*lev*). And the *nefesh* supervises from within the liver (*kaved*), which, as we know, controls the blood's composition. (The first letters of these three central locations are מל"ך (king), referring to the phrase: כל בני ישראל בני מלכים, all Children of Israel are sons of kings.[47])

When we are conscious, we are aware that we operate on these three levels simultaneously. This is one of the unique attributes of *bnei melachim*, sons of kings. This awareness stems from some unifying "I" that underlies all three. This "oneness" is like the air that makes its way from the glass-blower's lungs and mouth, travels the length of the tube, and ends up within the newly created glass utensil. It is the same air in three different capacities. So is man one unit of being, though his existence is expressed on three different levels.

This tri-level unity is more or less harmonious in the child. The reason for this is that he has not as yet significantly developed his *daas*. However, from the day of his Bar Mitzvah, he begins to notice, gradually but surely, that he sometimes acts in a way that there is disharmony between the three spiritual levels. (Actually, because the *daas* entered his being even earlier in

---

46. *Vayikra* 17:11.
47. *Shabbos* 111a.

small initial doses, he is not totally unfamiliar with his inner contradictions. It just never bothered him enough to mull over it.) Having acquired enough *daas,* he becomes sufficiently self-conscious to recognize that his thoughts do not necessarily correspond to his actions, nor are they always expressed by his emotions.

As increasing awareness of inner contradiction seeps into man's consciousness, he feels "split" within himself. The result is anxiety and confusion, and, in more severe cases, fear and emotional pain. Why is it painful? Because these new feelings contradict the deep-seated instinct that man's true nature is of oneness, a unity that miraculously expresses itself in the myriad details that compose man. This pain is man's basic reaction to having been disconnected from the Divine One (as described in chapter 2) since birth.

Of course, he does not make the connection between the primal cause and its effect. Nevertheless, there is a growing concern with this basic pain as it expresses itself in actions, emotions, and thoughts that often contradict each other. For example, if a parent wishes to show his love for his child, but the only verbal expression is criticism whenever the child misbehaves, the parent may become painfully frustrated. (Why can't I say "I love you"?) In this example, emotion and action are in disharmony. The emotion of love is somehow blocked, whereas negative emotions are more easily displayed by word or by action. Often these thoughts do not even express themselves in one's own consciousness. No wonder people long to return to childhood, when life flowed harmoniously, and to the ultimate embryonic period of bliss, when the soul was consciously connected to its Creator.

The Mechanical Lock Analogy

We may compare this three-level existence to a three-tumbler door lock. The lock, with the key inside, was inserted in its place within the door. Whenever the need arose to lock the door, one would simply turn the key, which in turn moved the three tumblers, allowing free passage for the key to move the lock's "tongue." When the key was pulled out, all three tumblers fell into the newly formed space, blocking the path to the "tongue" of the lock. Any other key might move one or even two tumblers, but the door will remain locked. Only the unique form of the original key can move aside all three tumblers, thus allowing passage to the lock's mechanism.

The analogy is quite obvious. Man's connection to God prior to his birth was free and unobstructed. Upon birth, however, the "key" is extracted, and this passageway becomes obstructed by three innate "tumblers" that fall into the newly vacated passage. These, of course, are the *nefesh, ruach,* and *neshamah.* Man must exert great effort to reopen the "hotline" with his Creator. All three "tumblers" must be moved in one direction to achieve this goal. This is quite a project, which takes a lifetime of work. This is the deepest meaning of the words of our Sages: *"Adam l'amal yulad"* (Man is born for strenuous work).[48]

The Nefesh

The metaphor that compares the *nefesh* to the air within the glass utensil requires further elucidation. Just as the compressed air expands the glass and gives it form, so is it limited by the solidity of the glass. Likewise, the *nefesh* is determined, to a certain extent, by the natural properties of the body within which it resides and to which it gives form. In similar fashion the *neshamah,* on the opposite pole of man's being, partakes of the properties of God to whom it is directly connected. Both

---

48. *Iyov* 5:7.

parts, the *nefesh* and the *neshamah,* are connected, at their opposite ends, to the middle "link" — the *ruach.*

Since the *nefesh* is limited by the physical properties of the body, all of which are subjected to nature and its God-given laws, it has no free will. The *nefesh* has no choice in its government of the body and its actions. Its counterpart, the *neshamah,* is likewise determined and unable to choose contrary to God's will. After all, it is firmly connected with the Almighty. While the *nefesh* is forced to pull man in the body's direction and its satisfaction, the *neshamah* by its very nature is forced to pull towards the spiritual satisfaction of uniting with God.

Against this "tug-of-rope" background, the *ruach* is the middle link, the mediator, the lawyer and the judge. Therein can we find man's freedom of choice, his free will. Centered in his heart, the *ruach* controls emotions and imagination with which it bridges the God-seeking *neshamah* with the body-oriented *nefesh.* Man's purpose therefore is to use his *ruach* to connect "Heaven" with "earth" in a smoothly flowing continuum. That allows the Heavenly blessings to reach man on earth, while the opposite also occurs. When the earthly beings connect with the higher beings by means of man's *ruach,* a cycle of give-and-take is closed and the world is a unified whole. Man is thus considered as "partner" of the Creator.[49]

The Infinite Nefesh-Ruach-Neshamah

We used the lock analogy to illustrate the three functions of man's spirituality. If the three tumblers truly depict the *nefesh-ruach-neshamah,* then we would easily identify their operations within us. Our actions would be ascribed to the *nefesh,* our emotions and imagination to the *ruach,* and our thoughts to

---

49. See Rabbi Eliyahu Dessler, *Michtav MeEliyahu,* vol. 1, p. 32 (*Kuntres HaChesed*).

the *neshamah*. If that were the case, however, we would lose the smooth sense of continuum that exists between these three components. In this hypothetical situation, it would be difficult, if not impossible, to activate all three in harmony and to one purpose. We would be unaware of their common and unifying source, which is God.

Therefore, we must surrender the simplicity of the three-part lock analogy and delve more deeply into the details of man's nature. We learn from our Sages that each of these major components is subdivided into a *nefesh-ruach-neshamah* of its own. For example, the *nefesh* is said to be composed of a "smaller" *nefesh*, *ruach*, and *neshamah*. This subdivision continues in each of these smaller components, on a smaller scale, and so on and so forth...ad infinitum.[50]

The idea is simpler than it sounds. Every component in man's nature is a link between that which is "above" and that which is "below." Therefore, that part which connects with the "above" can be termed *neshamah*, and that part which connects with that which is below can be termed *nefesh*. It follows that the middle part will be termed *ruach*. The conclusion is obvious: every detail within man's nature is composed of all three components in whatever scale we choose to view him. Therein lies the secret of man's continuous and harmonious consciousness in terms of a unified personal existence. Therein also lies the roots of the many contradictions between man's actions, emotions, and thoughts.

The Tree Analogy

A better analogy than that of the lock might clarify the above. Let us consider the branches of a tree. They branch off one from the other, becoming ever smaller, yet maintaining the same

---

50. Ramchal, *Kelalei Ma'amar HaChochmah* 15 (*Sefer HaKelalim*, p. 315).

physical properties as the main branch. Since they are connected internally, they all partake of the water that is ingested by the tree's roots. It ascends and reaches all these branches, naturally diverting its course through their inner structure. The water also causes leaves and fruits to grow on their extremities. It is obvious that if one branch, however small, were to be broken off, it would influence all the others to a certain degree. (The branch's significance is dependent on its position relative to the other branches on the tree.)

In a similar fashion, man's nature divides and subdivides itself in its powers of thought (*neshamah*), emotion (*ruach*), and action (*nefesh*). These three are found in various "amounts" in each and every part of human nature. Each thought directly influences the *neshamah* portion of each unit. Each emotion influences the *ruach* portion of each unit. Each action influences the *nefesh* portion of each unit. The result is a totally unique nature for every human being. No two people, however similar, could ever really be the same.

The tree analogy is actually the Torah's: "For man is the tree of the field" (*ki ha-adam eitz ha-sadeh*).[51] He is rooted in the Divine soil of the Creator. He therefore feels one and whole. Nevertheless, as he constructs his unique "branches" in endless subdivisions, he also feels divided and is often in self-contradiction when his thoughts, emotions and actions oppose one another. However, only by means of his unified core can he be aware of these contradictions.

The Unique Unit of "Life"

As explained above, each individual is perforce totally unique. The application of each of these three parts in whatever level is the direct result of man's choice. No two men are the same,

---

51. *Devarim* 20:19.

since each man chooses in accordance with his unique nature. This is what our Sages meant when they said: "Just as their faces are not the same, so are their minds (de'oteihem) different."[52] This uniqueness of being is not merely a vague philosophical notion. It infuses each of us with a very special sense of purpose or meaning. **Our lives are truly significant.** When we realize this truth, we experience a spiritual rebirth. Our previous melancholy state, in which we feel like worn-out cogs in an eternal cosmological machine, gives way to a state in which we are dynamic partners of God and His creation.

The uniqueness does not cease here. Our Sages explain that **every moment** of man's life is utterly unique and irretrievable. Every single minute is a product of man's choice, one of infinite possibilities, and therefore no two moments are alike. This is a fantastic thought! When we attempt to grasp what it means in relation to our lives, it can leave us breathless. No unit of my life is to be found in any other moment of my life, in no other person of my generation, in all generations past and future. This is truly mind-boggling! To grasp this idea is to feel the breath of God, so to speak. There are no words to describe the experience in which one is first aware of the meaning of **LIFE**.

Man's Uniqueness — in Practice

The practical application of the above is obvious. Every person is a world of his own. In this light we may understand the words of our Sages: "Do not judge your friend until you have reached his place."[53] Since, according to the ideas of his uniqueness, that is impossible, that means that there is only one judge of people. Only He who created all men can actually "reach his place." We human beings, on the other hand, must desist from

---

52. *Berachos* 48a.
53. *Pirkei Avos* 2:4.

our judging of others!

Secondly, since no two people are alike, then they may never have exactly the same problems. Even though their problems might be quite similar — after all, they stem from one common Divine root — they nevertheless branch out in different details and forms. That means that the solution for one could never be exactly right for the other. Only God, Who created all men, can give, through the Torah, those solutions which are perfectly fit for all.

Thirdly, every person has his own *tikun*, a unique life script that is his personal, divinely-intended goal. The significance of this idea is incredible for a person who, until now, saw himself as a speck of dust within an infinite non-personal cosmos. As a fully unique being, he discovers that he himself is an infinite world of his own, and yet he is still connected to others through his Divine core. He is partner in the continual creation of the world through his actions, feelings and thoughts. There is no greater solution to man's problems than to realize with all his being that, rather than seeing himself as a "fleeting shadow,"[54] with little or no significance, he is actually a part of the One and Only, one of "the sons of God."[55]

The Unique Self-Image

In chapter 1 we dealt with the question: "Who am I?" The answer, we explained, is that the child's comprehension of those reactions which he elicits from his parents, neighbors, acquaintances, etc. forms his self-image.

This self-image is constructed in an endless cycle comprised of three stages:

---

54. This term is taken from the famous High Holidays prayer, *Unesaneh Tokef*.

55. *Devarim* 14:1.

1. The self communicates (by word or action) to another being.

2. This elicits some response or reaction from the other to the self.

3. The self interprets this response as he wishes.

These three steps combine to form the basic unit or building block of the self-image. Each step is the product of man's free will, whether it is the initial action, the reaction, or its interpretation. It is obvious, therefore, that the self-image is the unique product of man's free will, for no two people can ever communicate, respond, and interpret in exactly identical fashion.

The uniqueness of the personality is mostly the result of the third phase of the cycle. This is because the interpretation is purely subjective, or at least less objective than the action and reaction which make up the first two phases. The end result, therefore, is often regrettable, if not tragic. For the self-image created in this manner is infinitely distant from the true "self" that God created. This chasm between the true self and the false self is discussed in the next chapter.

Chapter 5

The Construction of Man

The Relative World

"Man views the world through the glasses of his self."[56] With these words, Rav Dessler sums up the extreme subjectivity of our world. Despite its apparent objective nature, the world is observed by the subjective eyes of each and every person, and therefore is as subjectively unique as its viewer. Although this concept may seem familiar to many of us, it is nevertheless extremely difficult to actually accept and assimilate it into our mindsets. We have been accustomed since childhood to see the world as a fixed entity which imposes its objective reality on our senses, not as infinite alternative realities, all true yet very different.

For example, if a person had a difficult childhood which lacked warmth and nurturing parents, then he concludes quite logically — from his subjective point of view — that the world surrounding him is cold and cruel. He must stubbornly fight for survival; otherwise, he will lose and perhaps die. Thus, when, for example, he marries and experiences disappointment from

---

56. Rabbi Eliyahu Dessler explains the concept of *mishkafei atzmo*, glasses of one's self, in a poem: "The Roots of Strife" (*Shoresh Ha-machlokes*), in *Michtav MeEliyahu*, vol. 3, p. 305.

his wife, he is confident that the fault is totally hers, just as the world as a whole is at fault for his painful childhood. Likewise, he would tend to blame his employees for financial problems in the business, as he would blame Divine injustice for his maladies.

This person is suffering, yet he would reject out of hand the idea that **he is his own victim**. He would vehemently deny that his suffering is subjectively brought about through his **negative view** of the world. His world seems hostile and threatening. It would take great courage and fortitude to revolutionize his whole grasp of reality and to see the painful truth: that man is his own enemy...or friend. This difficult conceptual switch (from that of an objective world "out there" to a subjective world "inside") is what comprises the transition from spiritual childhood to spiritual maturity.

Who Is Rich...

Let us consider, for example, a practical application of the concept that the world is subjective in regards to money. Our Sages taught us that wealth is not dependent on the amount of money that a man amasses. "Who is rich? He who is happy with his lot."[57]

As long as we believe otherwise, that wealth is, for example, a million dollars, we must necessarily be disappointed when we reach this goal. The experience of other millionaires proves that they still feel "poor" relative to multimillionaires, who themselves feel lacking relative to billionaires, and so on. As long as there exists someone who is richer than us, we cannot feel that we are truly rich. Is no one rich then?

We must come to terms with the idea that wealth is not some external quantity of money, but a personal approach to

---

57. *Pirkei Avos* 4:1.

life. Only then will we discover true wealth. Only when we grasp both mentally and emotionally that what is doled out to us from Heaven is exactly right for us will we feel rich. We won't want more because we don't need more. What we receive is no more and no less than what we need, and therefore we can be happy. "Who is rich? He who is happy with his lot."

The Root of Our Problems and Their Solutions

Many of our problems are rooted in the false concept that they are created by the external circumstances of the world in which we live. We feel that we are constantly victimized, and "they" are the cruel and heartless exploiters. However, as this immature, though natural, concept gradually gives way to the more mature and truthful one, that our view of the world is subjective and relative to our inner values and judgements, many of the seemingly insurmountable problems begin to dissipate. If these problems were created by us, we begin to understand that it is up to us to solve them.

The internal mechanism that allows us to deal effectively with our problems is our *daas*. This *daas*, which was previously defined and explained, enables us to make the difficult (and often painful) transition from being the passive victim of external causes to the state of maturity. In this state of being, we accept full responsibility for all our internal processes, including our reactions to those external circumstances that we are powerless to change. Using our *daas*, we activate a dynamic connection between our inner state and the world around us. We thus create a harmonious continuum in both directions. Our *daas* is therefore the key to our well-being and happiness in this challenging and sometimes threatening world.

Daas cannot be gained all at once. Initially it is to be found, in minimal amounts, at the age of twelve (for girls) or thirteen (for boys). From that point on, *daas* is acquired through arduous work, both spiritual and physical, and that is justifiable. For by gradually acquiring more and more *daas*, man slowly frees himself from his perceived bondage to the external world. No goal could be more worthy of striving towards throughout life. This tremendous task is accomplished by means of the Torah and observance of its *mitzvos*. (This is also termed *daas Elokim* — the knowledge of God.)

Why? Why is Torah the necessary means to achieve this end? Why does Torah, more than anything else, develop our *daas* to the extent whereby we can solve lifelong problems?

To answer this question, we must first understand the process by which these deeply entrenched problems are formed. Although we have already seen that problems arise as a result of the false belief that they are externally caused, we must still find out why this belief is so common and deeply rooted in all of us. Only through total comprehension of the problem can we deal with its solution. This is analogous to winning a war by gathering critical intelligence concerning the enemy, its strengths, its weaknesses, its strategies, and future plans and goals.

He Who created the "enemy" also created the strategy for its defeat. All of this (and much more) He mapped out in the Torah. We must orient ourselves within this Divine "map" of our lives before we can make out its meaning for our future "moves." Or, to use a simpler metaphor, we must first use Torah to diagnose our sickness before learning (through Torah) how to treat it.

Habit: Friend or Foe?

We all possess and make use of a superb, God-given mechanism called habit. The concept is so familiar to us that we never stop to consider its purpose. Habit is always available for us, like the mind or the body, and we accept it as such, plain and simple. But upon further consideration, it appears that without habit, life as we know it would be simply impossible.

Habit is what enables us to learn. Learning — no matter what — requires that full attention be given to that which is to be learned. As long as our thoughts are fully occupied with the subject at hand, we are not free to learn something else. By repeating the process being learned, it becomes habitual, automatic, if you will, thus freeing our minds to learn something else.

Let us consider, for example, someone learning to drive a car. Initially he is quite bewildered when he attempts to operate all the components involved. A lot is required: total synchronization of eyes, hands and feet in various holds and positions, all of which can barely be accomplished without one-hundred percent concentration. The technical difficulties are compounded by the natural fear that an accident may result from his incompetence. However, things seem to improve surprisingly well from one driving lesson to the next. The hands "know" how to turn the steering wheel, the feet "know" which pedal to press for acceleration or brakes, and the eyes "know" in which mirror to look and when. Habit has taken charge of what initially required conscious deliberation. As a result, our new driver is less and less preoccupied with the processes involved in driving. His consciousness is increasingly available for other uses, such as listening to the radio, or thinking about subjects that are not related to the driving at hand. He may even learn something new by listening to an enlightening *shiur* on tape. Thus we see that habit allows the freedom of thought which is required for learning or doing new things. We develop in mind and action by means of this endless repetition which comprises the learning process.

On the other hand, habit can and does create severe problems. If an undesirable behavior, such as a sin against God or man, becomes habitual, then it becomes incredibly hard to stop it. The more it becomes a habit, the greater momentum it gains in self-perpetuation, and the harder it becomes to regulate it, let alone stop altogether. Whoever has attempted to break a lifetime habit of alcoholism, drug abuse, or verbal aggression knows only too well how seemingly impossible it is to break. In this negative context habit seems more foe than friend. As our Sages taught: "When one commits a transgression and repeats it, he comes to see it as permissible."[58]

Habit can be dangerous not only in connection with negative behavior, but even when applied to desirable behavior. An example of the negative influence of habit when it pertains to a *mitzvah* is the act of prayer. When first learning to pray, a person feels involved, full of concentration, and is emotionally moved. But as habit sets in, concentration becomes more and more difficult, excitement wanes, and boredom sets in. Prayer becomes dull and tiring, and the *mitzvah* is more confining and less liberating. To this end, we are forewarned by our Sages: "Do not make your prayer a fixed act, but rather a beseeching for mercy."[59]

Habits of Thought

The above examples are quite familiar. We are generally quite aware of habits that we have formed on the physical level of our lives. But we are usually **unaware** of habits formed in the mental spheres of our everyday living. The influence of these thought-habits is almost totally unconscious. That is all the more reason, therefore, that they control so much of our lives, for how can we be critical of these automatic thought patterns if we are unaware of them? Thus the "slave" becomes the "mas-

---

58. *Moed Katan* 27b.
59. *Pirkei Avos* 2:18.

ter." Habit is a gift from God that allows us to learn and grow by freeing the mind for further learning. But the tremendous power of habit, when unleashed and out of control, turns on its human master and subjugates him to a life of tormenting boredom and sameness.

When thought becomes confined to patterns governed by habit, emotions and actions likewise become habitual. As we have learned, man's three parallel levels — thoughts, emotions, and actions — are all intimately intertwined. We saw how any change in one level automatically influences the other two. Thus, habit all too often paralyzes man's freedom to choose what he really wants not only in action, but also in emotions and thoughts.

Because this bondage is initially unconscious, most people are unaware of their enslavement to preconceived axioms that were automatically internalized since childhood. It takes the maturity of *daas Torah* to realize that we were the innocent victims of the natural process of subjugation to habit. But as this realization dawns upon us, so does the desire to choose our lives with the freedom innate in our beings. However, desire for freedom alone cannot help us extricate ourselves from the bonds of habit. We need hard work and — as always — help from God.

To clarify, let us consider the following example. It is a widely held belief in today's non-Torah society that secular studies are a prerequisite for any person who wishes to be successful and happy in life. A child growing up in a home that accepts this premise unquestionably will unconsciously accept it as a "natural law," especially if society at large supports this concept as self-evident. Having internalized the notion that secular studies are a requirement for happiness, his future is predetermined in the sense that he must study within a framework of secular studies. His thoughts, emotions and actions are aligned along this habit of thought. Within this clearly defined frame of reference, he may choose what to study and where.

But it would be rare for him to stop and reconsider the truth of the basic belief that secular studies are a necessary part of modern-day life. It would strike him as odd to hear that this idea is no more than a premise postulated by general opinion of modern society. Having accepted the idea as absolute truth in childhood, when the critical faculty is barely developed, he would find it extremely difficult to reconsider this basic tenet of his life.

No wonder that thought habits developed in childhood become second nature over the years. The wonder is that man can somehow escape their bondage after reaching maturity. Nevertheless, it is a well-known fact that people **can** and **do** manage to change deeply rooted habits of thought, emotions and actions, and thus start their lives anew, so to speak. This possibility is applicable to all of us, and therefore it behooves us to further explore the wonders of this mechanism called habit. For if we truly understand its basic components, then we stand a chance of being its masters rather than its slaves. That is, if we know why we develop problems in our lives, mentally, emotionally or physically, then we may more easily deal with them and even solve them. This is *avodas ha-middos*, that arduous process of "cleansing" our personal attributes.

The Learning Process — A Microscopic View

Upon examination of the process by which we learn from our surroundings, a cycle can be detected, composed of four distinct phases which are repeated endlessly. Understanding these phases and their cumulative influence within the repetitious cycle is the key to understanding the mechanism of habit.

Phase 1: Sensing and registering an external stimulus.

Phase 2: Evaluating this stimulus by searching the memory for a similar experience, extracting it, and applying its evaluation (which was also memorized) to the new stimulus.

Phase 3: Reacting to the stimulus in accordance with the results of phase 2.

Phase 4: Cataloguing the **total** experience within the memory.

An Example of Habit-Formation

A common example of the process involved in habit formation would clarify these four phases. Let us consider the simple act of drinking milk that every newborn child undergoes from the first day of his life. He is hungry and therefore cries. As a result, he is offered a bottle of warm milk. The bottle, the nipple and the warm milk are sensed by his mouth, lips, and tongue, and after a week or two, by his eyes as well. This is the external stimulus that is sensed by the baby, marking the end of phase one.

Instinctively his mind progresses to phase two, in which he searches his totally fresh memory for a similar experience...and finds none.[60] The baby is, at this point, at a loss as to how to evaluate the milk bottle with the warm, white liquid inside. For lack of choice (he is hungry!) he boldly decides to try it out, and instinct takes care of phase three. And how satisfying it turns out to be! This feeling of happy satisfaction attaches itself to the experience of the bottle, milk, and the process of drinking it, and is catalogued — phase four — within the brain's memory cells. End of first cycle.

About four hours later, the baby is once again crying. He is hungry, of course, and the bottle is ready. This time the exter-

---

60. The Latin "tabula rasa" associated with the child was probably taken from our Sages in *Pirkei Avos* 4:20: "To teach the child can be compared to ink written on a new [blank] page."

nal stimulus is recognized in phase two. When the baby searched his memory, instinctively and in a split second, he identified and withdrew a memory whose stimulus — a bottle of warm milk — was identical. This memory also contained a positive emotional and physical experience, which was phase four of the previous cycle. The result can be analyzed as follows:

1. Present stimulus = previous memorized stimulus.
2. Previous stimulus resulted in positive experience.
3. Conclusion: present stimulus should likewise lead to positive result.
4. It must be worthwhile to drink the proffered milk.

And the baby drinks away. (Mothers happily attest to the fact that baby's enthusiasm for the milk increases steadily from one meal to the next.) Now, having drunk his fill contentedly, the baby will catalogue this second feeding within his memory. However, this time around, the feeling connected to the experience will be **twice** as strong! This is because, in addition to the actual drinking experience which proved to be a good one, the new memory inserted into the brain in this fourth phase also contained the previous memory, from the first cycle, which was also positive. So if, to simplify matters, we say that the first memory contained the feeling that "milk is good," and this conclusion was reached by the baby this second time as well — i.e. "milk is good" — both "good" messages will now be entered together and catalogued in a new memory cell, and the message is: "milk is **doubly** good."

Let us go through this cycle for the third time, in order to understand what is happening in the baby's mind. Around twelve hours after birth (more or less), this process repeats itself. This time, however, when the baby wishes to evaluate the milk offered him (phase two), he draws upon two separate experiences, each contained in its own memory cell. The first contains the message: "milk is good." The second contains the message: "milk is doubly good." Together they add up to: "milk is good three times over."

Now the baby is really enthusiastic about drinking the milk, and he is not disappointed. It is really good! This good experience (phase three) is added to the recalled memories ("milk is good three times over"), and it is catalogued in a new memory cell with the feeling that sums up the total cycle: "milk is good **four** times over!"

It doesn't take much to guess what memory content will be entered four hours later, when the baby is hungry once again. In this fourth cycle the message will increase to eight times "good." The next time the number will be 16, then 32, then 64, and so on. This is a simple arithmetic progression.

Within the first day of the baby's life, he has already formed a **tremendously strong bias** in favor of milk. (Figure out what those six feedings, one every four hours, did to his memory.) Of course, in real life these numbers might be a bit different, because negative experiences (such as a stomachache) can influence the overall value of the experience. But in essence what we have here is the self-reinforcing process called **habit.**

Habit-Power

As we saw in the four-step analysis of habit, its power stems from the self-reinforcing element due to repetition. It is so natural and basic to human experience that we normally don't question the validity of the results. For example, as the baby goes on drinking milk over the days and months, its beneficial value becomes as obvious as a law of nature. From his youthful point of view, if at first milk was a **means** to assuage his hunger, within a short time it became a primary **need** for life. Habit endowed milk with a significance for the baby's well-being which was far and beyond its initial value.

Therefore, if Mom were to discover that her baby is allergic to milk, and therefore must switch to another formula, she would have quite a problem on her hands. Baby would object — as expected — to this abrupt change in his daily routine. After all, the new taste has no parallel within baby's memory with which to be compared (phase two). His reaction would initially be to spurn the offered beverage with obvious distaste. But, being a baby, he'd quickly adjust to this unprecedented situation and, with typical baby courage, drink the "stuff" until it, too, becomes a delicious habit.

However, let us suppose that we were dealing not with an eager, newborn baby, but with a mature person who has, for thirty years, been accustomed to drink tea. He is now, for the first time, invited to drink coffee because there is no tea available. He would probably flatly refuse to even consider this possibility, unless he is one of those rare, experimenting types who enjoy the challenges of the unknown. After all, a thirty-year habit of drinking tea thrice daily becomes an unalterable "law of nature."

Thought Habits

Now that we have familiarized ourselves with the process of habit formation, we may more easily grasp the notion of thought habits and their powerful influence on our lives. Let us consider, for example, a person who has always believed that life is nothing more than random events, in which chance mutations cause evolution, rather than a supreme, infinitely wise God. This message had been fed into his mind since childhood as an "obvious" axiom of the philosophy of life, until it seemed no less obvious than any natural law, such as the law of gravity, for example.

If we were to introduce this person to monotheism, belief in one, ungraspable God, he would certainly deny its validity with total conviction. If, in addition, he had been brought up in an anti-religious atmosphere, he would ridicule the notion of a one, all-seeing, all-caring God. He would scorn this idea as an outrageous remnant of primitive belief. It would seem to his habit-formed mind a shallow and crude way of viewing man's existence, reminiscent of savage and uncultured tribes who roamed the earth many, many years ago.

This well-educated individual has been strongly, if subtly, brainwashed! He is the unwitting victim of typical (and natural) social coercion to accept as true whatever is fashionable and common in the society in which he grew up. Communist atheism is a case in point.

Then again, man can choose to form thought habits that are not common to his society. In this case he becomes "conditioned," for better or for worse, through his own freedom of choice. He may be aware of his supervisory role in this process of self-conditioning, in which case he enjoys the feeling of control. The more he controls his thought-habits, the easier it becomes to maturely select those social values and beliefs which are truly acceptable to his mind. The others he may — with his new-found power of thought-control — discard as useless for him, despite their popularity and social acceptance.

The Three Levels of Thought-Habits

We have seen that our spirit is composed of three levels, the *nefesh*, *ruach* and the *neshamah*, (ego, spirit and soul.) Thought habits are formed within each of these levels of consciousness, and their influences on us are accordingly felt as external, middle, or internal expressions. They may be good habits, desirable and beneficial, or bad habits, destructive or detrimental.

External thought habits, which correspond to the *nefesh*, deal with man's appearance and behavior in relation to his society. They may include, for example, a code of dress, a definitive attitude towards overeating, size, weight, hair style, modesty, etc. All these are external expressions of thoughts and emotions that have become habits, if not actual beliefs.

The thought habits of the **middle** level, corresponding to the *ruach*, deal with communication with one's fellow man. Here is the "middle-ground" between the external and the internal, for at this level man attempts to externalize his inner thoughts. This rather complex human "bridge" is called communication. What was completely private is expressed and made known to another. Examples of thought habits on this level are social acceptability, the value placed on wealth, career or wisdom, physical and emotional problems of communication, social dynamics, etc. Positive examples on this level may be: the ability to express emotions, coping with social pressures and stress, the ability to teach, listen, understand, empathize, identify, etc.

The **internal** level of thought habits deals with one's basic existential beliefs. Examples are: faith in one's life, in the general significance of life, personal goals, ethical and religious values, self-esteem, and, most importantly, awareness of identity ("Who am I?"). As discussed in chapter 1, self-identification is based on childish interpretations of reactions that we solicit from others, especially parents. This self-consciousness is purely subjective and often confused. Nevertheless, it is the basis of one's awareness. **It is the basic thought-pattern, upon which all other thought-habits, on all three levels, develop over the years.**

The Construction of Man

We have now acquired the conceptual tools needed to deal with the "construction" of man. To begin with, we can now understand how man is unwittingly his own worst enemy. He builds his self-image from the day he is born, using habitual thoughts and actions that repeat and reinforce themselves millions of times, every hour of every day throughout the years. Man unconsciously "brainwashes" himself, with the aid of external influences, to come up with something he can consider "me."

Another conclusion we can now draw is that this process of accustomed thought-habits is inevitable and, during childhood, unchangeable. It matters not whether a child's idea of himself is true or false, good or bad, noble or grotesque. He is at the mercy of this process of self-construction as dictated by his inner nature and external authority-figures. His critical faculty is still undeveloped during those crucial formative years. Therefore, all actions, words and thoughts relating to him are accepted as absolute truths. They are stored in his memory with all the emotional force and unquestioned authority of prophetic revelations.

This is God's will. By allowing man to construct a subjective — and therefore false — self-image, God enables him to reach that point at which he is equally drawn to good (which is his basic Divine nature), or evil (which results from a negative self-image). Freedom of will is meaningful only when the innate *yetzer tov*, the good will, is balanced by the *yetzer ha-ra*, the bad will. Only by neutralizing man's basic goodness during his formative years of childhood, thus allowing a false self-image to be formed (the *yetzer ha-ra*), can God bring us to the point at which we are free to choose. This choice is a constant daily battle between the habitual dictates of our self-image on the one hand, and the combined strengths of our actions, emotions and thoughts as supervised by our *daas* on the other hand. The struggle, however, is worthwhile, for we know that the fruits of our many victories, however small and seemingly insignificant, are waiting for us in the world to come. Thus, the battle itself becomes meaningful, an end in itself, enriching our lives while we inhabit this world!

It is true that we are the ones who created our false identities. And yes, we were all coerced by our basic human nature in this self-structuring process. We had no choice. God decreed and so it must be.[61] There is no way to justify this human "curse" of self-inflicted pain, unless we view it from the perspective that it is the only means to an infinitely joyous eternity. This physical world, with all its joys and sorrows, is merely a corridor through which we must all pass in order to enjoy eternity with our Maker in His heavenly palace. Without this overall view, it is easy to become frustrated and upset. Life becomes increasingly insufferable as awareness of its seeming meaninglessness deepens. Even suicide seems preferable. (This tragic conclusion is the logical result of existentialists, as portrayed, for example, by the hero of Albert Camus' "The Stranger.")

The Great Trap

The next stage in understanding man's subjective self-creation is a startling discovery: man's lifelong struggle to overcome endless obstacles is actually a wrestling match with **himself**. He is like a dog chasing his own tail. The obstacles that seem so frightening or insurmountable were actually created by him! This self-entrapment is a vicious process which is both intricate and cunning. It is a maddening "game" that is supervised by

---

61. We should take note that the concept of "Divine decree" (*gezeiras Shamayim*) has been widened to include not only physical aspects of our lives, but also our inner world, the construction of which was entirely out of our hands. This spiritual makeup of our *nefesh* was created for us by the circumstances of our childhood, and in accordance with the roots of our *neshamah*. Only by attaining *daas* can we change ourselves.

our well-known "friend," the *yetzer ha-ra*, the negative side of our self-image.

One of the most effective tools used by our *yetzer ha-ra* is the *panas ha-kesem*,[62] which, freely translated, means projector. Projection (a well-known psychological process) can be summarized by Rav Dessler's famous dictum: "Man views the world through the glasses of his self." In other words, everything — including problems and obstacles — is totally subjective!

Projection

Projection, as a concept, can be grasped quite easily by our minds. However, it is much harder for us to accept it in our hearts. This is because projection contradicts our basic common-sense belief in the absolute and objective reality of the world around us. Projection implies that our consciousness registers only those sense perceptions which we recognize from our subjective experience of reality. For example, a person walking through a field of daisies is not necessarily aware of them. If his mind is totally preoccupied with something else, he can be totally blind to the beautiful daisies surrounding him. He may be depressed or perhaps concentrating intensely on a certain thought. The result is that his external world is far different than that of the carefree children frolicking around him amongst the daisies, enjoying their beauty and freshness.

Let us consider another example. Assume that a person had been taught since childhood that lying is necessary for survival. It would be safe to assume, therefore, that to him, truth is a rational idea of common-sense living, rather than an actual dictate of his personal ethical system. Being truthful would assume the status of a luxury that cannot always be afforded in

---

62. This term was coined by Rabbi Shlomo Wolbe in *Alei Shur*, and it means "the miraculous flashlight."

this dangerous world. The consequence of this preconceived "law of survival" is that he interprets the success of others as a logical outcome of lying and cheating. He will not believe, despite all protestations to the contrary, that these people achieved success while remaining truthful. As in the previous example, in which the strolling man was unaware of the daisies around him, this "brainwashed" liar is unaware of the truth spoken by successful people of his acquaintance. His reality is actually the tint of his very personal and unique "glasses." What he believes cannot exist he simply cannot see!

Our Personal Movie

It is understandably difficult to truly grasp and accept projection as a fact of life. What has until now appeared solid and familiar suddenly seems vague and abstract. However, it is something we must all come to terms with in our own lives if we wish to live a truly fulfilling life.

Life can be compared to a movie, which we project on our personal screen of consciousness. Yet, we are rudely awakened at the end of the movie — as compelling and convincing as it may be — into the everyday world of the theater in which we are sitting. We may be disappointed to discover that what was emotionally stirring and fascinating was merely the creative product of some actors and their director. Such is our experience when waking up from a life which we believed was objectively real, and in which we played a dramatic role, only to discover that "all life's a stage." That which seems external is no more than our projection of our inner consciousness onto the natural "screen" that God created for our personal "viewing."

However, after the initial shock, we discover tremendous power and inspiration in the idea that we, in conjunction with our Creator, are constantly creating this world. When we make that fearful plunge into the icy waters of the unknown, we find ourselves swimming competently and joyously within the infinite creation of which we are an integral and dynamic part. Yet another overwhelming discovery is that we are eternally connected to God, part and parcel of His infinite, ungraspable Being. Simultaneously, we lose the fear of external threats, and our inner peace and security increase proportionately. Our previous blindness to the process whereby the *yetzer ha-ra* enhances its control over us now gives way to the awareness needed to take control over our lives and our habits, on all levels.

Like all existential truths, projection, too, is described in the Torah.

"...From You Is It Empty"

Moshe Rabbeinu warns Bnei Yisrael to command their offspring to strictly observe the Torah. Why? "For it is no empty thing from you (*ki lo davar reik hu mikkem*) for it is your life."[63] The word "*mikkem*" — from you — seems redundant, and thus calls for explanation. Our Sages comment in the Talmud Yersuhalmi[64]: "And if it's empty, from **you** is it empty." If you see the Torah as a system that is empty of meaning, perforce it is you yourselves who are empty. It is simply more convenient to identify your own deficiencies in others.

The Torah is teaching us that the accusation of emptiness has no bearing on the Torah itself; it serves to reveal the spiritual status of the accuser. It would be easier to understand projection as the process by which a man recognizes his deficiencies in others of similar nature. It is more surprising to realize that man projects his negativity onto whatever "screen" is available, even when, like Torah, there is no objective basis for this

---

63. *Devarim* 32:47.
64. *Pei'ah* 2a.

accusation. Thus, people may be completely innocent, yet the projecting accuser will find them guilty as charged, for they serve as **mirrors** to his personal existence.

This, then, is the conclusion. The whole external world, including all my acquaintances, especially those with whom I am intimate, serves as a mirror to my ego, i.e. my self-image. If I am empty — a thought which revolts me — then you, or even the Torah, must be empty. This false conclusion is necessary for me if I am incapable of confronting my own emptiness. Projection is thus not just a convenient balm, but a shelter of sorts for the oppressed, who lack the means of self-redemption.

Projected Hatred

Another example of projection in the Torah is found in the verse: "And you rebelled in your tents and you said, 'It is for God's hatred of us that He brought us out of Egypt...to destroy us.'"[65] Rashi points out: "And it is not He who hated you, but [rather] you who hated Him." This time the projection is not of "emptiness," but of hatred. Rather than admit that the children hate their Father, they accuse **Him** of hating **them**.

Even though this is not referring to vicious hatred (for this was a *dor de'ah,* an enlightened generation), it matters little. Projection is applicable in the finer points as well as the grosser ones. The common denominator is that when people cannot confront their deficiencies on whatever level, they project it onto others. Even God can be the victim of projection.

A person may project onto someone who, through his goodness, causes feelings of guilt or unworthiness in the recipient of his kindness. This, in turn, causes him to project these negative feelings onto the beneficiary. Let us clarify this a bit more.

---

65. *Devarim* 1:27.

"He Who Renounces Is Himself Renounced"

The Talmud relates a case in point. A Jew from the city of Pumbedisa in Babylonia went to another city named Nehardea. He entered a butcher's store to buy meat, and stood in line waiting for his turn. But, as his turn came up, he was forced to wait. The *shamash* (helper) of the city's rabbi, Rabbi Yechezkel ben Yehuda, had entered and was naturally served first. The visitor was indignant, and when he was told who the person was, he ridiculed his name in a very disrespectful manner. When Rabbi Yechezkel ben Yehuda heard of this, he immediately proclaimed *niddui*, ostracism, against this person. Furthermore, he declared this Jew to be a descendant of slaves.

The visitor from Pumbedisa retorted by pressing charges against the rabbi of Nehardea in the great Rabbinical court of the *Reish Galusa*, the "Head of the Diaspora." The presiding judge was Rav Nachman, the son-in-law of the *Reish Galusa*. Rabbi Yehuda, despite his lofty station, was forced to come and answer charges. When asked why he ostracized the plaintiff and why he denounced him as a descendant of slaves, he answered in the name of Shmuel: *"Kol hapossel passul"* — he who renounces [others] is himself renounced. Since the plaintiff was evidently accustomed to disparage others, and this became a typical mode of his self-expression when made angry, he thereby revealed his secret. The plaintiff is inferior **in his own eyes** and worthy of renunciation.

Furthermore, added Rabbi Yehuda in the name of Shmuel: *"Kol hapossel bemummo possel"* — he who denounces [others for a specific deficiency] is himself denounced for that same deficiency. In other words, if the criticism expressed towards others is often of the same nature, that reveals that the accuser is lacking in exactly that area. Therefore, when Rabbi Yehuda found out that the Jew from Pumbedisa was noted for calling people the derogatory name of "slaves," he felt fully justified in denouncing him publicly as a slave and revealing his lowly social status. The Talmud relates that the defense won the case, and the plaintiff, along with other typical "slave-callers," was shamefacedly renounced.

Secret Revealed

We have seen that the principle of projection was effectively used by our Sages to reveal a secret social scheme in which many families had participated. Their deception was revealed because of an interesting characteristic of projection: the projector is unaware that he is revealing himself. He has no idea that by repeatedly denouncing another for a certain evil, he is actually letting others know that he himself is tainted by this same deficiency. His secret remains such to himself alone. Even the unschooled in psychology can often sense projection, so obvious is the angry criticizer.

Similarly, the rebellious members of Bnei Yisrael unknowingly revealed their true colors for all future generations. By voicing their self-righteous claims against God and their paranoid accusations, they displayed their lack of faith to all. If they had realized this, they would have certainly remained silent. Even more startling is that it is very likely that since this was a *dor de'ah*, a generation of knowledge, their lack of faith was so minute that it was unknown **even to themselves**. Nevertheless, projection reveals even the most subconscious of beliefs.

We can conclude that there are two types of secrets revealed by projection. The first, as portrayed by the slave from Pumbedisa, is known to the projector, who tries to hide it from everyone and is shocked when he is found out. The second, as seen in the *dor ha-midbar*, is originally unknown to all, including the projector. Only when he repeatedly opens his mouth in angry criticism, is it made known to others. Yet it still remains a secret to himself.

The Characteristics of Projection

We find several characteristics of projection in the examples drawn from the Torah and the Talmud, as well as those, which we shall discuss later, that are drawn from everyday life. They apply whether the projector is conscious of his defect or not. The projector has no notion that he is revealing his defects.

His denunciation or criticism is usually strongly emotional and often bitter, cynical or derogatory. It seems that the intensely negative emotions that are blocked out by the projector concerning his own life are transferred en masse to the accused.

The projector seems to enjoy self-righteous satisfaction when belittling his victim. This feeling probably stems from his unconscious victory over the threatening emotions that would have made **him** the victim.

Although we all project all the time, the classical projector whose defect is eventually revealed is a person who has made criticism a habitual form of communication. It is almost second nature. The style of criticism also becomes typical, such as biting cynicism, angry indignation, cutting scorn or disparaging dismissal.

The one underlying emotion in all projectors, whether expressed or contained, is anger. It might even be suppressed to such a degree that the projector is unaware of its presence. By projecting, he liberates the tremendous emotional pressure of the anger building up inside, and he once again sidetracks his problems successfully... until the next time.

It is extremely difficult for the habitual projector to accept, or even to comprehend, the concept of projection. Even when he shows ability and desire to grasp this notion, and accept it as true, he is usually incapable of applying it to himself. This difficulty is quite natural.

If we add up all these characteristics of projection, we find that the projector has been pooling all his mental and emotional resources for many years to one purpose: to avoid coming to terms with self-criticism. He is terrified by the demons of his creation, so he hurls them in anger at others. To apply this knowledge of projection to himself, to gain *daas* of self-awareness, is frightening for him. To him it seems like a diabolical scheme for suicide.

Is the Projected Criticism Justified?

One of the characteristics of projection that we mentioned above is the overall sense of righteousness that is strongly felt by the projector. Is he truly justified, at least to some degree, or not? In answering this question, we find three different possibilities:

Since the projector is sensitive to his own defect(s), whether conscious or not, he must be likewise sensitive to those same defects when they are present in others. Therefore, in cases like these, the projector is justifiably revealing negative traits in others, even though his provocative and hurtful manner is certainly uncalled for. In such instances we are reminded of the saying of our Sages: *"Tol korah mi-bein einecha"* (remove the wooden beam from between your eyes).[66] Although you may have found defects in others, take a look at your own, which until now you have not been able to see. They were so close to your eyes, that, just like the bridge of the nose which cannot be viewed, so were your defects outside your line of vision. If you distance yourself from them a little, they will come into sight. As we are taught: *"K'shot atzmecha t'chilah"* (attend first to your own appearance).[67]

In a different situation, the projector is totally unjustified. He, and not the accused, is the deficient one. The hapless vic-

---

66. *Kiddushin* 70a.
67. *Bava Metzia* 107b.

tim merely serves as a blank screen on which the projector hurls his angry accusations. Such was the case with the slave from Pumbedisa. He was accustomed to labeling others derogatorily as "slaves," when there was actually no basis for these accusations. This was his way of cursing them out. His victims were like boxing bags on which he would vent his frustrations and anger, rather than deal with his own slave status.

In the third case, the projector is once again totally unjustified, but even more so than in the second case. The reason is that the accuser is emotionally connected to the accused, and this personal connection gives rise to his projection. The nature of this connection is what makes the accusation so unfair. In this case the projector had received benefits from the accused and gradually accrued a debt of gratitude towards him.[68] For several reasons this gratitude was not forthcoming and this caused pangs of guilt. These, in turn, gave rise to feelings of anger which expressed itself in the accusations of projection, stemming from the basic feeling that the displayed goodness was actually bad. (This is called *"lehachzir ra'ah tachas tovah,"* returning evil for good.[69])

This manner of projection was displayed by Bnei Yisrael in the desert. They replaced gratitude towards Hashem, who took them out of slavery in Egypt, with ingratitude and bitter complaints. Their hatred stemmed from the very personal connection that bonded them to their Savior, who took them through the Red Sea, and gave them the *man*, who made them His peo-

---

68. The indebtedness of the receiver is learned, for example, from Moshe, who was taken in by Yisro. The Torah says *"Va-yoel Moshe,"* meaning that Moshe agreed to live with Yisro. But the word *Va-yoel* hints at the existence of an oath, *allah*, that Moshe took to repay Yisro for his hospitality. Thus we learn that receiving entails indebtedness.

69. *Mishlei* 17: "He who returns bad for good causes bad to remain in his home." See also *Kesubos* 53a.

ple, and gave them the Torah. These innumerable acts of Divine love and mercy tallied up such a large debt, that, unable to "pay up," the wayward children simply projected their self-hatred onto their Father. Lacking any justification for their ingratitude, they naturally and unconsciously placed the blame on Him.

What Is the Natural Development of a Man's Life?

We are now able to connect the various related topics in this chapter, and take an overall look at the way man builds and creates his life. Our goal is to clarify Rav Dessler's statement (chapter 2) that our personal world is the product of our imagination. Based on this, we concluded that our personal problems are likewise the product of our imagination, even though they **seem** to arise from external reasons. Finally, we arrive at the next and final logical step: **that we ourselves, with God's help, can cure our own maladies.**

Let us enumerate the first two stages. Every human begins to identify his existence by means of his relationships with his parents. Every child absorbs the innumerable evaluations of his self-worth, both positive and negative, as he interprets them from his peers. The habits he forms, especially his thought-habits, become a "filtering lens" through which he views the world around him. He projects his self-image (including repressed, subconscious feelings and thoughts) on the "screen" of his surroundings. This projection becomes a practical means by which to avoid confronting painful experiences. As we saw above, one's deficiencies can be thrust onto others, thereby deflecting self-accusations and pain. As a result, the accuser feels justified in his role of the hapless victim of a cruel and merciless world.

This then is the meaning contained within Rav Dessler's words, that every person sees the world through the "glasses of his self" (b'mishkefei atzmo). If his childhood was warm, loving, harmonious and secure, then he views the world around him as a fascinating and promising stage on which to fulfill his ambitions and achieve happiness and contentment. His world is almost like a playground in the eyes of a small child.

But if his childhood was cold and forbidding, fearful or threatening, full of pain and injustice, then he may come to view the world around him as a dangerous jungle. He feels preyed upon by cruel lurking monsters, and his life is full of torment. His days are often annoying, dreary, boring, depressing, disappointing or terrifying, depending on the upcoming hurdle of what appears to him as life's endless race to oblivion.

This extremely negative approach to life is to be found only in more severe cases, where pain and suffering were the norm. Likewise, the happy and optimistic approach described above is, sadly, rare. Most people have a mixture of both approaches, just as their childhood consisted of both good times and bad. Therefore, the "glasses of the self" are different proportions of wonderful experiences and painful events and everything in between, which made up our childhood and the ensuing years of adulthood.

The Personal Life-Script

The endless repetition of our personal world-picture becomes a thought-habit. Our view of the world and our role in it is already solidified in childhood, as our personal interpretation of life's meaning is absorbed into the depths of our subconscious and conscious existence. Our self-image is thus built and reinforced accordingly. This world-view, unique to each of us, may be seen as our **personal life-script**. It quickly develops into the axis of our lives, around which we revolve, constantly reinforcing its values, both the good ones and the bad. The smallest, most mundane matters, along with events of great significance, are all absorbed within our personal life-script, and, in turn, serve as interpreters to future experiences.

Thus, the natural development of man is a constant reinforcing of his life-script. As each experience is assimilated, not only is it made to fit the preexisting view of life and self, but it also turns out to "prove" how true this view is. Now that this event is fitted exactly into the jigsaw puzzle of one's life, it can serve as the basis for accepting new pieces of life's great puzzle.

On top of this, we project onto others that which we expect to see, in line with our life-script. We receive, not surprisingly, feedback that matches what we expected. Our self-image and our life-script are thus strengthened even more. To better understand this process, let us look at an example.

Consider a child who is certain that he is the victim of his parents' indifference and neglect. He feels the pain of being alone. He suffers from the gnawing suspicion that he is unloved and, therefore, not **worthy** of love. Eventually this thought becomes knowledge. An existential conclusion has been intuitively reached: "I am unworthy of love, respect, or even attention." This negative self-evaluation is the child's self-image and serves as the axis of his personal existence.

In accordance with his poor self-image, this child quickly registers all of life's disappointments and burdens. Every failure or criticism is immediately accepted as a fitting part of his life-script. However, every pleasure or compliment is disregarded or disdained, an irrelevant and mysterious detail that cannot be accepted within his world view. Thus, school is a burden, friends are threatening, and home is a painful vacuum. Life seems like a cruel and painful series of trials and tribulations. His self-image and evolving life-script are constantly reinforced until they become set in stone. Even overt messages of appreciation by teachers, friends, or even his parents, are immediately interpreted as selfish means to take advantage of him. Any attempt to help is immediately under suspicion. Nobody can be trusted because this forsaken child is utterly certain that there is no one who appreciates him. And that is justified, in his innocent opinion, for there is no reason whatsoever that he should be of value to anyone. Furthermore, when he does concede that a favor was done to him, it arouses his anger for being victimized most other times, and his reaction (as described above) is to project this anger on those towards whom he feels indebted. Instead of expressing the gratitude expected by others, he remains silent or even scornful and bitter. The tragic results are further alienation of those who wish to help and support. The child develops into a bitter and isolated victim of what he sees as a cruel and meaningless existence.

Self-Burial

It is clear that, tragically, a person can actually "bury" himself in his own, self-made tomb. Every event and comment is interpreted in such a manner that he, the interpreter, is digging his own grave. This is the real tragedy because it is so unnecessary and based upon a terribly mistaken opinion of himself. All this pain and wasted life resulted from a gross misconception of other people's attitude towards himself.

The opposite is also possible. He may choose to exert his free will and escape from the magnetic pull of his masochistic life-script. He is free to raise himself, with God's help, on his own two feet, and slowly climb upwards on his personal ladder. It is not easy. It is one of the hardest things in the world. But it is possible.

Most people prefer the easier, well-trodden path of the life-script they constructed during childhood. Having chosen to follow nature's course, they are voluntarily imprisoned, **chained to this life-script**, whether it is positive or not. A child born into a warm, protective and harmonious home tends to develop an upbeat, optimistic life-script. By following its natural course, he would find himself increasingly capable in dealing with hardships or overcoming obstacles. Life as a whole would seem a pleasant and rewarding challenge.

But there are many exceptions to this rule. Even when the external circumstances of childhood **seem** ideal, the child may develop a negative life-script. For many reasons, both known and unknown, he will **interpret** his surroundings negatively, thereby creating pain and suffering within his personal world. For example, parental worry can be seen by the child as parental intolerance, warmth can be interpreted as weakness, and encouragement of independence might be viewed as lack of care. Once again we have an example wherein the child gradually blocks out positive experiences and registers mostly negative ones, thereby creating for himself a destructive, painful life-script. Only conscious effort to escape this self-made grave will enable him to find pleasure in life.

This unfortunate development is not as uncommon as we might think. We just tend to notice mostly those cases that are extreme. To some degree, though, we all unwittingly create our own hurdles, and then cry angrily when we fall painfully over them. This self-entrapment is a natural human trait from which we all suffer to some extent, each at his/her personal level of consciousness.

Of course, the nature of our childhood is influential in this matter. The harder our early experience of life, the harder is it to escape our life-script. This is because the negative self-image is doubly reinforced, both by external sources of pain (such as parental violence), as well as internal interpretations of personal unworthiness. In this case a person finds it twice as difficult to bring his free will to the fore, in seeking to escape the clutches of his life-script.

On the other hand, where childhood was more pleasant and supportive, the negative self-image is built more on misconstrued events and meanings than on actual aggressiveness or neglect. In this case, a person begins his escape from his life-script on a "higher" and, therefore, easier starting point. In both cases, however, this process is arduous — if rewarding — work.

In essence, we are all, to a large extent, the imagined products of our minds' interpretation of life's circumstances. These structures may be likened to trees. Some are tall and deeply rooted in the ground. Others are shorter and less rooted in the earth. There are those whose roots are very deep, in contrast to their insignificant height. We may also find tall trees whose roots are not deep at all. They all have one characteristic in common: their traits were initially determined by God's will. All grew and developed (or fell) in accordance with nature's rules.

Children, like trees, grow and develop and sometimes fall without much choice. Their homes are their roots, for better or for worse, and they grow up more or less in accordance to the messages that they received regarding their worth. All children are initially completely at the mercy of their *yetzer ha-ra*, and are forced to react accordingly. They have no choice but to structure their self-image on the reactions that they receive from their parents, siblings, teachers and friends.

This natural development serves as the basis for the future growth that strengthens the roots of one's personality, as he uses his freedom of will to fulfill his destiny. Using his *daas*, he must choose between living more fully or remaining in a "spiritual daze." At this point he begins his personal *avodas Hashem*, service of God, in the spirit of the Torah: "See that I have given unto you today life and goodness, and death and evil...[so that] you shall choose life...."[70]

---

70. *Devarim* 30:15.

Chapter 6

Man's Freedom of Choice

"And You Shall Choose Life"

During childhood, the self-image is constructed without an effective *daas*. This unique attribute enters into play — if at all — at the age of Bar Mitzvah, (13 years of age for boys) or Bas Mitzvah (12 years of age for girls). Therefore, every child without exception projects his shortcomings on those people with whom his relationships are meaningful: his parents, family, and friends. Their reactions reinforce his self-image, and he thereby builds his own identity. This image becomes deeply rooted in his consciousness by force of habit, and thus he is the unwitting victim of this natural process of "self-brainwashing."

The logical consequence is for the child to create a life-script for himself in accordance with his self-image. He naturally subjugates himself to this script, unaware that he has the choice to change its contents. The force at work, of course, is the *yetzer ha-ra*, the evil inclination. His duty is to escape this self-made prison, be it ever so "pleasant," and elevate himself above the limitations that his life-script placed on him. In other words, he must utilize his *daas*, with the help of Torah, and exercise his innate freedom of will. "And you shall choose life"[71] — this is the commandment to choose the greater life which is potentially

---

71. *Devarim* 30:15.

ours. What does this mean for us? **Overcome our habits of thought and action, as stipulated by our personal life-script.**

Saints and Sinners

We may conclude, in light of this Torah injunction, that one who continues to blindly follow his personal life-script without attempting to live real life is considered dead. This idea is referred to by our Sages: "The righteous who have passed away are alive, and the evildoers, even as they live, are dead."[72] Spiritual death, then, is the gradual surrender to the quicksand of the limiting life-script that evolved over childhood. In this context, death is not defined by transition from this physical world to the next world of afterlife. Likewise, life is actually a freedom from the bondage of the initial life-script, which may continue both in this world and the next. It all depends on our observance of the Divine commandment to choose life.

Thus, the terms "saints" and "sinners" take on very different forms than the popularly accepted definitions. The sinner in essence is he who does not employ his God-given free will to improve his life-script. Despite the pain and suffering involved, he refuses to believe that he has other options than those that he has always used to deal with life.

Saints, on the other hand, have taken charge of their lives. They too started off with a limiting life-script. However, they refused to accept its contents as inevitable, and, using their free will, they gradually and arduously worked their way out of the negative limitations of these scripts. With the guiding help of Torah and its observance, and the wisdom of our Sages, they increased their happiness and improved the quality of their

---

72. *Berachos* 18a.

lives. They can truthfully be called *bnei aliyah*[73] (those who ascend). This idea is referred to by the prophet Zechariah: "And I shall give you paths to tread amongst those who stand still (angels)."[74] In other words, whereas angels, lofty as they are, remain static for all of existence, you, who are human, are capable of "movement" from one level to another, for only you have free will.

We may summarize, therefore, that righteousness is not determined by observance of commandments alone, either by quantity or quality. The essential criterion is the amount of successful effort invested in improving one's life-script. This gradual and difficult change is true spiritual and personal evolvement. This ascent is not always a conscious one. But the effort expended is very conscious! Our awareness of this effort allows us to evaluate ourselves, more or less. We know whether we have been struggling to change and grow spiritually. We can often look back and realize that we have changed somewhat. Former habits of thought, expression or action have gradually made way to new and improved manners of thought, expression, or behavior. This, of course, was brought about by observing God's will, learning and applying Torah to our lives. Nevertheless, our spiritual paths are totally unique. The reason is that each of us received a different spiritual basis from where to begin his ascension. Each home offers each child a uniquely individual starting point from which he may evolve over time. **Therefore it would be totally wrong to evaluate ourselves in relation to others**. Only God knows the truth about our righteousness.

---

73. *Sukkah* 45b.
74. *Zechariah* 3:7.

The "Point of Choice"

The starting line for the war against the *yetzer ha-ra* is termed by Rav Dessler the "point of choice" (*nekudas ha-bechirah*[75]). This war, which is none other than the struggle to escape our self-created life-script, begins anew each day. The point of choice is likewise different from day to day and even from one moment to the next. Actually, every second of our conscious lives we must choose whether to improve our spirituality or remain where we are.

Rav Dessler explains that the area below the point of choice is controlled by acquired habits, either good or bad, and is therefore automatic. These represent our present life-script. In contrast, the whole area "above" the point of choice is — at present — inaccessible, for better or for worse.

Most people live their lives below the point of choice. Those who never struggle with their *yetzer* at the point of choice may be considered unrighteous. Thus, the vast majority of people are **not** unrighteous, because they do struggle to change their lives from time to time. On the other hand, those few who **constantly** struggle to "raise" their point of choice by waging war on their bad habits may justifiably be called righteous. Even when they sometimes lose or fail ("Seven times may the righteous fall and get up"[76]), they remain righteous. Small wonder that there are so few righteous people in this world.

The vast majority of people are inconsistent in their spiritual paths. At times, when they feel strong and optimistic, they struggle quite valiantly, and even successfully, to change their self-image through a change in their lives. This stage is called *aliyah*, ascent. But, as always, after every *aliyah* comes the *yeridah* — descent. At this stage, most people surrender to their old

---

75. *Michtav MeEliyahu*, vol. 1, p. 111.
76. *Mishlei* 24:16.

habits, and view their ascent as a temporary stage at the most. They feel weak and helpless to maintain their former state. This simply and unfortunately reinforces the feeling that one is imprisoned within his life-script.

The Level of Pain

It is easier to just "ride the streaming river" of our personal life-script.[77] All the parts fit each other almost perfectly. Everything is so familiar! This extremely complex human machine is well used and oiled frequently, so it performs as we expect it to and have grown accustomed to.

For example, a child whose parents often criticized him lived his life at an emotional pain level of 6 (when pleasure is defined as 0 and the greatest pain is 10). This child's life-script includes an average daily dose of emotional pain at scale 6. He is not conscious (in his early formative years) of this pain, nor does he have any notion that life could be different. For him the existence of pain at this level seems, after so many years, quite normal. It is so familiar, in fact, that any change in this pain level would seem abnormal.

Therefore, if, for example, we suddenly began complimenting and praising this person, thereby changing his pain level to 2, how would he react? Chances are that he would feel insecure, if not bewildered. Perhaps anxiety would arise. This stressful situation could also be achieved by **increasing** his pain level to 10. What is important to note is that his reaction of discomfort or anxiety would result whenever his accustomed pain level is changed, whether it is for better or for worse. Although this example is oversimplified for the purpose of demonstra-

---

77. The streaming river is an analogy used by Rabbi Yisrael Salanter in *Igeres HaMussar*, that depicts the powerful hold that habits of physical satisfaction have on us.

tion, nevertheless, my experience confirms that this holds true within the complex and often unconscious state of every human being.

I have also noted, time after time, that this person, whose customary pain level has been significantly changed, will unconsciously attempt to return to his "normal" level — that which is appropriate to his life-script. If, for example, he suffered pain at the increased level of 10 one day, he might compensate by running away and joining his friends for a wild night. This pleasurable experience (level 1, let's say) would bring him back to the average, level 6. At this point he'd return home feeling somewhat satisfied at having "taken revenge." However, in truth, his satisfaction stems from having returned to his normal pain level of 6.

Return to Life-Script by "Giving Bad for Good"

If, however, this individual received pleasure, which reduced his pain to level 2, what can he do to bring himself back to level 6? After all, this state is unpleasant for him and must subconsciously be changed. The answer is that he would offer *ra'ah tachas tovah*, bad for good. Rather than show gratitude, he would hurt the very people who gave him pleasure. His ingratitude seems surprising, but for him it is (subconsciously) the "right" thing to do. His justification is the unconscious threat to his life-script. This imbalance must be righted.

Therefore, his conscious feeling is to distrust the motives of those who give him pleasure. He interprets the compliment, the hug, the promotion, etc. as a self-serving act meant to extract some favor from him. This person is projecting his personal limitations onto those who offer to help him. In short, when offered to improve his life-script, he will manipulate the situation to maintain his status by refusing well-meant offers. He "returns bad for good."

The Difficulty in Improving the Self-Image

A more specific example may help to explain more fully the dynamics of this process of ingratitude. Let us imagine an adult —
call him Reuven — who angers quickly and aggressively whenever his wife, Sarah, dares to comment critically. His cutting re-
torts are totally disproportionate to Sarah's mild remarks. She is
well aware that Reuven's sensitivity to criticism stems from a
difficult childhood in which he suffered from highly critical
parents. Therefore, she must carefully weigh each and every
word if she wants marital harmony.

On the other hand, whenever Sarah compliments Reuven
or expresses her love for him, he usually dismisses her scorn-
fully and derisively. Her efforts at affection and intimacy are all
too often blocked by indifference. In response, Sarah fluctuates
between frustrated alienation and growing despair. Whichever
way Sarah acts towards Reuven, whether with criticism or compliments, she is turned away and rejected. Whichever way she
looks at the situation, she can't win.

Reuven's angry reactions are easy to understand when Sarah is critical. After all, his bears an open emotional wound that
was festering even before their marriage. However, Sarah cannot grasp why Reuven turns down her open offers of affection.
Why does he cynically misinterpret her compliments? It does-
n't make sense that, having suffered from lack of love and affection as a child, he should turn it down so blatantly. Logic
dictates — so Sarah thinks — that Reuven's need for love is so
strong that he would do anything to satiate his unquenched
thirst, rather than exactly the opposite. Isn't that what marriage
should mean: the opportunity to compensate for what was
lacking in childhood, and to build on this strengthened basis?

The answer that we can offer Sarah is that she is perfectly
justified in assuming that Reuven wants and needs love, appreciation, warmth and affection. In fact, he had needed it for so

long before they got married, that he simply cannot allow himself to feel just how much he needs love. It's much too painful. His negative response to Sarah's affection reveals his deep, almost unconscious secret. Reuven is "dying" for love! But he had suffered so many rejections that he unconsciously surrendered himself to a loveless existence. To accept the love for which he yearns but gave up on is to reawaken his hopes…and the chance of the pain and suffering of rejection. So Reuven chose to spurn all love and affection. This unconscious choice was the logical path for him, for it was less painful than the alternative.

Repression

As a child, Reuven suffered years of rejection and criticism. His tolerance reached a critical level, beyond which he would not have been able to function effectively. At that point, Reuven activated an innate God-given defense mechanism which is called repression. The pain is gradually repressed to the unconscious part of the child's mind, thereby permitting him to continue his "normal" existence. This subconscious storehouse of pain and frustration, among other repressed emotions, is what Rabbi Yisrael Salanter referred to as "the dark powers." As discussed previously, our behavior stems mostly from these dark powers.

The basis of this repressive mechanism is revealed by the Torah: "For bribery will blind the eyes of the wise, and will distort the words of the righteous."[78] Rav Dessler explains that any sort of bribe will blind and distort, but the greater the bribe, the greater the distortion. He continues by proving that there is no greater bribe than man's desire to please himself. This self-love (even when misused or misconstrued) is innate to human nature. Therefore, **every** human — be he as honest, truthful or

---

78. *Devarim* 16:19.

righteous as Moshe, or wise as King Shlomo — is partially blind. If the smallest penny given as a bribe can sway the wise and the righteous from objective truth, how much greater must man's blind prejudice be when the bribe is of the most valued currency: self-interest.

Therefore, when pain and suffering reach a threshold at which man's mental health is jeopardized, he "blinds himself" in order to function effectively and remain outwardly normal. His self-interest bribes his own mind to disregard the pain completely, relegating it to the abyss of his unconscious.

Back to Reuven. Over the years, Reuven began to gradually blind himself to the constant pain of censure and rejection. Every time his sanity was threatened by an overload of pain, he would automatically switch on his repressive mechanism, relegating the overflow to the unconscious. He developed a thick skin. The more Reuven employed this Heaven-sent safety valve, the thicker his skin became. By the time he married Sarah, it was more stone than skin.

What resulted is an emotionally disabled person who is totally insulated from his feelings. Within his self-built protective "coffin" this wounded, suffering man-child called Reuven manages to put on an outward show of existence. Threats may cause him to suddenly lash out in anger, or he may retreat even further, in order to distance himself from outside threats.

It is now understandable why Reuven loses control when he feels threatened. Even when Sarah comments mildly, she may be pressing that hidden button within Reuven's subconscious that touches his raw nerves, and he lashes out. But why must he reject affection?

The Fear of Pain

Reuven dealt with accumulated pain by repressing it. Self-blindness was his primary form of defense. Therefore, Reuven became used to withdrawing from any situation which threatened him with the pain he tried so desperately to avoid. Any action or word that touched upon this pain caused distress. Therefore, any action or word that **threatened** to reawaken the hidden pain was likewise to be avoided. Even if the stimulus was affection or love, it had to be dismissed immediately if it may bring up the repressed pain.

As a result, the **fear** of pain accumulated in Reuven's consciousness and was also repressed, **in addition to** the repressed memories of pain. The reason that the fear was repressed is that just as pain becomes unbearable at some point, so too does fear of pain. Without the defense mechanism of repression, the fear of pain could force Reuven to "freeze up" and become totally incapacitated. Thus, the nature of the stimulus is irrelevant if it even touches upon the fear of pain.

Rejection of Appreciation

The reasons behind the way Reuven reacts to Sarah's overtures of affection and appreciation are now clear. When she compliments him, he cannot smile and say "Thank you." He acts in the exactly opposite manner. He may either ignore Sarah completely, or screw up his face and utter some cutting remark. If she would show her appreciation by buying him a present, he might characteristically retort: "Why do you keep throwing away our money?" Or if he receives a new leather wallet for a birthday gift which he really needs, he might say: "I can get this at half the price. You should ask before you buy!"

The inevitable consequence of Reuven's reactions is the cooling of his wife's ardor and her distancing herself from him. Of course, this causes her much suffering. She cannot grasp this Dr. Jekyll – Mr. Hyde transformation that makes Reuven so callous and uncaring. Why is he so cruel? Is something so wrong with Sarah? If he once loved her, now he seems to hate her.

Poor Sarah! If she only knew the truth about her husband, she would have saved herself a lot of anguish and heartbreak. If Sarah knew that Reuven is reacting from his own wounded personality, she would probably have remained loving and compassionate, if from a distance. She certainly wouldn't have hated him as he seems to hate her. Life with Reuven would be bearable if Sarah could make sense out of his irrational behavior.

Sarah must grasp that every affectionate overture towards her husband, in word or action, activates an unconscious need to recoil from any stimulus that may elicit the repressed pain of his past. Even fear of this pain suffices to "press the button" of rejection by cynicism, scorn or whatever other means is available. When, for example, Sarah offers Reuven a compliment, she activates a series of deeply repressed memories, such as:

"I feel loved when I receive a compliment."

"I need as many compliments as I can get."

"Instead of getting compliments, I'm getting criticism."

"This hurts more and more. It's unbearable!"

"I'm afraid of suffering more rejection whenever I turn for affection or appreciation."

"It's best for me to deny the need for love in whatever form, so that I am protected from further pain."

"I must immediately reject compliments and affection."

These thoughts became internalized over the years, and the action and reaction evolved into an automatic response. Reuven held at bay all those who wished to become intimate, especially his wife. These reactions reinforced Reuven's emotional position, and his condition deteriorated as behavior and thought patterns became more and more ingrained.

Pain Levels

However, there are times, usually when in great distress, that Reuven does allow himself emotional intimacy. He might even accept a good word now and then with modest acknowledgement. He is not totally obnoxious. Sometimes he seems like a different person. Why is that?

Once again, habit is the key. Emotional pain, as discussed, can be measured on a scale of 0 (no pain) to 10 (excruciating pain). Now, let's assume that Reuven's childhood was characterized by a daily average "dose" of pain at level 6. Reuven is so accustomed to living his life on this level that a sudden change of this "normalcy" threatens his security. This threat, as we have seen, is the fear of touching on the repressed suffering of many years.

Therefore, when criticized or belittled, Reuven's pain level is increased, and he reacts in whatever means available to him to reduce the level back to 6. He might lash out angrily or run away to cool down. In both cases he reaffirms the secure pain status of 6.

Reuven likewise reacts negatively when offered affection, which reduces his pain level to 2 or 3. He must bring pain back into his life in order to return to his emotional stability of scale 6. However, there is one situation which allows Reuven to receive affection without prompting him to rebuff it. That is as follows: If this affection is offered to him **when he is suffering more than usual**, then it is accepted as logical and forthcoming. Say he has a terrible toothache that effectively increases his day's pain level to 9. In this case, he'd willingly accept comfort, affection or anything else that would aid in reducing his pain back to level 6. It is simple arithmetic:

$$\text{pain}(9) + \text{pleasure}(3) \div 2 \text{ (for average)} = \text{pain}(6)$$

This is why there are times when Reuven accepts affection

and appreciation. Rather than feel threatened in these periods of greater-than-usual distress, he is happy to receive the pleasure of love and warmth which brings him to his emotional security of level 6. Knowing this offers Sarah the chance to safely express her affections. She need not fear rejection when Reuven is in greater pain than is normal for his life.

But obviously this is not a permanent solution to Reuven and Sarah's marriage. However, there is some consolation for Sarah when she realizes that in the past she had completely misread Reuven's rejection of her or words of appreciation. His love for her is **masked** by fear of pain of rejection. Actually, Reuven needs **her** no less than she needs **him**. He is simply a slave to the emotional and behavioral patterns of his past.

"L'fum Tza'ara Agra"[79]
(Reward Is Proportional to the Effort)

Healing Reuven is no easy task. Both Sarah and Reuven must invest much effort to change ingrained patterns of thoughts, emotions and actions. For Reuven especially this change is quite difficult. But it is possible. He has the choice whether to invest tremendous energy to achieve this goal, or whether to remain as he is. The latter option is obviously the easier choice. In the long run, it is also the bad choice, because his suffering will continue and may even increase.

This question of choice between hard work that results in a higher quality of living, and the "easy" life of continued habits is an issue that confronts us all. Even those of us who consider themselves to be more balanced and emotionally stable must deal with this choice almost on a daily basis. We all have that area "above" our point-of-choice which we believe that we cannot attain. However, our Sages prod us and say: "Always must

---

79. *Pirkei Avos* 5:22.

one say, 'When will my actions reach those of Avraham, Yitzchak, and Yaakov?'"[80] We are thus encouraged to be *bnei aliyah* (those who ascend). This arduous work is what we were born for, and our rewards will be proportionate to the energy that we invest in this lifelong task. We simply have to choose, again and again and again....

We know that the Ramchal defines this world as the corridor to the next world, *olam ha-ba*, in which we receive our rewards. That means that our life in this world is the means to achieve the greatest pleasures in the next world, in proportion to the "work" done here on earth. As we have seen, there seems to be no task more difficult than to change one's self-image and life-script. With the help of Torah and its observance it can be done, but the daily choice between tapping our Divine potential and continuing the life of habit is always strenuous. This struggle forces us to deal with our present limitations, our failures, our pain, and our guilt feelings. We must consider our disappointments, our anger, even our hatred. To use this world as a corridor for the rewards of the next world is to bear the fear of possible pain that tends to paralyze us on whatever level we are, and stay forever within our familiar line of defense.

This is *avodas Hashem*! And now we can understand why there are so many good and innocent Jews who simply continue on and do not work on themselves. Then there are those who do attempt to solve their problems with the aid of Torah and nevertheless fail to improve their situation significantly. As we are taught, "The imprisoned cannot free himself" (*Ein chavush matir atzmo mi-beis ha-asurim*).[81]

There are solutions, one of which is offered in this book: Torah Therapy. After diagnosing our problems, in general and in

---

80. The Midrash *Tanna D'vei Eliyahu Rabbah, parashah* 23.
81. *Berachos* 5b.

detail, we may use this type of therapy, which is simply intensive application of Torah principles and the wisdom of our Sages, to escape our self-limitations. Our self-image and the resulting life-script need not bind us forever. We have an exterior force to liberate us: God's prescription and His ever-helping hand. All we must do is to reach out **our** hand and "bring Torah down to earth," in our limited capacities. This is the subject of the second section: Torah Therapy.

Part Two

Torah Therapy

Rabbi Yehudah the son of Rabbi Chiyah said: Unlike God's quality is man's quality. Man's natural quality is to offer medicine which benfits one and harms the other. God's quality differs. He offered Torah to Israel, which is a life cure to his whole body, as it says: "a cure for all his flesh."

(Eiruvin 54)

Introduction to Part Two

Why Therapy?

Why do people come to therapy? Is there one common problem which can be identified as the basis for the innumerable motives that move people to seek professional help? We are not referring to the basic unconscious human drive to reconnect with God, which was discussed in the previous section. We are looking for one simple answer that is common and **conscious** to all mankind.

The call for therapy seems to stem from negative feelings such as loneliness, anger, sadness, frustration and fears. When they become unbearable, we are driven to seek help. Let us examine these motives from close up.

Usually, the conscious motive is a problematic relationship with some other person, or with society as a whole. These problems are characterized by difficult communication, which is a result of emotional problems. These verbal barriers, rooted in emotional problems, are expressed as misinterpretation of the meaning of the words that are exchanged. This miscommunication, in turn, discourages openness, and conversation becomes more limited and more stilted, until eventually it may peter out altogether. This interpersonal barrier involves much pain (anger, hurt, frustration and fear), until finally it can be borne no longer. We seek help.

It is rare for an individual to seek aid in communicating with himself. Although this is probably the basic problem for most of us, we are usually unaware of it. Rarer still is the person who seeks help because of communication problems **with God!** Most of us do not make the connection between concentration problems during prayer and psychological problems. It is unfortunate that so many Jews neglect their basic religious needs just because personal therapy seems irrelevant to them. The tendency is to let things improve over time, with constant effort at improving one's observance of the *mitzvos*. Perhaps more hours of learning are needed, or more *shiurim* in Torah, more Chassidic songs and warmth...but to go to therapy — Heaven forbid!

The sad fact is that very few *bnei aliyah* (those who ascend in Torah and its observance) are aware that emotional problems are the direct result of being disconnected from God. This unconscious separation of cause and effect into two distinct realms is the reason why their tremendous efforts to do God's will do not include solving their personal emotional problems. Nevertheless, after seeking help for a more superficial issue, such as a strained relationship with one's employer, one usually reaches much deeper levels. Through therapy and introspection, he eventually deals with his communication with God, his family, and himself. All are interlinked and therefore important for his well-being and *avodas Hashem*. The key link is between himself and God. Only a serious attempt in solving interpersonal problems can bring us to the root of all problems: our "selves" vis-à-vis Hashem; the created and the Creator.

What Is an Emotional Illness?

The practical aspect of Torah Therapy demands that we must first define the anomaly we propose to treat. The world of psychology offers many definitions for the degree of emotional imbalance necessary to consider it as an illness. There are those who propose to define a criterion for normality, such as "the ability to function within one's social framework." Therefore, any conduct that strays from this norm may be considered to be symptomatic of some emotional illness. Then there are those who deny any absolute criterion for judging one's normality, and say that only very severe disorders can be considered illnesses. Another interesting definition of emotional sickness is that it is an interpretation of reality which is not commonly accepted.

Obviously, it is no easy matter to define emotional sickness. Only He who created man is truly able to define his condition as healthy or sick. This definition is revealed by the Torah as a condition that is determined by *daas*, knowledge-in-depth. Lack of *daas* causes sickness. Health is to be achieved by gaining *daas*.

This is illustrated by the following statement of the Rambam: "He whose *daas* is full of pride and takes honors unto himself, and feels thereby respected, sins and is a *shoteh* (foolish or crazy)."[82] In other words, *daas*, when blemished by pride, is the cause of egocentricity, which brings sin, and that makes man a *shoteh*.

What is a *shoteh*? Our Sages say that a *shoteh* is, among other things, a person who sins. *"Ein adam oseh aveirah ela im kein nichnas bo ruach shtus"* (Man does not commit a sin unless the spirit of *shtus* has entered him).[83] A chronic *shoteh* is considered to be lacking in the *daas* that is required to fulfill *mitzvos*. Like a child under thirteen, or a person who was born deaf-mute, the *shoteh* is freed of responsibility because his *daas* is underdeveloped. The chronic *shoteh* is more familiarly known as the mentally ill.

---

82. Rambam, *Mishneh Torah, Hilchos Lulav*, 8:16.
83. *Sotah* 3a.

However, it seems that most of us are — at times — "mentally ill." Since sin is digression (*shoteh=soteh=*digress) from the way of Torah, then every time we sin, we express (and reinforce) some mental/emotional illness. Our *daas* is temporarily lacking, and that makes us temporarily "insane." Those few who do not digress may be said to be truly healthy. It sounds odd that most of us are considered temporarily insane, but that is because we unconsciously agree and identify with the **non-Torah** approach that draws an arbitrary line between normal and insane. In contrast, our Sages point out that we all suffer from emotional instability to a certain degree, as is characterized by sporadic lapses into lack of *daas*, namely, sins. Since we are sane most of the time, i.e. our *daas* is functioning satisfactorily, we are held responsible for our thoughts, words and actions.

In conclusion, we find no clear demarcation between ourselves and those who are obviously mentally ill. We are simply more in control because our *daas* lapses less frequently. But the fact that most of us occasionally digress from doing God's will is testimony to some underlying mental or emotional malady from which we all suffer to some extent. Since we all transgress from time to time ("There is no righteous person in the world who does good without [any] sin"[84]), then the only distinction between us and the chronically mentally ill is a matter of degree. It may be difficult to accept this definition, but only the most conservative and timid would deny its simple truth.

Proof of Our Universal Emotional Illness

What is the common denominator of all sicknesses, both physical and mental? Pain! All illnesses are imbalances of natural states that result in pain. If the pain is chronic, then it becomes

---

84. *Koheles 7, Sanhedrin* 46b.

suffering. Therefore it is logical to use the presence of pain or suffering as characteristic of illness.

If the cause of pain is something like a thorn stuck in one's finger, then the illness is short-term. The imbalance of nervous energy in that finger is quickly repaired by taking out the thorn. However, if the thorn had entered the flesh so deeply as to make it impossible to extract it, then the nervous imbalance will continue for days or even weeks. As a result, the pain becomes more "natural" and accepted as part of life (at least until the thorn will somehow dissolve).

Let's assume, for the purpose of this example, that this painful thorn gives rise to infection once a month for a day or two. The "normal" pain, to which our subject has accustomed himself during the passing weeks, suddenly increases for a day or two. He is reminded of the "sickness" he harbors: an intrusive thorn, deep within his flesh. The everyday imbalance of the finger's nervous energy is painfully brought to his attention by the increased imbalance of the infection. In other words, the infection is a temporary symptom of an underlying sickness, and the pain became "natural" and virtually unnoticeable.

This permanent thorn is analogous to the chronic human condition: separation from God. This is our lot: a constantly painful state from the day we were born until our day of judgement. As explained in section 1, this is our normal predetermined condition, meant to serve as a starting point from which to reach unity with our Creator. This "human condition" gives significance to our lives, for, without it, there is no reason to get up in the morning. Our lives are a constant effort — usually unconscious — to try and dig out the thorn, and the pain is always there.

We are always trying to reunite with God, even though we often think there are more mundane purposes to our lives. Every action that brings us closer to Him makes us healthier and happier, for we are decreasing our pain directly. On the other hand, every action that draws us away from Him makes us less healthy, thus increasing the pain proportionately.

We may conclude, therefore, that we are all emotionally or mentally ill to some degree. This internal imbalance may erupt in physical symptoms. But more commonplace are the symptoms of sins, which may be described as digressions from the God-given path of health. The eventual pain that results from sinning is the deeply felt disappointment, usually unconscious, of once again losing the path back to our Gan Eden. But the reverse happens when we observe *mitzvos*. We are healthier deep inside, and therefore happier, having made one more step back to our personal Eden, even though all this may be deeply unconscious.

The conclusion is obvious. Our state of health is dependent solely on our freedom of choice (as explained in the previous section), which is the expression of *daas*. We alone are responsible for our choices between *mitzvah* and sin, between good and evil, between health and sickness. This human attribute of controlling our freedom to choose is broadened and deepened with the aid of Torah.

What Is Pain?

Now that sickness has been defined in a way that applies to some degree to all people, we are prepared to define pain itself, which is truly common to all of mankind. There is no fundamental difference between physical pain that is registered by the brain upon receiving messages from the nervous system, and mental or emotional pain that is felt when we are lonely, hurt and depressed. Pain is the basic element of all imbalances of the human organism, whether short- or long-term.

Ultimately, pain is that familiar feeling of powerlessness and inner weakness. We cannot make it disappear. Its presence is overwhelming. We are hurt and frustrated.

This description of pain may be easily accepted in the sphere of emotional illness, but it seems strange to apply it to the sphere of physical illnesses. When we think of physical pain, we easily recall the familiar jolt of a sharp, nerve-produced sensation. It seems totally and utterly physical.

However, upon further consideration, we find that even physical pain is rooted in our mental/emotional status. We all know that we are sometimes unaware of a bruise or some other painful physical trauma if we are involved with, or concentrating on some other subject. The opposite is also true: the more we are involved with the pain, the greater it seems to grow. Therefore, **awareness** of pain, on whatever level, is a mental-emotional phenomenon. That means that even physical pain is basically a product of our **minds!**

The Treatment of Pain

Having reached some understanding of sickness and the pain associated with it, we may draw a conclusion regarding treatment of sickness and alleviation of pain. Treatment must be oriented towards the patient's emotions. More specifically, treatment must deal with one's self-image, within which his emotions are rooted, as well as with man's connection with God, which is the basic component of his spiritual makeup. If, as we have seen, all illness is rooted in the initial rupture in the "life-line" connecting man and his Creator, then treatment must perforce seal that rupture. Therefore, reconnecting man with God and with his own higher self is what health is all about. As the innate lifeline with God is repaired and revitalized, so does the pain gradually disappear. The means for implementing this cure is the Divine medicine: Torah.

The gradual healing through Torah and its observance is what Torah Therapy is all about. Actually, there is nothing novel about this method. Ever since the Torah was given at Har Sinai, this God-given cure was freely available to all takers. What Torah Therapy does is to emphasize certain aspects that are, sadly, unknown or unclear in our day and age — such as the vital connection between laws *bein adam la-Makom* (between man and God), and laws *bein adam la-chaveiro* (between man and man). Both paths are ultimately one.

If health is to be achieved by "opening" our connection with God, then it is no less dependent on an open, free-flowing connection with parents, family members, all Jews and all of mankind. Progress in one area should and does affect the other as well. Being in contact with others, breaking down our interpersonal barriers and building up relationships with other people helps us develop our connection with Hashem once more. The treatment should be initially easygoing and step-by-step. Our Sages teach us: "If you attempt to grasp much, you shall fail. But if you reach for a little, you shall succeed" (*Tafasta merubah lo tafasta; tafasta muatt tafasta*).[85]

Therefore, treatment begins with current problems of communication, especially with those people who are less rooted in one's past, such as employers and friends. Gradually, treatment deepens to include those who are much more deeply involved with the patient, such as parents and siblings. Obviously, the longer the relationship, especially an intimate one, the deeper the problems, and therefore the more difficult are they to solve. In all cases, Torah Therapy applies the precepts of Torah and our personal connection with God to these interpersonal problems.

Three-Level Therapy

When we begin to define our relationships with others (which

---

85. *Yoma* 80a.

influence our relationship with God and with ourselves), we find three basic levels. The external level is composed of newer relationships, which are easier to deal with because they are more obvious and less entrenched. They are often the conscious motive for consultation.

Examples of these are friends, partners, neighbors, parents-in-law, bosses and employees. Problems in these relationships may sometimes be overwhelming, such as a deepening feud between business partners, or a strained relationship with the next-door neighbor. Usually, these problems are resolved by seeing them as symptoms of deeper problems, and by dealing with the latter, the solutions to the initial problems become evident. (For example, a son-in-law's aggression towards his wife's parents may be reduced by giving him the independence that he fought for against his domineering parents.)

The middle-level relationships include our family (except for our parents), old friends, neighbors and acquaintances from childhood. These people influenced our development to a large degree, for better or for worse, for two reasons: They showed up early in our lives when we innocently accepted as true all that was offered. In addition, they figured in our lives over a long period of time.

The third and deepest level of relationships is with our parents. They are so deeply rooted in our conscious and unconscious that they deserve a chapter of their own. The everlasting bond with our parents will be discussed in the chapter on *kibbud av v'eim*, the commandment that deals with respecting one's parents.

What about the marital bond? On which level is it to be found? The answer is simple: on whatever level is reached, starting from the most external. Usually it is determined by two components: time and effort. How much time have the two been together, and how much have they invested in the marriage. At first, the marital bond is relatively superficial, even as it is exciting and all-encompassing. Gradually, the relationship deepens into the second level, and ultimately — after many years — into the third and deepest level. At that point, the marital relationship parallels the deep bond one has with his parents.

From "Easy" to "Difficult"

In dealing with personal problems, we start off with the easier, more obvious, first-level problems. As mentioned before, these lead to second-level and third-level problems, which are deeper and, therefore, more significant. For the same reason, solutions are usually attained on the first level, even as deeper problems are dealt with. In most cases in which relations with parents are problematic, they are the last to be resolved, if at all.

For example, a man may seek advice in how to deal with his boss, and eventually realize that the problem stems from his fear of his superiors, such as his older brothers. Then he may realize that the root of his fears is his father's callous disregard for his well-being as a child. By this time, chances are that our man has improved his relationship with his boss, who now seems less threatening (after our man has realized that the problems are his own fears). As insight enlightens and awareness expands on all three levels, he can also make peace with his brothers and even his father.

In most cases, the harmony achieved is far from perfect. True peace is barely attainable after a lifelong struggle. But the rewards of the effort we invest in **improving** our relationships are immediately visible and tremendously gratifying. The quality of our everyday lives changes — sometimes dramatically — from day to day.

Ball and Knife

The multi-layer dynamics of psychotherapy can be likened to a three-layered rubber ball. Man's ego, the center of this ball, is initially surrounded by the innermost layer, his relationship with his mother and father. The second layer, his relationships with his siblings and childhood acquaintances, "wraps" itself around the first layer. Similarly, the third and last layer encircles the second. This third layer is the most obvious one because it is external.

Now let us imagine a knife whose long blade is narrow at its tip, but begins to widen more and more as it approaches its wooden handle. When a person comes for therapy, he begins to cut into the "rubber ball" of his relationships in order to solve his present problems. Using his own strength and at his own speed, he thrusts the "knife" into this three-layered ball. As the tip of the knife enters the outer level and descends into the second and then the third level, towards the very center of this entity, the blade widens the gash more and more, starting from the "outside."

What this analogy demonstrates is the multi-layered nature of the problem and its solution. To effectively deal with current, primary-level problems, we must often "cut into our living flesh," wherein lie the roots of these problems. As we attempt to solve these deeper problems, especially those connected with our parents, we gradually solve the **external** problems with increasing ease. But what is obvious is that no problem can be completely solved without uncovering its roots in the deeper level of our being.

Most problems are not solved completely on any one of the three levels. Improvement is noticeable but gradual, and many new problems may arise, for life is a never-ending challenge. "The present is a constant source of challenge," says Rav

Dessler.[86] Even as one solves his problems with his boss, for example, he is at a loss when it comes to dealing with his non-cooperative secretary. Or, one might reach marital harmony after years of strife, only to discover that the problems are still basically unsolved. What had been achieved was external accord through temperance and self-regulation — which is, in itself, no small feat.

Magnifying the "Ball" of Communication

If we were to enter our deepest layer of communication — the center of our "ball" — and magnify it, we may discover a deeper level of communication with...ourselves! Most people can notice — with a little effort — that they are constantly conversing with themselves and with others **in their minds**. We discover through self-awareness that communication problems with parents, siblings or partners are reflections of conversations which we hold with ourselves. Those internal dialogues, usually unnoticed for all their constant presence, are the basis of our communication with those around us.

Thus we discover that our personal "ball of relationships and communication" is composed of four layers, rather than three. The deeper layers are more basic and also more difficult to change. The primary layer of communication with ourselves might be readily available for scrutiny and awareness, but it can be so inflexible when it must change! In this layer lies our self-image, which is deeply ingrained after many years of viewing ourselves through the eyes of people around us. It might seem that at this depth of our being, not much can be changed... until we discover an even deeper layer of communication.

The deepest level within the magnified center of the "ball"

---

86. *Michtav MeEliyahu*, vol. 3, p. 306.

is actually invisible. The center of a ball is a point that — by definition — has no dimensions whatsoever, and is therefore indiscernible. That point within ourselves is our Divine origin, the eternal link between ourselves and our infinite Creator. Our soul is constantly connected to God through this center of our being. This imperceptible "line of communication" is the root of the four layers of communication surrounding it.

The ball analogy demonstrates why our Divine link with God is the basis for all our relationships. A ball is spherical. The definition of a sphere is that all the points are equidistant from one point (the center) in three dimensions. Thus, the visible sphere is determined by the invisible point within its center. Likewise, our "ball of relationships" is defined and brought into existence by the Divine center within us. God is constantly creating the world for us, both within and without. He, however, remains unperceived by His creations. He creates and maintains existence. He is above all existence. Hence He is not to be grasped in any sense by those whose existence He enables. But He may be approached by one and all. Our most basic line of communication is with God, within the center of our beings.

Switching Direction in Communication

We are now better prepared to understand the idea that our orientation can be reversed. During childhood, we all formed the habit of orienting our thoughts and communications towards those around us. These were our lifelines, or so we thought. Now, through Torah and *mitzvos*, through maturation and awareness, we can reverse this process. While maintaining healthy relationships with those around us, we orient our dependencies "inwards," linking our lifeline with our ever-present Creator.

Let us follow this process in more detail. At and immediately following birth, the child creates his primary layer of communication with his mother, and then with his father. From about the age of two, he constructs a second layer of communication around the first, composed of his relationships with his brothers and sisters, other family members, old friends and acquaintances, teachers and other dominant figures, all of whom deeply impress the growing child. Over the years, a third layer develops, overlaying the second and first, which is made up of newer relationships, including present ones. As the third layer expands with newer and more numerous acquaintances, the first two layers "sink" deeper and deeper into man's unconscious. External relationships occupy our attention more and more, and the deeper relationships with our parents and family become more firmly entrenched within our psyche. They seem eternal and unchangeable, a natural part of our existence. These "facts of life" are the raw material from which our communication barriers are built.

If we find it difficult to communicate with those around us, we may likewise find it difficult to communicate with God within us. We expend much energy in our preoccupation with our external relationships, and thus have little strength left to converse with our invisible "Center." Nevertheless, that is exactly where we must orient our thoughts and emotions, because our goal is to reestablish our lost communication link with God. We have learned that — **consciously or not, every person is constantly seeking to be unified with the Divinity within his soul.** This goal gives meaning and significance to our lives.

Is this change of direction, this mental/emotional reorientation, feasible? Is it perhaps limited to the chosen few? "Of course!" is the answer to the first question, and "Of course not!" to the second. It is inconceivable to propose that our Divine Creator is so cruel as to throw us out of the Gan Eden and forever lock the doors, denying us the chance to return.

There are two basic ways by which one can reunite with God. One is the method proposed by all non-Jewish religions, which, as we shall see, has a major drawback. The other method is that which is proposed by the Torah. Torah Therapy, obviously, aims at assisting man to reunite with God through Torah and its observance. This God-given formula is foolproof and therefore healthy for all of mankind.

Connection with God, without Torah

Yes, connection with God can be achieved by non-Jews. The non-religious Jew, as well, may feel this same connection. This might initially seem strange, for we are taught that life without Torah is spiritual death, similar to fish without water.[87] How can the non-observant be included among those fortunate about whom the Torah states: "And you, who are devoted to God, your Lord, are all alive today"? Albeit every being that exists is of necessity connected to God through its very existence, there is no awareness of this eternal bond without the God-given tool of Torah. So how can a Torah-less person feel close to God?

The answer lies in the multi-layered nature of man, within whose center resides the Divine connection. When man switches his orientation from the external spheres of his relationships with the world to his central innermost point of existence, he discovers God. The reasons for this reorientation may be a desire for asceticism, in which all external pleasures are to be shunned. Or it might be motivated by the loss of hope and desire in finding meaning or significance in the world "outside." The ascetic saint is a noble figure in many religions, since he is

---

87. *Berachos* 61b. Rabbi Akiva offered this metaphor to Papus ben Yehuda when asked why he taught Torah at risk of death, after the Romans decreed that it was forbidden.

"realized" in his union with God, after eschewing the earthly bonds of this material world. For the same reason any man — even the simplest — may suddenly discover his inner Divinity when faced with death. In the midst of a life-and-death struggle, such as a furious battle, in which people are getting killed and everything external seems meaningless and insignificant, he may look inwards for the first time and discover his eternal unity with God. Only that inner spark of existence can somehow be grasped, and — at least for that moment — the man is truly religious! His life is in the hands of God. The world outside ceases to exist for the time being.

The "Jewish Connection"

Torah Therapy emphasizes the need to connect with God **by dealing correctly with the world around us.** It encourages us to use Torah to improve our lives in general, and specifically our relationships. The goal is to connect ourselves to God through love of His creation; we learn to love Him by loving the people around us. "Love your fellow man as yourself"[88] must be fulfilled in all its details before man can be considered holy. this therapeutic model urges us to practice, and not just discuss, all of the *mitzvos*, especially those between man and man. Observance of *bein adam la-chaveiro* is the only way we can break down the emotional walls separating us from those around us. By giving and receiving love, we learn to love life and living. **And through loving life we learn to love the One who gave us life and allowed us the pleasure of loving.**

By gradually severing the emotional bonds of "tied-up" relationships, we build new healthy bonds with God, as well as with those who are dear to us. We free our parents, partners and friends from our suffocating dependencies, and we rees-

---

88. *Bamidbar* 19:18.

tablish our total dependence on God alone through the central, utterly private connection deep within us. Our weakened ego is gradually refreshed from within, at the same time expanding and embracing the significant relationships which were denied entry in the past. As our trust in God increases, so does our capability to give love to those around us and receive their love in return.

The road to God without Torah is short but long. With Torah it is long but short. This lesson was taught to Rabbi Yehoshua ben Chananiah by a small boy, when he asked him the way to the city. Rabbi Yehoshua chose the "short but long" road, only to find himself entangled in underbrush and unable to reach his destination. He traced his steps back and decided to take the "long but short" road, and reached the city easily, although it took a while.

The path to God without Torah is short but long, because man tends to get entangled in interpersonal relationships, which may cause him to "cop out." His Creator, however, intended otherwise. Man's goal is to enjoy his earthly life as a servant of God, receiving and giving love from within and without. The road is long, but, with Torah, it is made "short" and smooth by being clearly bounded, straight and true. Taking the path of Torah means we near our destination day by day.

Torah Therapy encourages us to take this path, paying special attention to increasing harmony within oneself, with God, and with those who surround us. This is man's goal in life, the reason for which we were created, and can be very difficult at times. We must struggle along this path while simultaneously expressing our free will and choosing between good and evil. This is what ensures us of our rewards in *olam ha-ba*. The road is long and tiring. Torah, *mitzvos*, and the wise directions of our Sages are what support us and enable us to live fulfilling lives of interpersonal harmony and a loving and secure connection with God. The material world fuses with the spiritual, and we thus find happiness in the simple acts of closeness with both man and God. Therefore, "He with whom his fellow man is contented is a source of contentment for God as well."[89]

---

89. *Pirkei Avos* 3:13.

Chapter 7

The Principles of Torah Therapy

Permission to Heal

He who created man also created the very maladies that plague him. However, this enables Him to promise with certainty that "all the sickness that I have placed upon Egypt, I shall not place upon you, for I am God your healer."[90] On this basis, it behooves all those who suffer, physically or mentally, to seek help from the one and only healer — God. All efforts to alleviate the sickness by other means, human or otherwise, natural or artificial, could be viewed as disrespectful, apart from their futility. It may even increase the suffering instead of diminishing it.

The Torah thus teaches us, "*verapo yerapeh*"[91] (loosely translated to mean "the healer will heal"). It grants permission to human beings to heal one another. As such, they become "tools" in the hands of God, through whom He delivers help and health to those who suffer. This is the first principle of this therapy, and underlies the entire system. Man cannot heal man. What he can do is to **offer aid in opening the lines of connection between man and God, thereby allowing God's blessing to be received by man.**

---

90. *Shemos* 15:26.
91. *Shemos* 21:19.

117

This approach is empirically recognized by many medical practitioners, religious and irreligious. Many doctors will agree, at least privately, that the patient's recovery is no more due to the doctor's efforts than his original sickness. At most, the doctor increases the rate of recovery, decreases the pain involved, and offers solace and strength. Sometimes he does just the opposite.

That the true healer is God alone is emphasized repeatedly in Torah Therapy. The Torah Therapist, therefore, is no more than a messenger, albeit one who is entrusted with extremely important messages. The patient initially tends to view the therapist as his savior, yet he is reminded, at least in later discussions, that only God saves, and we humans are mere messengers. For better or for worse, the therapist cannot claim credit for whatever happens. Recovery or increased suffering is between the patient and his Maker. All cries for help must be directed to the true address, to God. Every session therefore includes the reminder that prayer to God is a must. We beseech Him for recovery "among all fellow sufferers of Israel."[92] All gratitude for recovery is likewise directed towards God first and only afterwards to His messengers: humans, herbs and medications, hospitals and so on.

Identifying the Healer

Even when the healer is fully cognizant of the fact that he is only the means by which the Divine Healer allays man's suffering, the **patient himself is usually in the dark**. This is one of the symptoms of all sicknesses which — as explained — are the result of painful separation from God since birth, and the consequent frustrated attempts at achieving peace and happiness

---

92. From the optional addition to the *berachah* in *Shemoneh Esrei: Refa'enu Hashem*....

through the external physical world. Therefore, all true cures and full recoveries are dependent on the patient's realization that God is the One Who both brings the malady and heals it. (There are some patients who, despite their firm belief that God is the only true healer, have not recovered from their sicknesses, the reason being that this is not yet "common knowledge." That is, the righteous must suffer because of the unrighteous. This will continue until all of mankind recognize that He Who decrees the sickness also provides its cure.)

However, this lesson cannot be taught from the start. The patient is usually unaware of it, and would feel spurned and "brushed off" if the therapist would express the idea that God is the only healer and that we must connect with Him and "heal ourselves," so to speak. Moreover, if the patient is an observant Jew, he might very well feel provoked by this statement and take it as condescension.

To further clarify, let us return to the sphere analogy. The "knife" of awareness begins to cut into the emotional layers from the outside. Initially, the patient wants to deal with problematic relationships in the present. These lead on to the deeper layers surrounding the ego. Only when the deepest layers of self-consciousness are dealt with in therapy can the knife of awareness continue to the very core of our being, to our Divine spark of connection with God. It may take a week, a month, a year, or several years. But only when the patient finally reaches the point at which he recognizes that his basic problem is a faulty connection with God is he able to assimilate the first principle of therapy: that God bestowed all maladies, and He alone can heal them. The Torah Therapist is only the means by which the cure may come about. As the knife deepens and widens its entry, so does this principle increase in significance, until it becomes the central point for recovery.

Thus we see how the subjects discussed in the sessions begin with everyday relationships and gradually evolve into the deeper relationships with parents, with the self, and finally, with God. Most attempts to hurry and skip one or more stages in this progression, in order to save time, will be ineffective and are usually harmful. Moreover, it seems that many of the emotional problems that block healthy communication and cause painful relationships stem from overeager parents and educators. In their understandable desire to instill the basic truth that God is the only true address for all needs, they often forgot the "means" to this "end," i.e. those methods of teaching which are tailored to each individual. "*Chanoch la-naar al pi darko*"[93] — educate the youth in accordance with his [individual] path. These wise words of King Shlomo must guide us in therapy, no less than in the classroom. By gradually taking the patient from one level to the next, at his own pace, Torah Therapy allows him to mentally and emotionally experience an expansion of self-consciousness. This reveals to him that his personal problems are external expressions of problems in communication and connection between his self and God. By dealing with the root of his problems, he naturally solves the external problems which were the initial motive for seeking help.

Truth — God's Signature

The second principle of Torah Therapy — which is also quite widely accepted (if not always practiced) in other schools of therapy — is the affirmation of truth as the only basis of health. The emphasis is on the patient's awareness of what is true or false in his life. For example, is he **truly** calm and peaceful, or is he actually angry and hurt deep within his heart? As we saw above, we often tend to deny or avoid confrontation with our negative feelings, as a defensive response to the social need to

---

93. *Mishlei* 22:6.

appear "normal." Even if this denial is unconscious, it is nevertheless untrue, and must be expressed. Despite the pain involved, the truth is the only means towards recovery.

Unlike other forms of therapy, however, this method stresses the significance of truth as a means of fulfilling our personal goal of cleaving to God. Truth is one of God's "characteristics," which, when emulated, enables us to grow closer to Him. We are instructed by our Sages: "As He is merciful, so must you be; as He offers sustenance, so must you...."[94] They also teach us that "the signature of the Holy One Blessed Be He is **truth**."[95] In this spirit, the patient is encouraged to open himself to the truth and share it, rather than continue wearing the masks that so many people use to avoid being themselves.

One is justified in asking the following question. How is one supposed to know "his truth"? After all, he has come for help because, more often than not, he is **unaware** of the deeper truths within his being. How can a person, who for many years disregarded "uncomfortable" facts of life until they became totally concealed from him, be encouraged to emulate God's attribute of truth? This may be a noble idea, but it seems more theoretical than practical!

However, the answer is to be found in the precise language of our Sages. Truth is described as God's **signature**. A signature is one's external characteristic, which can be found on the envelope of a personal letter. The letter's contents are folded and concealed within. But the sender can be identified by his unique signature, imprinted on the envelope.

God's "letter" to us is enclosed within the "envelope" of our daily existence. His "signature" is the instinctive need for truth that we recognize deep within ourselves. This common bond

---

94. *Shabbos* 133b.
95. *Sanhedrin* 64a.

with our Creator is a constant force that eventually drives us to open the "letter" of our lives. Its contents are God's words to us. This is Torah. It takes no small amount of courage to confront our need for truth and open the "envelope" of our lives. It is a slow and arduous process that sometimes becomes static and unmoving. It is also called "expansion of awareness," especially self-awareness. The natural tendency to search for the truth inside ourselves is God's signature in our lives.

This process of self-awareness is enabled by the "point of truth" (*nekudas ha-emes*), which Rav Dessler discusses.[96] This point can never be extinguished and is our bridge to God. For these two reasons — its constancy and its quality — we are justifiably expected to be truthful to ourselves, to expand our self-awareness, and to consciously bridge the gap (from our point of view) between ourselves and God. That means that from a limited subjective frame of reference (our personal lives), we are obligated by the Torah to expand our awareness and build ties of honesty with ourselves, our fellow man, and with God. Thus, we start out with the **love** of truth, and we realize our potential with the **product** of truth: love of life, man and God.

"Exercising" the Point of Truth

To benefit from the point of truth we possess, we must exercise it on a daily basis. Rav Dessler makes the analogy between our qualities, specifically the *middah* of truth, and our muscles. Muscles, by their very nature, must be used daily in order to maintain their elasticity. Otherwise, they gradually become dysfunctional until they atrophy. A person may slowly grow accustomed to carrying the load of an atrophied muscle to the point that he is unaware of its existence. By normal standards, in

---

96. *Michtav MeEliyahu*, vol. 1, pp. 52–58.

which all muscles function harmoniously, he is considered a cripple. Like all cripples, he must somehow compensate for the unused muscle by exerting other muscles above their normal level. This may lead to other problems, crippling him further.

This holds true for the quality of truth as well. It must be exercised in order to function at its peak. When this personal "open line" with God remains unused, it gradually "atrophies" until it is all but forgotten. The point of truth becomes just like a dead muscle that is carried around for years. Sadly — for this is the case more often than not — we were not encouraged in childhood to be honest with ourselves or with others. Our point of truth gradually fell into disuse, until, like a vestigial organ, it disappeared into our subconscious. We compensated by playing the game: "Everything's okay!" This game of pretense and falsehood eventually became "natural" and expected, and therefore "true" for ourselves and accepted by our figures of authority.

This game gave rise to the need for egocentric manipulation. After all, we have to survive in this "world of falsehood" (*alma d'shikra*). Every day, week by week, over years and years, the point of truth becomes more and more concealed within us, quite forgotten and even denied. It seems to have atrophied itself out of existence.

But it is always there, under the surface of our everyday lives. Once in a while we feel the drive for honesty and openness, or even complete truthfulness. The "atrophied muscle" of truth lies dormant, like a seed deep within the earth, yet sometimes sprouts and reveals itself, usually in response to traumatic events. When these events threaten our daily routine, and the very foundations of our "normal" lives grow unsteady, our fa(ade begins to crumble. The need for honesty and truth becomes more and more pressing until we rediscover the "signature" of God within our hearts. We reassess our existence. We reevaluate our personal ethics and beliefs. In light of the newly awakened power of truth, we courageously scrutinize ourselves under its glaring light. What is true? What is false? And we start reorganizing our lives and aligning our existence in accordance with the answers given by our point of truth.

What we had thought extinct turns out to be alive and well. The presence of honesty gradually yet increasingly makes itself known, as a disused muscle slowly becomes rehabilitated. Slowly, a complete overhaul of preconceived notions, prejudices and biases, and "natural" false fronts is made. In response to events that shock our normal lives, we tend to reassess our beliefs and existence, even before realizing that these are Divinely inspired aids to reawaken us.

The new perspectives based on the point of truth can be felt, among others things, in our relationships. Harmful relationships are discarded, and good ones are improved and strengthened. This new openness allows us to reopen clogged lines of communication, as well as to create new ones. We "make contact" with a friend, with ourselves, with our parents, and then with God. As the point of truth is exercised more and more, we become more efficient in direct and open communication with those surrounding us. We realize the previously unperceived characteristics in those who are dear to us. We relate directly and honestly to others, even to the bank teller, the postman or the office clerk.

Slowly, we change our daily lives. As our false fronts gradually dissolve, we find increasing pleasure in being more open and honest. Others find pleasure in us. We are thus approaching the directive issued by Rabban Gamliel that one should be "*tocho k'varo*."[97] Roughly translated, that means that one's external appearance should equal his internal state of being. In other

---

97. *Berachos* 28a. To be truly the same inside and outside is almost im-

words, one must be honest and truthful in his relationships with others. We strive to be open with each other, without fear of expressing our feelings, both good and bad (provided we don't hurt or provoke). We try to be honest with ourselves and with God. As the point of truth becomes more active, we feel an increasing life-flow streaming from deep within us, from our very soul, to all of life around us. Even the material world is part and parcel of this harmony, serenity and happiness. Through the "signature" of our Creator, we gradually open our hearts, only to discover the Divine "letter," which teaches us: "And you who are devoted to God, your Lord, are all alive today."[98]

Truth — Avodas Hashem (Devotion to God)

If the reactivation of the point of truth was initially prompted by our personal need to solve our problems, including our connection with God, this personal emphasis expands somewhat over a period of time. We find ourselves in a **giving** mode. Using the point of truth as our focus, we inevitably switch from taking to giving. We modestly offer our help in an effort to make the world a better place to live in (*tikun ha-olam*). As our awareness expands and includes others, we realize that we are expressing the divinity within us. This internal "holiness" inevitably overflows and touches those around us.

The natural change of emphasis from the personal to the general is rather unique to this type of therapy, compared to other therapies such as gestalt or transactional analysis (that aim at bettering one's personal world). Only through Torah is

---

possible. The fact is that hundreds of wise and righteous *Tanaaim* were kept out of the *Beis Midrash* of Yavneh because they could not meet this requisite. What could we say about our generation?

98. *Devarim* 4:4.

individual betterment **synonymous** with the general good. By focusing on our personal point of truth and using it to improve our lives, we are actually doing God's will and improving the lot of mankind. From our small personal world, we reach out to embrace our fellow man **without thinking about it**. There is no Messianic idealism with egocentric aspirations in this approach. Torah Therapy simply encourages us to grow internally, and leaves the external to "natural overflow."

This idea (that honest self-scrutiny is also a step forward for all mankind) is — as always — to be found in the Torah. We are taught that a person who eats of impure animals becomes impure himself. The word *v'nitmeitem*[99] (and you shall be impure) is written without the letter *alef*, and therefore may be read as *v'nitamtem*, which means "sealed off." This, in turn, refers to the parallel impurity of one's heart or spirit. What is an "impure" heart? The answer, says Rabbi Shlomo Wolbe, *z"l*, in his *sefer Alei Shur*,[100] is a heart **whose contents are sealed off from its owner's awareness.**

If lacking awareness is the spiritual counterpart of an impure body, then the expansion of awareness, or simply self-awareness, is the spiritual counterpart of a pure body. In this light, we may find deeper meaning in the Torah's words: "You should be holy for I am holy."[101] Since holiness involves self-purification, then this obligation to tread in the path of God refers, among other things, to self-awareness. In this context God's command may be obeyed in very practical terms, for we are all involved with ourselves.

We can conclude that this involvement with our consciousness is a cornerstone of *avodas Hashem*, service of the Lord. Ac-

---

99. *Vayikra* 11:43.
100. *Alei Shur* vol. 1, p. 136.
101. *Vayikra* 11:44.

tually, this mental and emotional activity is popularly known as *cheshbon ha-nefesh*, or spiritual accounting. It is referred to in the Torah in these words: *Al ken yomru ha-moshlim bo'u cheshbon.*[102] Our Sages explain the verse to mean that those who wish to rule their inclination must make a spiritual accounting within their world.[103] Using our point of truth and Torah as a guideline, we make account with ourselves on a daily basis, thereby improving our personal lives as well as benefiting the world around us.

This second principle of Torah Therapy, emphasizing truth and honesty, is part and parcel of our belief in God and Torah. It is not just a technique for self-improvement, as it would have been if this method were a branch of psychology or psychotherapy. As an integral part of Judaism, this therapy is a "language" with which the Torah Therapist reaches out to help his fellow man. The basis is that of equality and a common goal: service of *Hashem*.

"Adam L'amal Yulad"[104] (Man Is Born to Toil)

Now we may understand a third principle of Torah Therapy, which is the requirement that the patient invest unceasing effort in his own therapy. He must work hard, even at the expense of certain emotional pain, to improve his quality of life. This element of Torah therapy is quite foreign to all other therapies. The Torah's approach to the improvement of one's lot is in stark contrast to that of all other schools of thought. For a Jew, therapy is an **obligation!**

In the world of psychology, the word "therapy" implies that a person is lacking or sick, and is encouraged to seek help

---

102. *Bamidbar* 21:27.
103. *Bava Basra* 78b.
104. *Iyov* 5:7.

rather than suffer needlessly. The tacit assumption is that he, and he alone, is responsible for his health, and therefore is free to choose whether or not to come for help. He is at liberty to end his therapy at whatever stage he wishes, even at the expense of aggravating his situation. His life is his own, and therefore he may do with it as he wishes.

Torah Therapy is not an addition to the gallery of psychotherapies from which a person may choose as he sees fit. Rather, it is a concentrated expression of what the Torah requires from every Jew: improvement in the sphere of *middos* (attributes), and in his relationships with others, *bein adam la-chaveiro*. Having sworn to obey the covenant between God and His people, our forefathers passed on to us the moral heritage to do God's will as written in the Torah. This is the essence of Torah Therapy (and most of its techniques).

Of course, we still have free will to choose whether or not to obey the Torah's injunctions. But we are obliged to improve our relationships with others, with ourselves and with God. The fact that this requires hard work makes it no less obligatory. On the contrary, it makes it even more attractive in terms of the rewards. The harder the work, the greater the benefits (*l'fum tzaara agra*[105]).

This unique approach in therapy is practically applied from the very first session. Like other psychotherapies, the focal point of Torah Therapy is the therapeutic session, the dynamic dialogue between the therapist and the patient. Unlike other psychotherapies, however, this method stresses the interim between sessions as the actual medium for change and work. Since its basis is the requirement that each and every Jew invest effort in improving his quality of life within the context of his *avodas Hashem*, the Torah Therapist gently prods the patient to

---

105. *Pirkei Avos* 5:22.

work on himself between sessions. Psychotherapists, in contrast, are quite wary of demanding, however diplomatically, that the patient actually work on his own. It is sufficient that the patient chose to come to the session. Hopefully, its effects will gradually be felt in his life outside of the session. This approach is justified since the basis for the psychotherapeutic session is the purely voluntary motive of the patient.

In Torah Therapy, however, both the therapist and the patient are (ideally) motivated by their faith. The obligation imposed on all Jews to obey God's will is the underlying foundation — the session is merely a helpful aid. The working process is a constant everyday mission, whether or not one turns to therapy for help.

Therefore, the emphasis in Torah Therapy is on the "homework." Each session is partly devoted to checking on old "homework," and to suggesting new assignments, usually while reassigning the old ones. As a result, the real insights occur during the interval between sessions. These sessions serve to open the eyes and heart to what was previously completely, or partially unperceived. Lack of awareness is spiritual blindness. For one's sight to return, there must be more effort exerted than merely coming to therapy. The real work starts at home. Initially, the "homework" is not stressed. However, as the patient gradually grows in strength and efficiency, the weight of the therapy increases in the direction of constant daily efforts on his own. Therefore this technique may justifiably be considered "short-term therapy."

The Therapeutic Wonder

The fourth principle of Torah Therapy is the emphasis given to the spoken word as a primary tool for internal change. Of course, speech is significant in that it is unique to mankind as an expression of human mental and emotional capacities. This is described by the Torah: "...and He exhaled within his being the soul of life, and he became a living spirit."[106] The last two words are translated by *Onkelos* as "speaking spirit" (*ruach memalela*). In other words, the human *daas* (which combines mental and emotional components of his spirit) is expressed in speech.

Speech, in turn, is the medium for any human contact other than physical. However, speech is much more than just a means for connection between two or more people. There is a metaphysical aspect to it as well.

When we speak, we express our thought and/or feelings. These are quite mixed and unclear within our minds and hearts. Therefore, before they can be expressed, they must be defined, or — if you will — given boundaries. The need to communicate forces us to try and express our thoughts in words, and these, in turn, must be composed by us as we attempt to make order inside our minds and hearts. The process of speech is in essence a process of defining our thoughts or making boundaries between them. In other words, the need to communicate forces us to clarify our ideas for ourselves, and only then can we communicate them. It turns out that our first communication is with **ourselves**.

Perhaps this is the reason that the Torah describes speech as *hafla'ah*, which means "wonder." To understand what speech entails is to be struck with awe and wonder. (Rambam also used this term — *hafla'ah* — when naming the sections of his *sefer*, *Yad HaChazakah*, that deals with laws concerning speech: including oaths, *nedarim*, *hekdesh*, etc.) The Torah states: "...a man or woman who would *yafli* to make a *neder*...."[107] Rashi explains the word *yafli* as meaning *yafrish*, gives tithe, or takes out

---

106. *Bereishis* 2:7.
107. *Bamidbar* 6:2.

a part of himself.

It is hard to think of a greater miracle than the human ability to "take out part of himself" when he speaks. One may well wonder how it is that he is capable of choosing among thousands of semi-formed ideas, thoughts and emotions, and then immediately giving them clear and bounded expression, while simultaneously employing his brain, vocal cords, mouth, tongue and lips. Using his Divine spirit, man can direct his lower self to turn the spiritual into the physical. It is as if he is skimming the waters of *tohu va-vohu*,[108] and then creating from them a unique and distinctive world. (This analogy to God's creation of the world is not accidental. As we shall see in the last chapter, man is considered a "small world," which he creates in partnership with God.)

Tikun Ha-Olam (the World's "Completion") through Speech

The power of speech is one of man's basic tools for bringing the world to its completion or wholeness. It is stressed in the learning of Torah. We are told, *"v'higadeta l'vincha"*[109] — and you shall **tell** to your son; *"v'shinantam l'vanecha"*[110] — and you shall **teach** it to your sons. It is also emphasized in the realm of prayer, such as the obligation of saying *Shema Yisrael* out loud. This is common knowledge for the observant Jew. It is less well-known that speech is a powerful tool in therapy. When used wisely, it can improve and enhance a man's spiritual world and, in turn, the world as a whole.

King Shlomo, the wisest of men, long ago pointed out the therapeutic value of speech as a means for ventilation. *"De'agah*

---

108. *Bereishis* 1:2.
109. *Shemos* 13:8.
110. *Devarim* 6:7.

b'lev ish yash'chenah,"[111] he taught — worry in man's heart should be talked out. These words are explained by Rashi, in the second meaning given there, as referring to the value of expressing one's anxieties to someone else in order to obtain good advice. Experience teaches that even before receiving advice, there is great benefit in revealing one's worries and sharing one's heavy thoughts with another empathic person. But there may be further advantage in ventilating anxieties.

As mentioned above, talking is the process of extracting some of our blurred ideas and defining them. This process also serves to externalize the thought and thus get rid of it to a large extent. Anxieties or worries that are expressed verbally are also exorcized from us, if not completely, then at least partially. To the degree that they leave us, our spirits are lightened.

The process of *tikun* through speech refers not only to our personal world, but, simultaneously, to the world at large. Since this improvement finds expression in better conduct and positive actions, then it follows that the world around us benefits from our personal *tikun*. The macro is inextricably bound with the micro, just as the body as a whole is influenced by the health of each of its parts. Torah encourages us to "save" the world by working on ourselves.

The Mouth — Spout or Funnel?

It is becoming clear that the mouth, as the medium of speech, is of greater significance than we have assumed until now. This is alluded to by the prophet Yirmiyahu in his words, "Their faith was lost; it was cut off from their mouths."[112] These last words seem redundant. If Bnei Yisrael lost their faith, obviously they wouldn't express it! *Metzudas David* offers two seemingly para-

---

111. *Mishlei* 12:25.
112. *Yirmiyahu* 7:28.

doxical answers concerning this:

How is it known that people have lost their faith? When their mouths produce speech that is lacking **expressions of faith**. In this case, the mouth serves as a spout, or — if you will — a loudspeaker, that gives voice to the silent words of the mind and heart.

Even when faith is lost, it may be gradually restored by "mouthing" words of faith. In this sense the mouth serves as a funnel which receives from the outside and directs the flow towards the heart and mind. The author of the *Sefer HaChinuch* tells us that our hearts are led by the deeds and acts we do. We may likewise suggest that our **words** can influence our emotions too. This is popularly referred to as self-suggestion, and is made all the more effective when expressed out loud and in words.

Torah Therapy uses the mouth both as a spout and as a funnel. When there are negative feelings and thoughts that are internal blocks to communication, they are given expression and expelled by using the mouth as a spout. The spiritual poison is pushed out. At the same time, positive words of spiritual and personal value are repeated out loud by the patient, with the distinct purpose of imprinting their contents deep within his heart. The mouth now acts as a funnel, receiving values which are initially external, but gradually become internalized.

How Is Daas Expressed?

The mouth can be viewed as the crossroads between the mind's mental capacities, originating in the brain, and the powers of emotions and imagination, originating in the heart. When these uniquely human forces come together, they are called *daas*. The spiritual expression of *daas* is *ratzon* (will) and its physical expression is speech. For this reason, the development of a person as a *bar-daas* can be assessed, to a large extent, by his speech.

Conversely, when a person consciously attempts to elevate the content and form of his verbal expression, he draws forth the nobler parts of his mind from one end, and the more elevated emotions of his heart from the other. These forces converge within his *daas*, and the result is that the external words, expressing his ambition for improvement, are now made internal, part and parcel of one's being. His **will** is thus elevated even as his words reflect this *aliyah*.

The Therapist as a Patient

The fifth and last principle of Torah Therapy is that the therapist must himself be a patient at all times. For, as we said above, we are all ailing spiritually and mentally, as evidenced by our sins. (Health, we defined, is doing God's will, which is always to our benefit. When we transgress His *mitzvos*, we perforce become unhealthy.) Since "there is no righteous person who does good without sin," the therapist must also be treated, righteous as he may be. As our Sages teach us, "a prisoner cannot free himself from prison."[113]

The Talmud tells the story of Rabbi Yochanan, who healed his friend, Rabbi Chia bar Abba, simply by offering him his hand, curing him completely. But when Rabbi Yochanan fell sick, he was healed not by himself, but by his friend Rabbi Chanina, who likewise gave him his hand and put him on his feet. Obviously, the healer needs someone else to heal him. Why this is so the Talmud does not say.

---

113. *Berachos* 5b.

The Power of a Bribe

Rav Dessler in *Michtav MeEliyahu* offers the answer as it appears in the Torah: "… for bribery blinds the eyes of the wise and distorts the words of the righteous."[114] He explains that even a penny, when given as a bribe, is capable of influencing the heart and mind of a judge, irrespective of his stature. The largest bribe, and therefore the most influential, is man's love for himself. Just imagine how great the power of the bribe is when a man is supposed to judge — and "treat" — **himself!** Whether he tends to favor himself, or even when he judges himself harshly, it is inevitable that he will sway from the truth. He is only human!

Therefore, the Sages required that each person choose a rabbi for himself. "*Aseh lecha rav*"[115] is a maxim that applies to every Jew, great or small, for he must hear from another that which he is incapable of hearing from himself. This too is learned from the Torah: "In accordance with the Torah that they [the wise men of your generation] shall teach you… so you shall act, [and] you may not veer from their words [neither] right [nor] left."[116]

In other words, one of the basic tenets of Judaism is the acknowledgement of the higher authority of our Sages, specifically of one's personal rabbi. Self-bias is a very strong force. We are blinded by the natural bribe of our concern for our welfare. Therefore, even a rabbi who is the authority for others must himself turn to some other authority for guidance and "treatment." All people are ultimately guided by the One, Whose authority is unquestionable and Whose will is Torah.

As a result of this approach, both therapist and patient are

---

114. *Devarim* 16:19.
115. *Pirkei Avos* 1:6.
116. *Devarim* 17:11.

on equal footing. The relationship between them is essentially egalitarian. Although the obvious difference is that the former offers and the latter accepts, it does not preclude the possibility that they switch roles. The teacher often learns from his student even though, being wiser and more learned, he usually teaches and the student usually learns. In any case, the teacher is himself a student of other teachers.

This state of learning and receiving guidance is basic to all Jews. Therefore, it is incumbent on the Torah Therapist to make this equality clear to the patient. We are all students of our rabbis and therefore of God. What we accept we may pass on in the name of our teachers. The patient likewise is encouraged to counsel those who are dependent on him, such as his children. This is more than permission; this is his obligation. The common denominator of all is: **we are the servants of God**.

Chapter 8

Honoring One's Parents

Parental Respect and Therapy

One of the most emphasized *mitzvos* in Torah Therapy is the obligation to honor one's parents. The issue of parental respect and honor must be addressed from the start of therapy, for all problems ultimately relate to our relationships with our parents. This emphasis becomes more obvious and therefore more pronounced from session to session, to the degree that the correct observance of this commandment is used to assess one's improvement in therapy. Why is this so?

Upon close inspection of our relationships with people around us, especially intimate ones, we always discover that our relationships with our parents are highly influential. The significance of the emotional connection with one's parents cannot be overly exaggerated.

It is evident that patterns of behavior and emotions which we formed in our early years vis-à-vis our parents tend to repeat themselves time and again — with variations, of course — with our spouses, children and friends. Inadvertently, we copy these models of our childhood relationships, even though we may sometimes strongly prefer to change them.

Parental "Dress" (Levush)

The special bond with our parents is clarified by Rabbi Yitzchak Luria, the famous Ari *z"l*. His teachings were written down by his student Rabbi Chaim Vital. The Ari explains the *mitzvah* of "Honor your father and mother"[117] as follows:

"His father gives him [the *neshamah*, soul] his [part]...which becomes a sort of covering for him, that serves to guide him in this world, to observe *mitzvos* and to learn Torah. For the newborn is small and how will he know by himself how to follow the way of Torah and *mitzvos*, if not by means of that part of his father's soul that aids and guides him in this direction. Likewise, his mother gives his soul [a *levush*]...such that **everything that man does in this world includes part of his father and mother**, for they are his aides and guides in this world, by means of this *levush* that covers his soul, as mentioned. Furthermore, all the gifts that are offered him from Heaven may be received **only by means of this covering**. Thus is the partnership of the parents with the newborn clarified, and so [we understand] *kibbud av v'eim*, [the commandment of] honoring one's father and mother...."[118]

This explanation of the obligation to honor our parents needs clarification in one area: what is *levush*? Our direct experience of our parents' role within our "inner dialogues" allows us to translate the word *levush* as the internalized parent figure of both father and mother. Besides "hearing" our parents' voices with our "inner ear," we also seem to view things and evaluate them through the eyes of one or both of our parents.

It is common knowledge that values instilled in us by our parents from early childhood continue to guide us through the years — for better or for worse — unless we make a great effort

---

117. *Shemos* 20:12.
118. Rabbi Chaim Vital, *Shaar HaMitzvos, Shemos* 20:11.

to change them. We learned in the first section that as children we lacked the critical faculty of *daas*. Therefore, we innocently internalized their words over the years. We also had their faces imprinted on our minds, along with the authoritative and unquestioned tones of their voices. Therefore, even when our parents are very distant in our lives, or even after their deaths, they are continuously present **within our minds and hearts**.

What we have just learned from the Ari *z"l* is mind-boggling. This parental *levush* of both parents is not only constantly by our side, for better or for worse; it also serves as a **screen** through which we experience the world outside us or within us. This is a staggering idea! Whatever we feel or think or sense must necessarily be filtered and translated by these internalized figures of authority. We seemingly have no mind of our own, unless we term this *levush* as "our mind." Having made our parents an internal filtering system, we must deal directly with them, in person and in our minds, in order to influence the way **we experience ourselves and our world**. This is what the commandment to honor our parents is all about.

Working with Imagination

Based on the new understanding of *kibbud av v'eim*, we may reach the logical conclusion that, to obey this commandment, we must deal predominantly with our "internalized" parents. Actually, we really don't have much choice if we want to choose our own way of life. As sons and daughters, we wish to take the good that we internalized from them and filter **out** those elements that seem negative to us. Of course we must honor our parents in person and not just in theory. But our attitude towards them is directly influenced by our attitude towards our internalized parents.

The external expression of this attitude towards our parents is very low-key compared to the emotions we experience "within." The real dialogue with our parents is constantly going on in our minds and hearts, both consciously and unconsciously. And whether this dialogue is of a fixed nature or a dynamic one (depending on our choice, as we shall explain), it is the only medium by which we experience our existence. Our parental *levush* is our personal lens through which we view the world, ourselves and even God.

With this new comprehension, we can now understand the words of the Malbim in his explanation of the fifth commandment, that of *kibbud av v'eim*. He refers to the words added to the commandment: "*u-l'ma'an yitav lach*,"[119] (so that it shall be better for you):

> In the second *luchos* "so that it shall be better for you" was added, because there are people who believe that the world is more evil than good. They therefore despise their lives and curse their parents for having brought them into this world of suffering (as may be understood from the *pasuk* in *Mishlei*: "He who curses his father and mother shall have his candle extinguished by the heart of darkness"). Therefore, the words *u-l'ma'an yitav lach* were added, [to teach us] that by honoring your father and mother and **thinking that life is good, it really will be better for you.**

In a few terse words, the Malbim brings up the problems concerning our filial obligations to honor our parents, and the solution to these problems. There is a causative connection between our experience of the world and our attitude towards our parents, who **brought** us into this world. It is almost like an equation: if our life experience is bad, then our feelings towards our parents are negative, even to the extreme degree of cursing them. Likewise, if our experience of this world is good, then our attitude towards our parents is positive. But how can we

---

119. *Devarim* 5:16.

change a negative attitude to a positive one?

Here is where the Malbim reveals the "therapy" offered by Torah. The words *l'ma'an yitav lach* — so that it shall be better for you — contain the answer. The Malbim brings the *pasuk* from *Mishlei*[120] to show that the negative behavior of cursing one's parents causes a process of spiritual deterioration. The light within one's soul gradually dims until it flickers out in the heart of darkness.

The opposite is no less true when we honor our parents. By observing this *mitzvah*, we make our lives brighter and more enjoyable. By acting and thinking positively in regards to our father and mother, we actually feel better about ourselves and the world in general. *U-l'ma'an yitav lach* contains this equation:

$$\text{life} = \text{parents}$$

By changing one side of the equation, we naturally change the other as well. Just as deprecating our parents results in deprecating ourselves and making our lives miserable, so too, by honoring them we honor ourselves and find life more and more enjoyable and meaningful. The choice is ours.

The Role of Imagination in Observing Kibbud Av V'eim

We have even more to learn from the Malbim. With one word he answers a difficult question. How can we change the above parent-life equation? On the surface it seems preordained and unchangeable, a fact of life that God decreed for each of us, whether we like it or not. Especially after learning from the Ari z"l that we are forced to view our existence solely through the internalized "eyes" of our parents, this question becomes critical. We seem to be firmly trapped within our existential prison, whose bars were constructed by our parents. But then, they too

---

120. *Mishlei* 20:20.

were prisoners, and their prison was constructed likewise by their parents, and so on and so forth, stretching back to the very beginning of time.

The answer lies in the exact wording the Malbim used. "By honoring your father and mother and **thinking** that life is good, it really will be for you." The Malbim is revealing the Torah way to change both sides of the parent-life equation. The parental side is changed by observing the commandment of honoring our parents, even if its fulfillment is initially relatively superficial. The life side of the equation is changed simultaneously by **thinking or imagining** that life is good. Today this is termed "positive thinking." Thus the Torah teaches us that we are definitely **not** imprisoned within the *levush* given to our souls by our parents. We are empowered to change this "screen" and, consequently, our lives by changing our attitudes towards our parents in thought and action, (which is what this *mitzvah* entails), and likewise changing our attitude towards life and ourselves. Our hearts are influenced by our actions as well as our imaginations. Our lives are essentially in our own hands.

The power of imagination was discussed at length in the first part of the book. Now, in reference to the commandment to honor our father and mother, we see its practical application. Likewise, all *mitzvos* include the two basic elements of action and thought (or imagination). Only by applying these two elements simultaneously can we effectively change our lives. Our subjective existence is the product of our "hearts," which, in turn, are influenced by thought and action.

Imagination Versus Reality

The difficulty in changing our thought patterns regarding our parents and our lives is the seeming contradiction between the present reality and the desired imagined existence. At first glance, the idea of changing our attitude towards our parents by employing our imagination seems a naive one. Why fool ourselves? Aren't our lives — and our parents — exactly the way we see and know them? Are we supposed to regress to childhood fantasies?

The fact is that we are accustomed to viewing the external world as real, and treating the internal world of thoughts and imagination as false and unsubstantiated. Our senses receive clear and constant images, sounds and smells, thereby building our faith in a "natural" unchanging world of physical reality around us. Our minds, however, are in constant flux. We therefore attribute the term "reality" to the constant world of nature, and "unreality" to the mental and emotional constructions of our hearts and minds. This, of course, is God's plan for us. We are led from childhood to regard the external world as reality and the internal world as imagination. (In fact, the etymological roots of the word "imagine" all relate to "likenesses" and images, that is, creating a mental image or likeness that is not actually present and real.)

The Malbim's suggestion to **think** that our parents are honorable and that life is good seems like daydreaming, if not an outright distortion of the truth. If this is one's approach to the words *l'ma'an yitav lach*, he shall have to make do with the usual interpretation: that it shall be good for you in the next world (as payment for this important *mitzvah*).

However, the Malbim is not alone in his understanding of what the Torah advises us regarding the practical use of one's imagination. The Chayei Adam also identifies the imagination as a primary tool in observing the commandment to honor our father and mother.[121] He explains that the *mitzvah* is observed on three parallel levels: thought, speech and action. He goes on to prove that the most important of the three is **thought**. How

---

121. Rabbi Avraham Danzig, *Chayei Adam* 67:3.

can parental honor be observed in one's heart?

The answer of the Chayei Adam is as follows: "That is to say, he honors them in his heart, for they are important in his eyes and his heart. In other words, he must **imagine** that they are great and respected personages, even though others might not regard them as important at all. And this is the basis of honoring, for if this is absent, then 'in his mouth and lips he honors me, but his heart is distant from me.'"[122]

Thus we learn that there is a straightforward obligation to observe one of the most important *mitzvos*, honoring our father and mother, by use of the imagination. Reality, as seen by others, is irrelevant. We must create a positive life-script in our mind's eye, making our parents figures of nobility and significance, and learn thereby to honor them. The Torah's injunction to honor our parents refers to our **internal** spiritual existence, not to the external "objective" view of life.

Conclusion

We saw at the beginning of this chapter how our lives are inextricably bound up with those of our parents. The result, we explained, is that all of our communication problems and interpersonal blocks are rooted to a large degree in our relationships with one or both parents. The logical conclusion is that we are obliged — for our own sakes — to better our lives by improving our relationships with our parents. The way to do this is by observing *kibbud horim* (parental respect) by use of our imagination, **as well** as in actual fact. The end result of this spiritual journey is *l'ma'an yitav lach*.

The means by which we must fulfill this *mitzvah*, our imagination, is the expression of our minds and heart in tandem, i.e. our *daas*. This is where the option of employing our freedom of

---

122. *Yeshayahu* 29:13.

will comes in — no small task. To effectively use our imagination we must overcome deeply ingrained habits of thought, feelings and action, which, as children, we felt were true and natural. Now, as adults, we must use our *daas* to reconstruct our lives on a positive and optimistic basis.

This is arduous and slow work... but extremely gratifying, as the Torah promises. Gradually we supplant the darkness of our lives, and let the light of love glow stronger and stronger. By honoring our parents in our hearts and minds, and not just in action, we connect to them on a healthy basis and, **through them**, to all those we love. Life becomes more beautiful, for we have achieved — to some degree at least — *l'ma'an yitav lach*, "for it [life] shall be good for you."

Chapter 9

Researching the Past — Mituk Ha-Dinim

The Past That Underlies the Present

An important element in treatment through Torah Therapy is the discussion and understanding of one's personal history. The past, in and of itself, is **not** the main point. As Rav Dessler writes:[123]

> The past consists of mere memories,
> The future is just wishful fantasies,
> The present — avail yourself within it,
> It is your life, filled with challenges.

The past is important insofar as it serves the present. We need to research the past to more fully avail ourselves of the present. To enhance our life from day to day, we must sometimes clear up "unfinished business" from the past. This is no small feat when we are emotionally blocked in our relationships. As discussed above, these blocks were influenced greatly by our childhood and our relationships with our parents. Our life-scripts are rooted in the past, and thus the past must be addressed if we wish to change our lives and achieve harmony in the present. Of course, later relationships also serve to hinder

---

123. *Michtav MeEliyahu,* vol. 3.

this process. The difficulties we experience in the present are enough to warrant our dealing with their roots. Yet this is difficult in itself.

This is not to say that we must always research our personal history in order to improve our present mode of life. There are times when this is superfluous. There are also times when it might be risky or even dangerous. If the present problem is relatively simple, specific or straightforward, then practical advice is sufficient to overcome it.

For example, a young couple might find themselves in a deteriorating relationship, the future of which is laden with doubt and worry. At first glance, the situation is complex and rooted in personal problems. However, it sometimes turns out that what is lacking is no more than practical guidance to the "mysteries" of married life. This ignorance initiated a series of disappointments that led to heartbreak, coupled with accusations, and mixed with loss of self-esteem, remorse, guilt and second thoughts. Having reached a painful impasse, the young couple turned to Torah Therapy as a last resort. They received intensive counseling, and, in a short time, rebuilt their relationship on a positive and harmonious basis.

The Threatening Past

More often, we come across situations that preclude dealing with the past, not because they are simple, but because they are complex to the degree of being threatening if past memories are "brought back to life." The patient (or couple) is obviously suffering in the present because of previous emotional problems, especially with one or both of his parents, which he or she managed to cover up over the years. Childhood experiences of pain, guilt, frustration and anger had been efficiently — or at least sufficiently — bottled up in the unconscious. These powerful emotions — both then and now — are unbearable. If allowed to surface, they may cause an explosion and a traumatic cessation of the present way of life, problematic as it is. Deep depression or destructive rage may result from reliving these difficult memories. That is certainly not the purpose of the therapy. As important as the past is, serving as the basis of the present, it must remained "sealed" as long as the patient is not ready to benefit from it. There is no *mitzvah* per se to deal with the past.

How do we know whether the past is too threatening to be dealt with? When can we be assured that reliving difficult experiences with our parents or others will actually aid us in our present relationships? Let us turn to our Sages and their *daas Torah* to learn the answers to our questions. If living is to be found in the vibrant present, and dealing with past experiences of pain may lead to trauma, perhaps we should desist from bringing up the past altogether? Who says that the end justifies the means? Perhaps this approach was unintentionally borrowed from general psychotherapy, and runs counter to Torah values.

Chesed and Din

In order to answer our question from the Torah point of view, we require a basic understanding of two opposing qualities called *chesed* and *din*. Both are used in conjunction by God to regulate the world. *Chesed* may be defined as the quality of infinite love, translated into action. *Din* may be explained as the quality of justice and retribution which bounds and limits the grace and love that God bestows upon the world. The combination of both qualities, in varying forms and proportions, is termed *rachamim*, mercy.

A simple example may illustrate these ideas. A father's love for his child is sometimes expressed in punishment, when the child needs a heavier hand to control erratic behavior. If, for example, the child runs heedlessly onto the street after a strict warning to hold his father's hand, he must be firmly punished, lest he endanger his life in the future. Although from the child's point of view his father is cruel at that moment, what he is actually receiving is a dose of mercy, even though it hurts. Thus *rachamim* is expressed by the father, who, filled with love and responsibility, must sometimes curb his *chesed*, and apply *din* towards his child.

In similar fashion God regulates our lives. His purpose — from our limited point of view — is to grant us inifinite love and goodness. However, like small children, we are incapable of accepting His gifts because our egos stand in the way. Therefore, in His mercy, He allows us to gradually "work" on our egos (our *yetzer ha-ra*), and, in proportion, discover His infinite love for us. We must strive to overcome the spiritual darkness into which we are born, in order to discover God's Divine light. This darkness is the result of the quality of *din*.

Middas ha-din is used by God to hide His constant presence. We are left feeling alone, isolated and disconnected. This is our basic existential pain, which, as discussed above, is required for our benefit. We have already seen (in chapter 1) that this disconnection is present from the moment of birth, when the "umbilical cord" that connected us to our Creator is severed. The attribute of *din* intensifies over the years by stressful problems of all sorts, especially in interpersonal relationships. Our seeming isolation is enhanced on all levels; physical, emotional and mental. Existential questions, such as the purpose of life and self-identification, are the inevitable result. All these are *dinim*, which serve to weigh down on our souls, hiding thereby the ever-loving presence and guidance of God.

From Darkness to Light

Rav Dessler tells of a true story about a Jew who was concealed in a dark, hidden cellar during the Holocaust. Terrified of leaving, he spent the years in total blackness, but his basic requirements for food and water were readily available. When the war ended, the Allied soldiers discovered his hiding place and brought him out to street level. When he reached the street, he screamed in terror and pain from the searing light of day, and quickly returned to the familiar darkness of his cellar. It took much persuasion and gentle prodding to gradually reaccustom him to the light of day.

This phenomenon is referred to by Kind David in *Tehillim*: "For sun and protection is God, our Lord."[124] The sun is the source of heat, energy and light for our world, without which nothing can live or grow. But this blessing can also be a curse, for the sun can also scorch. For example, if a person was to go to the beach in the beginning of the summer after a long winter, and his skin is white, he would have to be careful. His purpose is to enjoy the sun, not to suffer from it. Therefore he would have to minimize his initial exposure to the sun's rays, and allow his skin to tan gradually from time to time. Shade must be used more often at the beginning if he wishes to avoid sunburn. The sun is a warm blessing as long as man knows how and where to limit its use.

To summarize, the process of enlightenment, coming out of darkness and into the light, must be one of many wise and gradual steps. This is true of the spiritual world, as well as the physical world. The process of leaving the darkness of isolation and loneliness and discovering the Divine light of God must be a gradual, step-by-step process, unique to every individual.

"For Sun and Protection Is God, Our Lord"

The Torah attributes several names to our Creator. According to

---

124. *Tehillim* 84:12.

the principle "as His name is, so is He," the names refer to different aspects with which God deals with us. The name God (*shem havaya*) refers to the aspect of love and mercy (*rachamim*). The name Lord (*Elokim*, meaning the all-powerful ruler) refers to the aspect of justice (*din*).

King David makes the analogy between the sun and God (the aspect of mercy), and between protection from the sun and the Lord (the aspect of justice). In loving us infinitely, God is also merciful in that He combines His love with *din* **in order to protect us.** It is amazing to discover that *din*, which is often painful and seemingly negative, is actually beneficial and merciful. It serves to protect us from the sudden glare of God's Divine light.

We saw above how the many "problems" which confront us from childhood create a "blind," through which we are viewed by God, even as He is concealed from us. However, when we "wake up" and attempt to discover His all-pervading presence, these same "problems" serve to protect us from the sudden revelation for which we are unprepared. The spiritual path of Torah is long and arduous not because God is hiding from us, but because He mercifully creates challenges for us with the sole purpose of strengthening our spirits as preparation for His revelation.

It is difficult — and sometimes painful — to rid ourselves of bad habits of thought and action and to acquire new ones. But this very same difficulty enables each one of us, in his own unique way and at his own time, to gradually be strong enough to live with God at his side, so to speak. The fruits of our labors are in proportion to the effort we invest. Therefore, this amazing process of "sun and protection," of *chesed* and *din*, is uniquely personal. Even when we fall prey to the trials with which He challenges us, there is benefit in it for us. For after every fall (*yeridah*) there is a comeback (*aliyah*). "Seven times the righteous person falls, and he rises."[125]

For this reason, we are forewarned by our Sages not to reach too high or too fast in our desire to come closer to God. We should climb — not leap — lest we fall. A famous example of tragic consequences is the Talmud's description of the four great rabbis who "entered the *pardes,*"[126] the mystical *kabbalah,* from which only Rabbi Akiva exited peacefully. Of the other three, one renounced his faith, another died, and the third lost his mind. The Divine light they discovered was too great for them to bear. The lesson to be learned is that one should first go through the "lower" spheres of *halachah* and Talmud, in depth and in practice, before delving into the mystical secrets of the Torah. Their light can be searing.

The Dinim of the Past

We are now equipped to deal with the question posed above. When — if at all — is it appropriate and beneficial to "dig up" the repressed pain of the past? We understand that the many events that we suffered both in early childhood and later on as well, which were painful or traumatic, were really *dinim kashim* (hard experiences), accumulating one "on top" of the next, much as the layers of an onion overlap to form a hard exterior. Inasmuch as this external covering protects the inside, they must be uncovered for us to eat the food inside. In order to realize our internal freedom to unite with God, we must peel away the many layers that protected us in the past. In the present, they deny us from "connecting" with those we love and, simultaneously, with our God. This is the greatest challenge offered us by our Creator. It is also quite painful, especially at the start.

---

125. *Mishlei* 24:16.
126. *Chagigah* 14b.

Let us consider the following example. Shmuel suffered for years from the domineering attitude of his employer. He had been the object of much criticism, disparagement and even ridicule. His anger and frustration, having been suppressed for years, are finally threatened to erupt. Although fear of losing his job enabled him to restrain himself, he had reached a breaking point. After years of managing to get along by suppressing his negative feelings and turning the other cheek, Shmuel was about to explode.

The repressed emotions began surfacing, and Shmuel agitatedly started attacking his employer behind his back, especially at home. His usual wariness when speaking of others (so that he not transgress in *lashon ha-ra*) was forgotten. If in the past he described his boss as opinionated and not too friendly, now he cursed him as a tyrannical egomaniac. He became depressed and started neglecting both his job and his family affairs. He was encouraged to seek counsel and, with great skepticism, he agreed.

Shmuel gave vent to his grievances and received an empathic ear. He was encouraged to describe his emotions in as much detail as possible, rather than rant about the shortcomings of his boss. Finally, he accepted the suggestion to write a letter to his employer, describing these emotions, with as little accusation as possible. With this letter in hand to bolster him, Shmuel confronted his boss at a preplanned appointment, and — for the first time — told him the truth.

As expected, the initial reaction wasn't pleasant. But Shmuel felt cleansed and relatively at peace with himself. To his surprise, the boss "toned down" and continued to employ Shmuel, to everyone's benefit.

Another Layer, and Another, and...

The work situation gradually improved. Shmuel became more

confident and more honest with himself. He realized how fearful he had been of expressing his negative emotions. At this point, Shmuel became aware that he had been harboring grievances against his wife, who also tended to be domineering towards him. For the first time in his life, he admitted to himself that, despite his love and appreciation of his wife, he had accumulated unexpressed anger and grievances towards her. Now, having removed the external layer of negative emotions towards his **employer**, he found himself dealing with the next layer that concerned his lifelong **mate**.

This project was much more difficult and confusing. To honestly deal with all his feelings towards his wife, negative as well as positive, Shmuel needed much courage, strength, patience with himself and understanding. However, after he had begun to discuss this layer (in order to strengthen his marriage), he eventually discovered a deeper layer.

Shmuel came to grips with the long-repressed knowledge (that, nevertheless, was always there at the back of his mind) that his father was often painfully domineering and insensitive towards Shmuel. There were many moments of emotional pain and anger. It became apparent that much of the anger towards his wife was a **reflection** of his frustration and rage towards his father, carried over from childhood.

At this point Shmuel discovered many more "in-between layers" in his relationships with friends, relatives, associates at work and so on. The quality of these relationships revolved around the central axis of a domineering personality (that created bad feelings), or that of a non-domineering personality (that caused good feelings). All of Shmuel's life became more comprehensible in this light, much like a picture which is revealed when the many parts of the puzzle fit each other to become one whole creation. What was once so confusing and composed of innumerable parts and pieces scattered around haphazardly is surprisingly simple and logical when the key to the puzzle has been found.

The Primal Layer

When the innumerable pieces of our lives' puzzles start falling into place, we feel great satisfaction. The mystery of our personal life is finally revealed. But that in itself does not really change the **quality** of our everyday existence. Although understanding is critical, it is not a solution in and of itself. Shmuel felt that although he had progressed significantly in improving his relationships, there still was one more layer that had to be dealt with. This "primal layer" was blocking the natural flow of life between Shmuel's ego and his soul, and, as a result, between him and God. This primal layer is composed of Shmuel's attitude **towards himself**.

Shmuel has reached the point at which he must address those basic, "primal" emotions which had been stirred up by his employer, his wife and his father. He must relive, in a sense, those moments of painful solitude, in which his efforts at uniting with God **through** his mother and father[127] were frustratingly thwarted. Over many years, so many moments of hurt and disappointment had been "swept under" his threshold of awareness as a means of survival. Now he must awaken these repressed emotions in order to cleanse his ego and reunite with his soul and his Maker.

These emotions of being unloved, disparaged, despised or insignificant are the raw material of the primal layer. This layer blocks the natural flow of life from God, through the soul, to the ego. No wonder Shmuel was still unhappy with life, despite his commendable progress. Where the connection with God is blocked by feelings of worthlessness, there can be no true hap-

---

127. See previous chapter on the *mitzvah* of honoring our parents.

piness. For the same reason, his ability to accept love from his wife, parents, children and friends is limited to the degree that he loves himself.

Let us stop for a moment and summarize that which we have learned from the simplified — but typical — case history of Shmuel:

An external layer of a communication block forms around an inner layer.

The internal layer is more painful because it is more deeply rooted in one's life, formed in an earlier period, and present for a longer duration of time.

For this reason, we are incapable of dealing directly with the inner layers of our lives **before** having faced and accepted the contents of the outer layer. The reason, we have learned, is that pain is insufferable unless we deal with it in small doses. Thus we strengthen our tolerance, allowing us to deal with the more painful, deeper layers of our lives.

The deepest layer — and the most painful — is that part of our emotions and thoughts that deals with our self-worth, our faith in our personal lives, the purpose of our existence and our connection with God.

The Therapeutic Process According to Our Sages

We now understand why researching one's personal history may be risky or even dangerous. If a person has not consciously dealt with emotional problems on the superficial levels of his life, then awakening memories of turbulent emotions from inner levels may easily upset whatever delicate balance is somehow maintained in the present. As the emotional stability of the present breaks down, the emotions of the past may overwhelm in implosive or explosive reaction, causing anything from depression and apathy to aggressive violence. If the past must be reached in order to clear up the present, it must be done gradually by peeling the layers from the "outside," starting with the present, towards the "inside," the distant past. Only by putting together the puzzle of our lives are we capable of consciously addressing the ultimate questions of our existence: Who am I? What is the significance of my life? Who is God, and what does He want from me?

This process — treating present pain and suffering by reaching deeply into ourselves — is termed *mituk ha-dinim*, the "sweetening of our sufferings." It can be achieved only by going to the root of one's *dinim*. In the words of Rabbi Chaim Vital, the Ari *z"l*'s foremost pupil, *"ein ha-dinim nimtakim ela b'shorsham"*[128] (the *dinim* can only be sweetened in their roots). What is the meaning of "roots"?

We have already seen that *dinim* refer to all the problems and pains that detract from our life's pleasure and happiness. These *dinim* are bitter, and we naturally have no desire for them. In fact, we do everything in our power to get rid of them. We certainly didn't ask for them, and, when they arrived, we could hardly bear them. Sometimes we even wonder about God's fairness and justice — why must the righteous suffer while the wicked have it good? Quite often we ask: "Why do I have to get the short end of the straw?"

We may have learned to answer these questions in terms of Divine justice (*kapparas avonos*[129]) or beneficial guidance by God (*gam zu l'tovah*.[130]) However, we usually don't have the will or the knowledge to fully comprehend these mystical concepts. If we **were** able to grasp them, we would find that this comprehension "sweetens" our *dinim*. This understanding must be as

---

128. Rabbi Chaim Vital, *Shaar Ha-kavanot*, on *Rosh HaShanah*.
129. See Rashi, *Sotah* 6b.
130. *Taanis* 21a.

emotional as it is rational. The **heart** must merge with the **mind** for true understanding to take place.

The result is that instead of the emotional bitterness that accompanied our *dinim*, a new "sweetened" attitude of acceptance and justification emerges. The frustrations and grievances that made our suffering unbearable give way to the calm surrender of understanding. The pain is tolerable even when it is still there. The desperate cry of "Why?" is replaced by the amazed "Aha!" of sudden insight. We, the children of God, must sometimes suffer in order to grow, and each of us gets exactly what he needs, no more and no less!

The Sweetening Daas

What is the human faculty that enables us to "sweeten" our *dinim*, thereby making our suffering tolerable and meaningful? *Daas* is the agent for this seemingly miraculous transformation. We have already learned that this faculty combines the rational with the emotional, the *chochmah* (wisdom) with the *binah* (understanding). This *daas* was completely absent from our lives in its early stages, when, as infants, we absorbed *dinim* uncritically. When we suffered, the hurt was absorbed in its pure form, undiluted by understanding. Lacking a developed mind to activate our *daas*, we could not blunt the painful experiences by rational justification or mature acceptance. This was the general situation during most of our childhood years, since, as we saw, *daas* develops very gradually. By Bar Mitzvah time, we had acquired it sufficiently to justify our responsibility for observing *mitzvos*. This newly acquired capability is also the spiritual tool for "sweetening" our suffering.

However, it must be **consciously** employed. Otherwise, we remain children in relation to our *dinim*. The sad fact is that there are many adults who are like children, for they refrain from using the *daas* which lies latent within them. *Daas* allows us to choose freely between doing God's will, obeying the To-rah, or disregarding it. Likewise it enables us to choose how we view our sufferings: as pure unadulterated pain, or as a mean-ingful way for God to help us on our personal paths.

The Torah teaches us how to employ this faculty of *daas*. We must direct our awareness to the three basic elements of our ex-istence: our fellow man, God and ourselves. We, the operators of our awareness, are, so to speak, at the apex of a pyramid, the base of which is defined by these three points: our fellow man, God and ourselves. By "beaming down" our awareness, our *daas*, towards one of these points, we strengthen our connec-tion with **all** three, for they are interconnected.

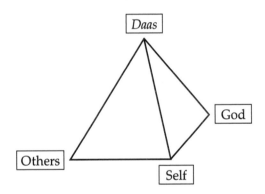

We can now define the process by which we deal with our painful *dinim*. We must reach the basic layer of our existence that deals with our relationships with ourselves, God and our fellow man. This is accomplished by using *daas*, which is the uniquely human possibility of viewing ourselves from a higher vantage point, the apex of our personal pyramid. This aware-ness is much more than simple "viewing." It is a conscious pro-cess of connection-in-depth. Perhaps we could even call this connection **love**. The result is a "sweetening" of our *dinim*. The frustration which was brought about by meaningless suffering dissolves. From our higher perspective we find significance in our lives. This new direction gives meaning and purpose to our *dinim*. The **bitterness** slowly changes to **sweetness**.

The Principle of Teshuvah (Repentance)

The process of increasing and activating our *daas* is a basic principle of *teshuvah*, the obligation to "return" and obey the Torah's commandments. Rabbi Nosson of Breslav writes the following: "A property of *teshuvas ha-mishkal* [repentance that is diametrically opposed to previous wrongdoing] is the necessity to retrace **those paths which had previously been negative**...and then he must turn away from them and cease [entirely] from treading upon them. And he must retrace these paths until he reaches the juncture which is all good, from which stem both the good and bad paths [referring to the sweetening of *dinim* at their roots — E.L.]...and **he must suffer great pain** while retracing these bitter paths until he reaches his [good] path in peace."[131]

Rabbi Nosson describes in detail the healing process of *mituk ha-dinim*. We must emply our *daas* in order to "relive" past events that, because of their painful nature, resulted in our treading "negative paths." When we make the effort to discover at which point in our lives we chose these negative paths, we arrive at their "juncture." At this point — the "root" of our *dinim* — we begin to understand how and why we chose the wrong road. We lacked the *daas* that we have now. We realize that, under those circumstances, we chose logically, if destructively. The painful results of treading the negative paths were inevitable. But they also served to finally awaken us to the realization that we had somehow chosen the wrong road.

However painful, our suffering was ultimately beneficial. It

---

131. *Likutei Halachos, Hilchos Purim* 1:3.

brought us to the initial point of choice between several options. Actually, at that time there was not much choice because we lacked *daas*. With maturity and the development of our *daas*, we may wisely choose between the good and the bad, thus changing the pattern of our lives.

We saw this in the above example, when Shmuel successfully managed to employ his *daas* in depth. He bravely confronted and changed his behavioral patterns. He realized over a period of time how he had let himself become victimized by domineering figures, who he would increasingly resent until he was forced to make a dramatic break-up. Shmuel unwittingly brought about his own demise. He would blame everyone except himself. Therefore he almost lost his job, and he was slowly losing his wife. As to his father, Shmuel had more or less written him off.

Depression set in. Shmuel's suffering became unbearable. Finally he turned to Torah Therapy and became aware of his self-destructive life-script. He recognized those many "junctures" at which he was faced with the choice to stand up for his beliefs or to submit quietly to the strong will of others. Time and again he had opted for the second choice. Then, he was unable to realize that he had any other choice, for this submission was an **ingrained habit** from early chilodhood. It was as automatic as breathing. No wonder Shmuel was frustrated and depressed. He was both his own prisoner and warden. He had believed until now that life for him meant suffering at the hands of domineering figures. He had no idea that he **himself** chose these people in order to deny his freedom of choice and serve their needs.

Tziduk Ha-Din (Justifying the Dinim)

Only after thirty-five years of painful relationships did Shmuel reach his breaking point. Until now, the frustrations were somehow more bearable than the fearful prospect of confronting his fears and painful experiences. Yet at last it built up, and one small disappointment was the straw that broke the camel's back.

At some point after starting therapy, Shmuel became aware, much to his astonishment, how he had led a life of errors and tragedy. Each session, his awareness — his *daas* — grew and became more penetrating. He understood that as a child he had been forced to hide his pain from **himself** in order to survive from one day to the next. This defense is **not** required for an adult, for with his *daas* he may react more constructively and beneficially when provoked. (This will be explained in the next chapter.) However, Shmuel continued the **habit** of repressing his needs and his pain, which distanced him from those he loved or needed. Thus, this defense mechanism developed into a vicious cycle.

Shmuel, upon being asked to describe what is happening to him as he gradually recognizes past mistakes and present options, would probably say that he is happy! This natural state-of-being was previously absent from his life. Now its presence is more often felt, making life seem promising rather than threatening. Happiness, optimisim, positive thinking — all these are gradually entering Shmuel's heart and mind, as he rebuilds his relationships with his boss, his wife, his self and God. He may justifiably see himself as "reborn."

In light of this new experience of life that contains meaning and purpose, the previous years of suffering take on a significance of their own. They are now perceived as a necessary preparation for the present life of enlightenment. The bitterness of the *dinim* has been sweetened. Shmuel now understands why we must all be born into an existence that is far from perfect. What he has gradually realized is that the Divine light of God's love cannot be digested unless we struggle to free ourselves from the bondage of darkness. Without the sufferings of our personal "exile," we have no notion of personal "redemption." When we try to grasp this Divine wisdom, we are inevitably awestruck!

This is *tziduk ha-din*. There is Divine justice underlying all our sufferings, for only through our pain do we reach our personal Gan Eden. But this is not just a generality. When Shmuel understood the significance of his past sufferings, he also caught a glimpse of the interconnection of all the many details that composed his life. He "saw" how God had maneuvered all the innumerable minutiae in order to bring him to this point of enlightenment. The realization that God juggles the infinite pieces of our personal "chess game" of life is mind-boggling. This is *daas* in depth, a mental and emotional explosion of the mind.

The Power of a Hug

Shmuel has another surprise coming. Our Sages reveal that there is yet another, "higher" sweetening of our *dinim* that is even more pleasureful. This too is attained through the *daas*, but this time, from a different part of the *daas*.

Daas is composed of the mind and heart, of the mental and the emotional. But the process of *mituk ha-dinim* that we described above emphasized the use of the **rational** part of *daas* as the first stage in changing our outlook on our sufferings. Now that the mind has accepted and justified, Shmuel is prepared **emotionally** to digest the significance of this enlightenment.

It is now the heart's turn, within *daas*, to continue the process. After the mind revealed to us that there is purpose and meaning to our sufferings, we gradually realize that **there is love** in our world. We no longer feel alone and lost. Our parents now seem no less human than us, and despite their shortcomings, they loved us then and now. Similarly, our partner in life loves us even though there might be problems that may seem insurmountable. Love is so powerful that nothing can stand in its way. Even the boss, however strange his method or character, appreciates our work. He is not such a bad sort if we choose to look at him more positively.

This is quite a change from the past. Love, at whatever magnitude, is slowly overcoming our previous blocks, and our attitude towards those around us changes radically. Our life is more and more suffused with empathy and, therefore, with optimism. Simultaneously, we begin to love the Divine humanity (*tzelem Elokim*) within us. This "honest" self-love overflows towards God, Who enabled us to reach this infinite goodness.

This idea is one of the many explanations that are given to the words of King Shlomo in *Shir HaShirim*: "His left [hand] is under my head, and his right [hand] hugs me."[132] This statement is generally understood as referring to the creation of the world, which combined God's left hand (*din*) with His right hand (*chesed*). It also refers to the creation of the Jewish nation and, analogously, to every one of God's children. The Divine combination of *din* and *chesed* also applies to the creation of man's personal life, if he only employs his *daas* in awareness of this "renaissance."

It is not a one-time affair, because man's creation is not merely the physical birth of man. It is also the cyclical, spiritual renaissance that each Jew experiences every year, starting with Rosh HaShanah. Let us try and understand the process of creation from the beginning of the Jewish year until Simchas Torah (22 days later, after Sukkos), in reference to the left and right "hands of God." This will enable us to understand the parallel process in our personal world.

Rosh HaShanah is the day of judgement, i.e. *din*. *Rosh*

---

132. *Shir HaShirim* 2:6.

means "head," and therefore "His left [hand] under my **head**" refers to the beginning of our year, characterized by God's judgement, **which is supportive**. He judges mercifully. His left hand is **under** our head. The judgement is mercifully postponed for the ensuing "ten days of repentance" in order to allow us to take stock of our situation. Our *daas* must work overtime in our final efforts at constructive retrospection and introspection. Where have we made mistakes in the past year? What can we do now to change things and improve our situation? The emotions are drained, but the mind is the major part of the *daas*, as it prepares our "case" for the last hearing before our Maker, on Yom Kippur. Then Divine justice is decreed, and we humbly accept it, for good or otherwise.

We emerge from this holy day with a deep feeling of gratitude, and even happiness, for we know that we have been heard by our merciful Father, and He continues to guide us in the path that, for each of us, is the most beneficial. In our homage to God as King, Judge, and Father, we feel His strength as supportive, rather than threatening. Our *rosh*, the head wherein lies the mind-half of our *daas*, feels how God's left hand is "beneath," holding and carrying it gently, and supporting its heaviness.

God's Right Hand

Having felt God's love through His merciful justice, we are now invited to open ourselves to His love as felt through His right hand. Our joy gradually increases day by day, as we become attached to Him through the holy days preceding Sukkos, culminating in the pleasure and excitement of Simchas Torah. In these days of happiness we are increasingly engulfed by God's presence. We are "hugged" by His right hand of Divine love.

This love is unconditional. It encompasses both body and soul. Our whole being, with all its human components, both good and bad, is encircled by God's protective and loving right hand. Through the Torah and *mitzvos* which He gave us on Shavuos, we have reached — by way of repentance — the harmonious unity of love between God and Israel. There is no boundary to unity. Although the supportive left hand of God was bound to the ten days between Rosh HaShanah and Yom Kippur, the loving hug of the right hand continues all year long. The right is always the stronger of the two hands. Therefore, the loving hug of God is **initiated** within the context of time, but **remains** with us for all eternity.

"And You Shall Love Your Fellow Man as Yourself"[133]

Shmuel also received one big hug. It started with understanding and pity for the "child" Shmuel, the chronic victim of circumstances. It then developed to a more mature comprehension of his entire life, as ordained by God for his benefit. The frustration and pain became meaningful as Shmuel slowly became aware of being reborn through these experiences. The result was a gradual process of "falling in love" with himself, his fellow man and with God. **What had been a supporting hand under his head has now become a loving hug as well.**

This hug is "external" and all-encompassing. Unlike the left hand that deals with the head alone (specifically, the introspective thoughts within), the right hand accepts Shmuel as a whole. The physical body, as well as the spiritual soul, and all that lies between, are lovingly included in this one big hug, for all of these are inextricably bound to the unique world called "Shmuel." With this in mind, Shmuel sits in the *sukkah* feeling protected by its leafy ceiling, commemorating the clouds of glory that enveloped and protected Bnei Yisrael in the Sinai desert.

───────────────

133. *Vayikra* 19:18.

Along with the wonder and happiness of finally beginning to love himself, Shmuel was surprised to discover a renewed love towards those who had become a part of his life over the years. He realized the truth in the words of the Torah: "And you shall love your fellow man as yourself." **As much as you love yourself, so can you love your fellow man, and no more!** Shmuel began to radiate his love from within towards those who surrounded him: his fellow workers, his boss, his wife, children and so on. They, in turn, reflected Shmuel's love back to him. There is positive energy going back and forth, propagating itself ever more strongly and positively. If we were to ask Shmuel at this point, he would say that his previous 35 years of misery were well worth the Gan Eden in which he is now living.

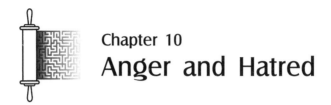

Chapter 10
Anger and Hatred

Anger Revealed

During the difficult process of uncovering the emotional layers that conceal and protect our sensitive ego, we experience many hard and painful moments. As we saw in the previous chapter, our everyday survival dictated to us — at least in childhood — that we disregard these painful events and, preferably, repress them and erase them completely from our consciousness. One of the major emotions belonging to this group is anger and its associate, hatred.

Have you noticed how easily and naturally children express their emotions, especially when they are very young? Their hearts are revealed by their faces. But as they grow older, they are less prone to express their emotions. Anger especially is unconsciously repressed. Why does the child repress the natural expression of anger, more than most other emotions?

This development is the logical result of the conditioned response. Most parents restrain their children from expressing their anger. They expect — and demand — that their children control this negative emotion. They are usually unaware that they demand this "maturity" in a domineering and often painful manner. They may say things like: "Control yourself, you silly child!" or "How dare you shout! Wait until I tell your father, and then you'll get what's coming to you." The child thus learns to conceal his anger, instead of bringing his parents' wrath down upon his head.

The instinct to survive dictates that the child will accept his parents' rebukes with silence. He learns to swallow his anger, while outwardly calm and expressionless. But, though invisible on the outside, it builds up inside in an ever-increasing pressure, churning emotions of frustration, wrath, hatred, self-disgust, remorse, etc. The need to repress his anger becomes second nature through habit. Even when encouraged to express these emotions, the growing child is incapable. At some point he becomes unconscious of the internal bedlam that he had repressed over the years. Whole sections of his childhood might be simply forgotten, erased from memory, due to this unconscious process.

But the increasing pressure must erupt, like a volcano, from time to time. This eruption is usually disruptive, if not disastrous. But it is healthy in the sense that it alleviates, to some degree, the painful pressure within...until the next time.

Accumulated anger becomes rage. Accumulated rage becomes hatred. Throughout there is inner turmoil and frustration. The explosions that erupt may differ in their appearance and degree. Sometimes instead of an explosion there is an implosion, which is a form of disconnection from the outside. The symptoms may be cynicism, criticism, disparagement or overt indifference. In all cases, the explosion of accumulated anger is very disproportionate to the stimulus. An innocent slip of tongue may set off an explosion that befits a World War III. The stimulus was merely the "straw that broke the camel's back." Or it might set off an implosion, which, to the external viewer, is an amazing metamorphosis. The subject is transformed from a mild, good-natured and rational person, to a seemingly autistic personality. He enters his "shell," excluding the whole world, or he runs away.

We are all familiar with our own anger. The only difference between one person and the other is in the degree of the anger and its external expression. All too often we refuse to acknowledge our anger to others and even to ourselves. We bring as proof of our inner calm the fact that our behavior is calm and rational most of the time. But what about all those times when we are accused of being indifferent, hypocritical, unemotional, or even cruel? Why are we often cynical, critical, disparaging or disgusted? Are we perhaps playing hide-and-seek with our anger?

Don't Be Angry! Control Yourself!

We saw above that parents naturally discourage their children from expressing their anger. They pass onto us what they learned as children: to **control** (i.e. repress) our anger. Repression is learned from outside of the home as well. Society as a whole sees anger as something negative, something that should be hidden.

At first glance, Torah also frowns upon the attribute of anger. Our Sages spare no words when discussing this negative and harmful *middah*. To hate is a sin: "You shall not hate your fellow man in your heart."[134] To be angry is to inherit hell: "He who is angry, all kinds of hell control him,"[135] and what is worse, "...even the *Shechinah* (Divine presence) is unimportant in his eyes."[136] These are just some of the many passages in the Torah that fiercely criticize the *middos* of anger and hatred.

They all seem to reinforce the social norm, expressed volubly by well-meaning parents, that we shouldn't be angry. We are taught as children that we are not supposed to cry, to rage,

---

134. *Vayikra* 19:17.
135. *Nedarim* 22a.
136. Ibid.

to show our *yetzer ha-ra*. We must control our emotions, and learn to understand and accept. Our parents drum into us that anger is bad, and by definition, if we are angry we must be bad people.

This attitude seems to be reinforced by Torah values. Anger and hatred must disappear if we wish our world to become better, for they wreak havoc all around. Life is worthless if anger and hatred control it.

It is no wonder that Rambam teaches that anger must be erased totally and forever. Other attributes, such as miserliness, for example, are not totally negative. They contain positive elements. Therefore to change miserliness, one must temporarily assume the extreme of the opposite behavior, and squander away his money. Eventually he is flexible enough to return to the "middle path," in which he is "generous."

Anger, on the other hand, must be eradicated.[137] We are allowed to demonstrate anger outwardly for educational purposes, but inside it must be absent. (Such was the case with Rabbi Yehuda, who would sometimes take a stick in his hand with which to threaten his children in order to instill fear in them. Thus he maintained his authority by showing anger outwardly.[138])

Thus we may conclude that the Torah's view of anger is totally negative. One should strive to completely erase any anger that he feels within his heart. Our parents were perfectly correct — so it seems — when they taught us that it is forbidden to be angry. Even if they didn't use those exact words, that was the message that came across to us as children whenever they reacted strongly against our expressions of anger.

---

137. Rambam, *Hilchos Deos*, 2:7.
138. *Shabbos* 105b.

Contradiction and Its Resolution

We are now faced with a stark contradiction. Our attitude towards anger, supported by the Torah and our Sages, seems to be in direct opposition to the psychological facts we described above. We saw how anger must be expressed, "let out," exorcised, or else it will become repressed into the unconscious. The result, we saw, is the erratic and damaging behavior of the oversensitive personality. Anger, the expression of which is forbidden, leads to stormy explosions or to autistic implosion. Repressing anger is an invitation to the "dark forces" (in the words of Rav Yisrael Salanter) to come and take control of our lives. To deny the value of expressing one's anger is to fall prey to the *yetzer ha-ra*.

Can this obvious truth be reconciled with the social, moral and halachic obligation to erase anger from our lives? Is it conceivable that Torah obligates us to act in a manner that threatens our emotional health? Can God demand us to obey *mitzvos bein adam la-chaveiro*, to love one another as we love ourselves, while simultaneously demanding that we should propagate the invisible seeds of evil and hatred by repressing all anger?

Is Anger Permitted?

To answer these questions, we must understand the *halachic* aspects of anger. Try as we might, we shall never find a halachic prohibition (*issur*) against being angry. If it were a sin to be angry, it must be explicitly codified in the Torah, the Talmud, or the Shulchan Aruch. Anger is the **natural** result of being hurt by others. How can human nature **per se** be considered sinful? The *yetzer ha-ra* is no less part of man's nature than his *yetzer ha-tov*. Therefore it cannot be forbidden and classified as sinful, for it is just as inherent to our lives as breathing is to the living body.

Yet, if anger itself is permitted, what is forbidden? The answer is: **its uncontrolled expression.** When anger takes over our lives, we damage and hurt others and ourselves. We blindly destroy that which we wish to build. In contrast, the Torah obligates us to construct our lives and help those around us through love and harmony. We disobey God when we let our anger destroy. We must do His will (and ours — if we stop to think about it), and eradicate the uncontrolled **expression** of anger, not anger itself.

Let us consider our relationship with our parents from the Torah's point of view. We are obliged to obey the commandment "Honor your father and your mother." We must demonstrate our gratitude for all the efforts they invested in our development. Nevertheless, many seeds of anger are sown at home, beginning sometime in our infancy and continuing for years. Despite their love for us, sometimes our parents are incapable of completely fulfilling our needs, just as **their** needs as children were not fully met by **their** parents.

It is natural for children to be hurt occasionally by their parents, and to experience the anger that is its natural result. (The fact that this is natural is no justification for hurting anyone, let alone children. We must do everything we can **not** to hurt a soul.) It is precisely because it is natural for children to experience anger towards their parents that we are obliged to respect them! This respect does not contradict the emotions of pain and anger. What it does is aim to **control** their expression. We are forbidden to lash out at our parents. If we are hurt and angry, we must deal with our pain without hurting others. Neither may we disregard ourselves, for we then become our own victims.

We often tend to feel ashamed of our anger. We were taught to feel guilty when we were hurt, rather than offended and self-righteous. In response, we generally repress our pain and anger. The fact that they are part of our all-too-human nature simply caused them to fester and grow until we explode. The Torah teaches us that we cannot afford to ignore the *yetzer ha-ra*, or its representative — the Satan. If we deny its existence, it merely lies in wait, constantly accumulating power, until it ambushes us one day when we are caught unawares.

The correct attitude towards Satan and the *yetzer ha-ra* is to keep them at a respectful distance by controlled "offering." This is exemplified by the goat which is offered to these negative forces once a year, on Yom Kippur. If we ignore our *yetzer ha-ra* completely, it may one day overtake and control us, instead of us controlling it. Rather, we prefer to remain true in our service of God while allowing the occasional controlled expression of anger as an outlet.

By not forbidding anger as a necessary emotion within our experience, we do not nurture it. By giving it some controlled expression, we allow our healthier emotions of love and respect to come into play. If we wish to obey the commandment to respect our parents, we must allow negative feelings to be recognized, **without** letting them take control. Repression of these feelings usually causes "deadening" of love and respect as well. What we need to forbid in our lives and those of our children are the uncontrolled expressions of anger, not anger itself.

Anger Reassessed

In this light, the words of our Sages take on new meaning. Why is internal hell the result of anger? We now know that it is because it is held within and finds no "safe" expression. The anger seethes and builds up pressure, pushing aside all emotions of love and harmony, until it is like a strange god, an idol. And when it erupts, it is savage in its destruction, hurting all those who are in the vicinity. No wonder this condition must be eradicated!

Therefore, when Mom snaps at her child, "You're not allowed to be mad at Mommy," she is actually damaging her child. True, he wanted candy and misbehaved when Mom said "no." There is no justification for kicking Mom. It is not his anger, though, which must be suppressed, but rather its destructive expression. She should say something like, "I know you're angry. You may kick the floor if you wish. But I forbid you from ever kicking me! And that's final! As for the candy, the answer is still 'no' because we haven't eaten yet." Anger is permitted. It should be vented in a controlled and planned manner. What is utterly forbidden is its uncontrolled explosion.

The True Situation

Unfortunately, the true state of affairs is that most children are not offered these ideal answers. Well-meaning parents are usually ignorant of the fine line between repressing bad behavior and repressing "bad" emotions. Even when they criticize bad behavior such as wailing, hysterics, aggressiveness and cruelty, they still don't allow for the presence of anger, frustration, wrath or disappointment. As a result, children learn to repress not only the negative expression of their emotions but also those emotions themselves. These negative emotions are, in their eyes, part and parcel of that which is forbidden. Children fear reprisal and parental anger not only when **expressing** their anger, but also when **experiencing** anger in their hearts.

Over the years, many children build a negative self-image around this axis of repressed pain and anger, which leads to guilty feelings, especially towards their parents. After all — they reason — we are bad if we are angry at them. A typical child's thought pattern might run like this: "I must be abnormal to harbor negative feelings towards my parents. Therefore I am unworthy of esteem and love." This becomes a well-known life-script and, as we mentioned above, is very difficult to change.

It is quite rare to find children who were allowed to express their anger as a legitimate emotion in a controlled manner. The reason, as discussed previously, is that the parents themselves were likewise forbidden to be true to their nature. The opposite extreme, however, in which the parents consciously attempt to educate their children in a better manner than they received, is quite common in this day and age. However, the permissive attitude of our generation as a reaction to the conservative and regimental lives of previous generations results in just as much damage to our children.

Many parents repress their instincts and allow their children to express their emotions, positive and negative, in any way they wish. These children know no bounds and regulations. They shout, scream, kick and tear, causing damage and pain to their parents and to others. More often than not, they eventually get what they want, if they keep at it long enough. This education, or rather lack of it, is no less detrimental to these children than the one described above. Regulations which draw clear lines between the permitted and the forbidden are required in tandem with the flexible and loving acceptance of natural emotions. **Anger is natural and therefore legitimate; its uncontrolled expression is a learned trait and is therefore forbidden.**

The Result: Hatred

How do we come to hate someone? Experience teaches that if we are hurt deeply enough and enough times by somone, we eventually come to hate him. In other words, repeated anger towards an individual or a society of people turns into hatred. (This may also serve as a simplistic description of fanatic bigotry.)

If the object of this evolving hatred is a child's parent(s), then he experiences emotional turbulence, tremendous confusion and endless guilt. This is due to the fact that he initially felt trust and love towards his parents. But, as years went by and he was hurt and made angry, this "primal" layer was covered by a "secondary" layer of pain and anger towards them. The thicker this new layer is, the less the former layer is conscious and expressed. In other words, the child now shows more fear and confusion towards his parents than he does trust and love. Eventually, as the anger becomes more intense, it solidifies into hatred. The child now becomes more withdrawn or more aggressive, showing greater signs of emotional disturbance. His basic position of a child who shows love and trust towards his parents is constantly challenged unconsciously by his feelings of anger and hatred. His emotional stability is precarious.

This emotional imbalance is composed of anger and hatred, of which the child is painfully aware, and innocent love and trust, of which he is often unaware. The result is the chronic gnawing of unrequited guilt. On the whole, there is endless confusion and unpredictable turbulence. Feelings of inferiority and self-hatred become more and more familiar to the child. From time to time this self-degradation erupts with tragic results, if not in childhood, then in adulthood.

This sad state of affairs is not confined to the individual. Nor is it a modern phenomenon. It effectively describes the reasons behind the destruction of the Second Temple. The Talmud states that hatred between man and man was the basic cause for its destruction. This explosive tragedy is the natural culmination of numerous personal insults and hatreds, accumulated over time.

Despite the fact that Torah was learned by Jews at that time, something was obviously missing. The Talmud states that the blessings of Torah, that must be said every day, were neglected. We interpret this to mean that learning Torah was more of a chore or habit than a joyous experience. As a result, Torah was not applied in practice to the degree with which it was learned. Specifically, the delicate area of personal interrelationships was more of an academic interest than a practical one. Instead of complying with the Torah's demands and loving one's fellow man, too many Jews (like Kamtza and bar Kamtza) hurt one another for petty reasons of pride and selfishness.

The solution to the problem, the way to building the Third Temple, is now quite apparent. We must exorcise anger and hatred from our hearts and replace it with love and forgiveness. Hatred-in-vain must give way to love-in-vain. This must be achieved by enough individuals so that it becomes a social phenomenon with sufficient momentum to sweep others enthusiastically and have them follow suit. If this state is not achieved, then God will bring it about through His intervention when the time comes to redeem us. But we shall have lost the opportunity to correct ourselves through our own efforts.

This world-wide revolution must, as always, begin at home. If our parents, in their innocence, did not realize that anger per se is natural and even healthy, then we are required to rearrange our concepts and attitudes. If they feared anger and hatred because of its destructive expression, we must respect it, by directing its expression towards those avenues which do not cause damage. We are obligated to improve our attitude and behavior regarding anger and hatred, as instructed by the Torah.

The Source from the Torah, with Help from Rambam

The Torah states the following prohibition: "You shall not hate your brother in your heart."[139] The last three words, "in your heart," seem superfluous. After all, hatred always begins in one's heart. It is a strong emotion, resulting from numerous

---

139. *Vayikra* 19:7.

painful episodes from a specific source. The accumulated anger towards that source, be it a person, a family, or a nation, becomes hatred. All this transpires in one's heart.

Our Sages learned from these words that hatred as a destructive force is to be found **only** in one's heart. Therefore, Rambam codifies this prohibition in the following manner:[140]

"He who hates a fellow Jew in his heart transgresses the prohibition of 'You shall not hate your brother in your heart'...and the Torah forbade only hatred **within** the heart. But if a person were to hit or curse his friend, even though that is forbidden, he would not transgress the obligation of 'you shall not hate'...When one person sins against the other, he should not harbor hatred towards him and remain silent, as it is said concerning evildoers: 'And Avshalom did not speak a word to Amnon, neither good nor bad, **because Avshalom hated Amnon**' [my emphasis — *E.L.*]. However, one must notify him [who sinned against him] and ask him, 'Why have you done so and so to me, and why have you sinned against me in such a manner?' For it is said [after these words of 'You shall not hate your brother in your heart'] — 'You shall reprove your friend'..."

He who was sinned against by his friend, and did not wish to reprove him or say anything to him since the sinner was very simple, or mindless [insane], and therefore he forgave him in his heart **without a trace of hatred or reproof**, this is a quality of *chassidus* (righteousness). [For] what the Torah forbids is [to harbor] hatred."

Torah's Solution

Let us understand these carefully chosen words of Rambam. He begins by defining hatred as a property of the heart, as is ex-

---

140. Rambam, *Hilchos Deos* 6:6.

plicit in the Torah. Therefore, he concludes, hatred is a trans-gression as long as this emotion remains within the heart. This is proven by the description of Avshalom who hated his half-brother Amnon **because** his hatred remained unexpressed.

We see that hatred remains in the heart as long as the person does not express his feelings. From here Rambam derives the proof that once expressed, hatred (as a sin, at least) disappears. Even if the expression of hatred is also a sin, such as hitting out or cursing the one who is the object of this hatred, the sin of **hating** one's fellow man disappears. In other words, a hate-filled heart is emptied of this negative emotion simply by expressing it, in any way. This "letting out steam" is not simply ventilation. It is a dynamic emptying of hatred from one's heart to the extent that from a "hate-full" person, he becomes a "hate-less" person.

Rambam then demonstrates, based on the words of the Torah, how hatred must be expressed **in a constructive manner**. The words "You shall reprove your friend, and you shall not carry sin upon him" oblige us to express our criticism. Yet we must not hurt in return. Therefore, concludes Rambam, we are forced to demonstrate **our** hurt, without being more provocative than to ask, "Why?" An even more delicate approach (probably needed more in this day and age) would be to simply say: "I am hurt by the tone of your voice/ the word you used/ your disregard/ etc."

The novelty in this approach, as Rambam learns from the Torah, is that the main purpose for reproof is **not** to improve the person who hurt me! It is for me to let the anger (the beginning of hatred) leave my heart. This point is clearly stated in the *sefer Lechem Mishneh*, one of the foremost commentaries on Rambam, in reference to the words quoted above. The author writes: "If he has hatred in his heart, he must reprove him **so that this hatred be removed from his heart**."

In other areas of moral conduct, we are responsible to warn and reprove our friends, since "*kol Yisrael areivim zeh la-zeh*"[141] (all Israel are responsible towards each other). Only in this case, when we are hurt by someone, is our responsibility first and foremost towards ourselves: to let the anger out of our system. Equally important is our obligation **not** to hurt anyone, because two wrongs don't make a right.

Any other form of confrontation must necessarily be hurtful. This is pointed out by the famous Tanna, Rabbi Tarfon, who says in the Talmud[142]: "I am doubtful whether anyone in this generation is capable of reproving [correctly] anyone else." If in the days of the great Tannaim, this ability — to reprove without hurting — was rare, how much more so must this be the case in our present day and age! Moreover, it is a known fact that the greater the intimacy between people, such as exists within a family, the greater the potential for hurting one another. Even when the reproof is perfectly justified, it wounds and lacerates, thereby weakening the delicate bonds of love and dependency.

Is it logical to suppose that the Torah offers a solution for ventilating our anger and hatred which is hurtful to others? Is it logical that reproof is a solution offered only to those few righteous people who can somehow rebuke others without hurting them? Neither of these possibilities makes sense! There must be some solution applicable to all of us, whatever our spiritual stature, that allows us to release our negative emotions without transgressing the laws of *bein adam le-chaveiro*.

To Reprove for the Sake of the Reprover

In this light we can more fully comprehend the Torah's attitude

---

141. *Rosh HaShanah* 29a — see *Rashi* there.
142. *Arachin* 16b.

through the words of Rambam. This point was stressed by the *Lechem Mishneh* mentioned above, who demonstrated that the act of reproving, in and of itself, is effective in erasing one's hatred towards the reproved. Whether or not the latter asked forgiveness is irrelevant.

Of course it would help greatly if the words of reproof found their mark, and forgivenss would be asked and given. It is extremely important for the person who was hurt to hear the other side say: "I'm truly sorry. Please forgive me." It is a prerequisite for reconciliation. Nevertheless, it is secondary. The immediate concern is to get rid of the hurt and the ensuing anger lodged within the heart. This is a unique and novel approach.

It is this largely unknown approach of the Torah that Rambam stresses as the solution to the paradox mentioned above. If we are obliged to reprove those who hurt us in order to empty our hearts of anger and hatred, yet we are forbidden to hurt back, then we have only one option. We must express **our** hurt feelings, **while consciously denying our natural tendency to condemn those who hurt us**. This initially sounds so strange and unnatural that it may easily be taken as a joke. The fact is that practically no one observes this explicit *halachah*. (Perhaps the reason is that if it's not learned as a child, then it is very difficult to learn as an adult.)

It takes great effort to receive criticism and reply immediately in such a controlled manner. But who says that we must immediately answer the person who hurts us? What if we answer back **when not in his presence?** After all, the point of reproof (as we learned from the *Lechem Mishneh*) is to let our hatred leave us, and it is only of secondary importance that it reach the ears of the person who hurt us. What if we say these words out loud in the privacy of our room, when no one, except God and ourselves, can hear us?

Freedom through Speech

This definitely sounds unusual to one who has not tried it. When practiced at first, it feels even stranger! But it works. Torah Therapy encourages the patient to alleviate the emotional pain of accumulated anger and hatred by voicing his "hurts" to the **imagined** presence of whoever hurt him in the past. Experience demonstrates that the pain diminishes to a large extent even when the accused is imaginary, and only the speaker's ears are hearing his own words.

A simple proof is to witness or — better yet — to experience this yourself. It is amazing how difficult it is for someone who was deeply hurt to voice his pain to the non-existent person, despite the fact that the whole scene is imaginary. The greater the pain, the more difficult it is to express it. But, in the same vein, once started on this therapeutic path of Torah, the greater the pain, the greater the benefit. To **see** this in action is to believe. But to **experience** it is to be filled with awe and wonder.

When, for the first time in many years, the patient expresses his fears and pain, his anger and hatred, the atmosphere becomes electrified. Whether in solitude or in the presence of the therapist, the presence of the imagined person can almost be felt physically. Painful emotions that had been held in check, or even buried, start spilling out, in a gradual crescendo of emotions and touching human drama, often accompanied with tears, and even heart-rending sobs. This is no mere imagination. This is reality. It stems from the deepest and truest reaches of the heart. Whether or not the events, memories or accusations are objectively true is completely irrelevant. The emotions are true, and it is these emotions of anger and hatred which must be exorcised like ghosts from his heart.

To undergo this experience is to realize that the battle for survival takes place more in our hearts than in the external world. For example, we may realize that our problems with our

parents today are actually emotional battles which we have
been waging with their **imagined** beings for the last several decades. We don't normally see them as they are, from an objective point of view. We see them through our internalized memories and emotions, as discussed above in chapter 8. Even after
their deaths, we may find ourselves "imprisoned" by them, or
— if we wish — loved and comforted by them.

As we unload our pain and frustrations on the imagined
person or persons whom we carried inside our hearts for so
long, we receive many insights. One of these is the comprehension of the idea, presented in the first section of this book, that
the world is more imagination than anything else. The external,
physical experience is the "raw material" of one's internal spiritual existence. Of course we influence and touch each other, for
better or for worse. But the **interpretation** of this experience is
purely personal and mostly imagination. Therefore, we allow
ourselves to become sick, through our emotional and mental interpretation of our daily experiences.

We can likewise bring ourselves to greater health with the
aid of Torah and its positive evaluation of life. With God's help,
we can take control of our emotions, living our lives in full even
when challenged by difficulties. Using the powers of speech
constructively, we can purify our hearts from negative feelings,
replacing them with those emotions that all people crave: love,
serenity, security and happiness.

Clinical Results

Given that this process is based on Torah and our Sages, it **must**
work. Granted, every person progresses with this at his own
pace. But all who try to accuse their imaginary "tormentors," especially when giving voice to their own pained emotions, come
away healthier. The benefits are immediate. But for long-term
benefit, this ventilation must become a habitual practice, like all

mitzvos of the Torah.

However, there is more than mere ventilation in this process. When done in the presence of the therapist, there is also a new awareness and learning involved. The patient is skillfully led by the Torah Therapist to reassess those experiences which created the pain that is now expressed. This is not necessarily a rational learning, for it is woven into the dynamics of the emotional confrontation with the imagined persecutor. For example, the patient might be asked to play the part of the accused. As strange as it sounds, he often represents him/her skillfully, thereby attaining insight into the minds of those who hurt him. This is a dramatic form of *mituk ha-dinim,* sweetening our pains, which was discussed previously.

For example, suppose Moshe suffers from negative self-esteem, lack of self-assertion and insecurity. It is no problem to trace his feelings of inferiority to the constant criticism that he received from a harsh father. He now suffers as an adult because of these negative beliefs, internalized as "whole and simple truths" when he was a child. In order to change, Moshe must deal with these false self-concepts at their roots, i.e. as "packaged emotional truths" thrown at him by his father. This involves coming to terms with the pain — and anger — caused by these accusations. As long as Moshe denies himself the right to confront his father, even in his imagination, and give voice to his feelings, he will continue to believe, deep down inside, that he is worthless.

Now Moshe is starting to let it out. His father is absent from the room, but present in Moshe's heart and mind. The stifled words and feelings start coming out, fitfully at first, and then in an avalanche. Even five minutes of this catharsis suffice to give Moshe a new, somewhat lightheaded feeling. This includes a strange satisfaction: Moshe has begun to **respect** himself for overcoming the natural fear, present since childhood, to express his hurt and desires. He feels newly mature. Then he understands that he has been holding onto his childhood for fear of growing up and experiencing futher pain.

He is also asked to play the role of his father today, as if he — the father — would be able to answer him with wisdom and compassion. Moshe hears himself saying to "Moshe" words like: "But I loved you then, Moshe, as I do now. I simply didn't know how to show it...and I always thought that you were smart and good...I'm sorry I hurt you...I really didn't mean to..."

Moshe is involved in emotional reconstruction. His self-evaluation gradually improves, and his insecurity slowly dissolves. By allowing his hatred to be heard (by himself, with or without the therapist) he became capable of readjusting his views on himself. With the aid of the therapist, he was able to reassess his father more positively, for the first time after many decades of painful separation. This will be discussed in further detail, but first let us reconsider our approach.

An Opposing Stance

Despite evidence to the contrary, there are those who vehemently oppose emotional ventilation. They maintain that words create reality, and therefore, negative words create negative reality. Anger, hatred and pain should be disregarded within one's spiritual existence. Being imaginary in nature, they will dissolve and disappear over time, absorbed — so to speak — within the texture of everyday life. If we give them form by mouthing these emotions, we give them life, until they occupy our thoughts constantly, and thereby change our lives for the worse.

This sounds right. It also feels right — perfectly right — when we propose, for the first time, to voice our pain and accusations to ourselves. The approach of mouthing our negative emotions runs counter to our basic beliefs from childhood: that by keeping these emotions inside — even from ourselves — we can somehow manage to survive living among those who hurt us. We naturally feel that to open our mouths to others, or even to ourselves, is to open a Pandora's box of troubles and needless pain. For years we exerted much effort to live peacefully. Are we now going to ruin our tentatively constructed relationships, like a bull in a china shop? It sounds and feels so wrong.

The Defense

This position is seemingly unassailable. It is founded not only on logic but also on emotional experience to which most people can testify. However, this only holds true until we actually begin practicing "you shall reprove" in the spirit of the Torah and Rambam, with the guidance of the Torah Therapist. There are two fallacies in the position of the opponents:

1. Accepted notions and experience are no proof against the validity of Torah. We must reassess and reevaluate these notions and beliefs, for Torah is eternally true.

2. The basis for the opposing view, that negative words "poison" the air which we breathe, is a non-Torah concept. It is taken from other nations and other beliefs. Granted, if a person constantly complains and expresses negative emotions, he may gradually drown in his own excess verbiage. But that is a far cry from the healthy voicing of one's pain and anger, at a specific time and in a controlled environment, as encouraged by Torah Therapy. When people speak of the destructive energy created by negative **words**, they are disregarding the poisonous energy, a thousand times more powerful, created by the negative **feelings** within the heart. Being undefined and not localized, negative emotions are truly a

fearful poison because they spread throughout our personality. All facets of our internal existence thus grow warped and tainted.

Of course we must strive to forgive and forget. Judging our fellow man favorably is an obligation, even when facts seem to point otherwise. We need to act with compassion and respond to bad with goodness. This is the *middas chassidus* which Rambam discussed in the section quoted above. But we also have to be truthful. It may be fairly easy to forgive some people. But it is no simple matter to be truly forgiving towards those who caused us to suffer, **even though we love them and they love us**. To reach the point when we can truly say "I forgive," we must first let the poison out.

Therefore, it is vital that we overcome our natural tendency to disregard the pain of the past. All our efforts to think only positively towards those who caused us suffering are futile exercises in self-deception. Time and again, we are forced to admit that our problems are still present, if not even greater. The more we try to deceive ourselves, the deeper we bury our pain and our accusations. As a result, our bonds become weaker and weaker, despite the love that was, until we are completely isolated from those who should be so meaningful to our lives.

Sweetening the Dinim of Anger

As we saw in the example of Moshe and his critical father, achieving spiritual health involves two steps:

1. Expressing one's negative emotions ("you shall reprove").
2. Sweetening the pains *(dinim)* by use of *daas*, with the aid of the therapist.

In other words, after voicing our pain and frustration, we are led to deal with them one at a time. Finally, we reach a point when the negative energy, inherent in our bad memories, starts to dissolve and disintegrate, both internally and externally. Concurrently, we can feel the wall which had been built between us crumbling, slowly at first, but then in a total avalanche. At this point (and not before, as the "opposition" would have it) we begin to think positive thoughts.

Having completed phase one in regards to a specific person, we are prepared to enter phase two, which is positive thinking. This does not mean, as is normally accepted, that we simply think positively of someone. Using our Sages (and the Torah Therapist) as guides, we must reenter the painful situations which we had supposedly "gotten out of our systems" (phase one) in order to evaluate them positively. This is *mituk ha-dinim,* sweetening of our pains, **at their origins.**

Sweetening Anger and Hatred

This second phase of dealing with pain and hatred is alluded to in the words of Rambam quoted above. When demonstrating correct reproof (which does not hurt the accused), Rambam tells us to ask, when we are hurt: "Why have you done so and so to me, and why have you sinned against me in such a manner?"

Let us think for a moment. Is this phrase worded in a style that seems natural? Is the sentence offered by Rambam a typical reaction towards someone who hurt us? Don't we normally retort much more aggressively?

When someone hurts us, we tend to call him all sorts of names, or accuse him of being egocentric, selfish, cruel or stupid. We hurl whatever words we can to sting him in return, taking revenge for the hurt and pain which we feel. It is rare to find someone who openly says: "I am hurt by what you just said." Equally rare is the person who asks: "Why have you hurt me in such a manner?"

Nevertheless, we are taught that this is exactly what must be said in order to "sweeten" the pain of rebuke or accusation. The reason is that when we are hurt we tend to dissipate it by turning upon the person who hurt us. We **disregard** our pain by focusing on the accuser and his faults. This, we feel, will be beneficial for us. But this natural tendency simply increases our frustration. If we wish to improve our mental and emotional health, we must **stay with our pain** and, within its context, address the one who hurt us. When we accuse without expressing our pain, we are being untruthful — and therefore unhealthy — to **ourselves**! This is alluded to in the words of Rambam: "Why have you hurt me in such a manner?"

Yet these words imply much more than that. The question mark at the end presumes an answer. This answer may be given directly by the accuser if he is present, or **by the patient himself**, using Torah Therapy to reenact the scene alone. In both cases the answer is very different from the emotional interpretation that the hurt person normally attributes — in "real time" — to the words or action that hurt him. Therefore, the result of the question is an understanding, however incomplete, that the word or deed was not merely a cruel act of causing pain. *Daas* is allowed to enter the scene and make some sense of what ensued. This is a simple form of *mituk ha-dinim*, sweetening of pain, which we may learn from the wise words of the great Rambam.

Entering the Shoes of the Aggressor

Understandably, it sounds like it would be rather hard to know the thoughts of someone who hurt us twenty years ago. Try and act out his words and actions? It doesn't seem possible! Nevertheless, experience demonstrates that we do not do too badly when we make a serious attempt. Whether reenacting the person as he actually was, or reenacting him in the ideal form that we would give him in our imagination (compassion-ate, understanding, sensitive, etc.), the words we make up for him seem to come from a deep source which echoes vibrantly in our hearts. Somehow, if we manage to overcome our initial discomfort at initiating this "forced" drama, we find ourselves extremely moved and powerfully involved in our ad-libbed, one-man play. We begin to feel ourselves entering his shoes!

The explanation for this phenomenon is derived from the comprehension of painful events, as discussed above. Firstly, our existence is primarily imaginative. "All the world's a stage" is so true that by acting out specific events, we actually relive them, at least at the emotional level. Secondly, we all have the inherent capability of knowing intuitively that which is true (Rav Dessler's "point of truth"), allowing us to understand our fellow man. Thirdly, the conscious attempt to represent some-one else forces us to surrender our opposition and assume some form of identification. The result is insight and compre-hension, stemming from a **totally novel point of view**.

We are commanded to judge our fellow man favorably. This is easier said than done, especially when applied to those who hurt us. Yet here we are presented with a personal experi-ence that does just that. By standing in the other's shoes, we somehow find ourselves judging him favorably, or at least not accusing him, as we are prone to do normally.

The result is a new insight into the dynamics of the difficult relationship. For example, when Moshe reached the point at which he was capable of assuming his father's role, he heard himself saying things like:

"Moshe, you know that I have always loved you. After all, you're my son...my eldest son...But I've been tense and ner-vous all my life, probably because I was orphaned and had a tough life, and I took it out on you. What I always wanted was for you, Moshe, to succeed where I had failed and when you

disappointed me...I...I got so mad at you...I'm sorry,
Moshe...I'm so sorry. I was sorry then too, but I couldn't say
it...I was so ashamed..."

Moshe had come a long way. He made the great effort
needed to obey the Torah's admonition "You shall not hate
your brother in your heart." By expressing his pain towards his
imagined father, he got rid of the spiritual poison that separated them both emotionally and physically for so many years.
Moreover, by "entering his shoes" and observing the commandment to always judge our fellow man favorably, he was
able to understand his father to a certain extent. The pain that
had been interpreted for years as derision and scorn became
"sweetened" and reinterpreted as a mistaken form of fatherly
love and hope for success. **The "mistake" had been in the expression, not the feeling.** His father was incapable of expressing his love and affection. He was limited to expressing his disappointment and anger. But now Moshe has matured. His father is no longer a one-sided, negative caricature of an evil
person. He is human and therefore multi-dimensional. Actually, he is not unlike his son, Moshe.

The Essence of Anger: TRUTH

As we near the end of our discussion of anger, which is the
building block of hatred, we may expand our view and deepen
our comprehension of this emotion. We may be surprised to
discover that the root of anger is something very positive! On
second thought, this is as it should be, for we are taught by our
Sages that all evil, even the most destructive, is "anchored" in
the Divine. It has no existence in and of itself. As evil as hatred
is, as repugnant as anger is, their root is holy. Even as we erase
hatred and anger from within our hearts, we must recognize
them as basically natural, and essentially normal emotions.
What we are doing now is "sweetening *dinim*" in a very general

and basic level — no small feat.

Hatred is composed of deep anger that is directed towards one person, group, family, etc. Anger was understood as the natural result of being purposefully hurt or pained. Why is that? Why should anger be considered a *natural* result?

To answer this question, consider a baby who wants to be held by his mother and played with. Finally she says: "No more, honey. It's bedtime for you." He cries in protest and frustration. When Mom nevertheless puts him to bed, disregarding his cries, we may see his face registering expressions of rage or anger, and finally succumbing to the harsh facts of life: we see resignation and...sleep.

Obviously, the baby experienced the pain of rejection. His facial expressions reveal the hurt of feeling unwanted, unloved and undesirable, even if only for that moment. The baby must feel this sudden change of relationship from his mother as unfair and unjustified. He does not know (at that moment) that she loves him and that he needs sleep. All he knows in his heart (because words are as yet absent from his mind) is that he is being **undeservedly** punished. No wonder he is angry!

If we project the unveiled emotions of the angry baby onto the more secretive adult, we would not be far off target. Anger stems from the **subjective** feeling that injustice has been done to us. The pain alone is not the reason. It is due to the fact that someone is purposely causing him pain that the sufferer **interprets** the pain as an injustice. The sufferer feels disparaged, scorned, put down and belittled.

This is unfair and untrue. Just as the baby feels that he has every right to demand attention and love, so the adult feels that he deserves to be treated as a worthy human being. When he feels attacked, he naturally responds from the **depths of his self-respect**. From his subjective point of view, he is perfectly correct. Are we not all rooted in the Divine? Are we not all built *b'tzelem Elokim*, in the likeness of God?

Thus it is clear that the root of anger is the feeling of injustice. The attribute of justice, *middas tzedek* — says Rav Dessler — is inherent in our being. It is a facet of the attribute of truth, which, our Sages tell us, is the "signature" of God. We human beings, created in His likeness, yet concealing our identity deep within, are His "signature." The truth is that we all deserve to be respected and loved. If we were required to be born into a difficult world of physical existence, we are essentially not at fault when we sometimes fail or fall. After all, the *yetzer ha-ra* is stronger than us, unless the Holy One aids us.[143] Therefore, anger can be described as a justifiable and natural (if destructive) reaction.

Tempering Anger

If we were to return to Moshe with this point of view, we could attain greater insight into his spiritual "transformation." What Moshe realized is not just that his father is human. Moshe himself, with all his anger and frustrations, is equally human. Moshe had needlessly suffered pangs of guilty conscience for hating his father. These tumultuous emotions were just as responsible for his decades of separation as was his anger. The pain of guilt is now sweetened too. Moshe can finally forgive himself for hating his father. He has absorbed the insight that his distorted vision of a one-sided, critical and cruel father was inevitable. He was only a child, without *daas*, when this image became a permanent fixture in his life. His frustration, anger and hatred were no less inevitable, for they stemmed from the inherent truth within Moshe that he deserves to be loved and

---

143. "And I shall remove your heart of stone from your flesh" (*Yechezkel* 36:26) is the basis for the *midrash Yalkut Shimoni, Hoshea* 14, in *siman* 532, to make this claim.

respected, not despised and rejected.

As these thoughts are absorbed over time, they gradually displace the negative emotions and the resulting lack of communication. Along with forgiveness towards both his father and himself, new emotions of understanding, compassion and identification are experienced and take root in Moshe's heart. Initially, this miraculous transformation is known only by Moshe himself. But his actions, behavior and speech betray him after a while. His wife is the first to feel the subtle changes. And of course, God, Who was with him the whole time, is now experienced by Moshe in a way which he had never dreamed possible. Life has a new glow....

This is the process, or part of it. It is not just theory. It is practical and applicable to everyone, for it is Torah, and Torah was given to be used and applied, not just studied. The light that it gives off within us is indescribable. "For the candle of God is the soul of man."[144] This candle glows within us forever. Torah Therapy is merely a practical application of Torah, with which to wipe the dust off the window panes that we had put up around our candles.

---

144. *Mishlei* 20:27.

Chapter 11

Guilt Feelings and Repentance

Resistance to Change

One of the greatest obstacles to improvement and growth is the belief that we do not deserve forgiveness. Sometimes we are so overwhelmed with guilt that we are positive that there are no more chances left for us to start anew. The sins of the past cannot be erased. For others there is grace and forgiveness, but not for me.... We view ourselves as stuck forever in the muddy mire of self-torment and bad deeds that cannot be undone.

Torah Therapy comes to help us help ourselves out of our personal quicksand, by applying one of the basic tenets of Torah — repentance — to our lives. The Torah Therapist leads the patient with empathy and sensitivity towards the astonishing discovery that he had believed that repentance, *teshuvah*, was available to all **except himself.** This is contradictory to our belief in an all-forgiving and gracious God. While learning and understanding the many details of repentance and the ensuing forgiveness, *kapparah*, it seems we neglected to include ourselves within its sphere.

Let us be more specific. For years we have been accustomed to connecting repentance and forgiveness with sins between man and God, such as observing Shabbos negligently, dressing immodestly, etc. As to sins between man and man, we merely

196

paid lip service to the obligation to repent for those sins that we seem to be unable to control. If we hurt another through anger, we "accept" it as a fact of life. We normally refrain from actually dealing with our low self-esteem, from which these everyday transgressions stem. Unconsciously, we often exclude ourselves from the difficult but healthy process of *teshuvah*. We therefore remain without *kapparah*, forgiveness.

For example, we might be very diligent in observing the many details of Torah, especially those between man and God. Therefore, when criticized for transgressing Torah in our relationships with those around us, we might retort angrily and hurt others. The reason for this reaction, we have learned, is low self-esteem and feelings of inferiority stemming from childhood. **Our background is not our fault. But our present behavior is definitely our responsibility.**

Torah teaches us to curb our instincts and control our habits of striking out and hurting others when **we** are hurt. Our *avodas Hashem*, service of God, becomes *avodah zarah*, idolatry, when we refuse to control our behavior. The master we are then serving is ourselves, or more specifically, our *yetzer ha-ra*. Being stuck in the quagmire of our anger and guilt is contradictory to our belief in change and improvement through repentance and forgiveness. True repentance includes the ability — and therefore the obligation — to change ourselves from within.

However, mere **will** to change and **desire** to improve are not enough. We also need outside help to pull us out of this emotional quicksand. The implements of our salvation are self-knowledge (*daas*), proper actions (*mitzvos*, and exercises suggested by the therapist), and help from Heaven (*siyata dishmaya*). Together, these form the basic fulcrum that can move and change our world.

Nosei Avon (Suffers Transgression)

One of the thirteen attributes with which God condones our transgressions is called *nosei avon*, meaning that He carries or suffers our sins. In other words, He lightens the load of guilt from our shoulders — guilt accumulated from past misdeeds, which cannot be undone — by carrying their weight Himself, so to speak. This is true *chesed*, grace, for the burden of our sins is removed for no other reason than that we repented for them. Suddenly we are free to move on and rebuild our lives, unencumbered by the past.

Of course, the conditions of true repentance must be met. Grace is not that simple to attain. We must confess to God and, if we sinned against man, before him as well. We must desist from our sins in the present, and truthfully intend to keep on refraining in the future as well.[145] If a person does not or will not meet these requirements, the load of sins, and the accompanying guilt, is his to carry. Gradually his knees start buckling underneath him, for the load only increases as time goes on. Eventually he will fall and drown in the tide of his deeds.

Rivka's Story

Let's take Rivka (false name but true story) for example. She has been carrying a heavy "sin" for the past thirty years or so. Despite myriad attempts at repentance, she constantly failed at "rehabilitation," and fell — almost happily — into the compulsion of her "sin," as if to spite

---

145. Rambam, *Hilchos Teshuvah*, 2:2. The Torah specificially requires verbal confession, but Rambam enumerates the stages of repentance as follows: 1) Refraining from further transgression. 2) Refraining from enjoyable thoughts about it. 3) Deciding in one's heart not to repeat this transgression ever again. 4) Regretting the past transgressions. 5) Allowing God to testify that all these thoughts are sincere and therefore the transgression will remain only in the past. 6) Verbal confession.

herself. Her guilt, self-hatred and self-criticism kept growing. Rivka's emotional storms about her compulsive habits were very tumultuous. One would have thought she was dealing with a sin of horrific proportions, like idolatry or murder.

In truth, Rivka's sin was merely that she neglected to take care of her body and her mind. For the past thirty years Rivka had been guilty of overeating. The accompanying "sin" of overeating was the "sin" of gaining weight. Food and Weight were the two ghouls of Rivka's nightmares. All the mitzvos which she fulfilled — and these were truly many — were of no weight or consequence relative to this greatest evil in Rivka's eyes and heart. She was aware that no such sin existed in the Jewish code of law, the Shulchan Aruch. Nevertheless, she felt like the biggest sinner in the world. Why is that?

Rivka was born to parents who survived the Holocaust. Their years of starvation had led them to acquire certain attitudes and principles towards food. They would skimp on food, and eat every crumb that fell from their mouths. No food was ever left uneaten, and food was never thrown away, even if it was spoiled. Rivka grew up under the impression that whoever is not thin is a criminal, eating more food than is necessary, at others' expense. Excess food leads to excess weight and is despicable, for it is excess waste. This was the gist of the gastronomic "Ten Commandments" that Rivka's parents drilled into her from early childhood. Food was to be eaten sparingly, to maintain bodily health. Anything else is pure evil.

During childhood, Rivka developed a tremendous craving for all the sweets and snacks that her friends would bring to school. Recess was pure torment as she stared and desired. Heaven forbid that she should eat to such excess! She would salivate just thinking about these forbidden fruits.

When Rivka finally left her parents' house for her own, as a married woman, she allowed her fantasies to be realized. She ate and ate and ate, and she grew fatter and fatter. Every day she chastised and hated herself more. Her life was a mess. Her husband was at a complete *loss, and nothing seemed to help. Even bulimia (binging and then throwing up), destructive as it is, could not stem her compulsion and the resulting weight gain. Rivka is truly stuck. Actually she is sinking...and she knows it!*

To Become "Unstuck"

Rivka may choose one of two options, each of which can free her from guilt and frustration. One is to force herself to return to the regulated eating patterns of her childhood, as her parents had dictated to her. The other option is to accept the fact that she must eat and thereby gain more weight, and to make peace with this fact of life. This would enable her to escape the vicious cycle of self-recrimination for a never-ending series of attempts at diets and immediate failures. By accepting her compulsion as inevitable, she might even come to control it to some extent.

Rivka has turned to Torah Therapy for help. The therapist must gently guide her to the realization that she is free to choose. After all, "everything is in the hands of Heaven except for *yiras Shamayim*, fear of Heaven."[146] This means that it is our responsibility, not God's, to observe those commandments which allow us to be physically and emotionally healthy. It is Rivka's choice, and hers alone, which path she chooses. There is also a third choice, which attempts to incorporate both and fails miserably. Rivka had been accustomed to being controlled

---

146. *Megillah* 25a. Most people explain this passage as referring to those *mitzvos* which demonstrate *yiras Shamayim*, fear of God, such as prayer, eating kosher and observing Shabbos. However, Rabbi Eliyahu Dessler in *Michtav MeEliyahu*, vol. 1 pp. 111–114, applies this idea to every moment of our lives in all areas. The reason, in short, is that we have the choice (free will) at every point in our lives between doing what our *yetzer* wants or what God wants. Therefore, if, as children, we were forced to sin, as adults, we choose to sin or not.

by the external powers of her parents, her physical cravings, the natural laws of weight gain and the fate that made her a victim. Now she must learn that she can choose, and that she had in fact been choosing all along.

At first glance, she is completely powerless to change her life-script. Just as her parents had no control over the events of the Holocaust and its consequences, so it seems that Rivka is destined to be forever torn between overeating and self-hatred.

Taking Responsibility

The novelty of the approach towards helping Rivka lies in the fact that she does have free will after all. She must realize that she — and only she — is responsible for her present state. First she must understand this revolutionary concept in her mind. Secondly — and much more difficult — she must realize this emotionally. She must accept responsibility for her choices.

The difficulty lies in the fact that Rivka found some consolation in the fact that her fate was not in her hands. As long as she could blame her parents, her physical and mental compulsions, or anything else, she was free to indulge her weakness, even though she hated the results. To assume responsibility for her life is to deny herself even this small comfort. It is much easier to simply go on as before, not realizing that she could change things. She might even resist considering this possibility, at least subconsciously.

Unfortunately, Rivka's plight is quite common. Every life-script contains certain elements that are similar to Rivka's mode of thinking. "I simply cannot change any more than I already have." Sounds familiar, doesn't it? Actually, we are afraid to face the challenge of exerting ourselves outside of the familiar borders of our lives. Rivka fears, albeit subconsciously, the challenge of actually escaping from her self-imposed prison. For the past several decades she has preferred to suffer the mental anguish of guilt and self-hatred, rather than face the unkown terrors of a different life. Her present life, hard as it may be, is familiar and therefore **secure**.

Change does not seem possible. Why should Rivka give up the security of her present life, when what awaits her seems full of terror? And even if she were to overcome her emotional blocks, what logical reason exists to persuade her that she has any chance of getting "unstuck"?

The Thin-as-a-Needle Opening

However, there has been a small, yet significant change. At age 30, Rivka seriously approached her Rabbi, who, despite his credentials as a *ben Torah*, preferred to refer her to the more experienced Torah Therapist. What brought about this revolution in Rivka's life? She had reached a point at which the pain and frustration caused her to think of suicide. It was unbearable. She did not want to give up her life, but neither did she see any hope to live happily.

At this point, the option to seek help came up as a plausible alternative. This novel thought was enough to stir some long-lost hope in Rivka's heart. She had made a small opening in her heart, as thin as the point of a needle. Yet, that is all that is needed for her to receive help from Heaven, as our Sages say: "Open for me an opening as thin as the point of a needle, and I will open for you an opening as wide as a grand hall."[147]

This initiative on Rivka's part was not really a rational act. It

---

147. *Yalkut Shimoni, Shir HaShirim Rabbah*, chap. 5, *siman* 988. This well-known condition for *teshuvah* is now understood better. This small opening is the brave decision on our part to face the fearful unkown by actively searching to improve our lives. Without this initial opening, there is no room in our hearts for God to offer us His blessings. Our hearts that are filled with water leave no room for the Heavenly wine to be poured in. Only by allowing our own cup to empty it-

was more an emotional reaction to an unbearable situation. This is referred to in the Torah in these words: "When you are oppressed, and all these [curses] will befall you...then you shall return...."[148]

Rivka is at the point at which she must finally take responsibility for her life. In considering death, she must reconsider life as well. And she must choose. What had until now been bearable and, therefore, preferable to facing the unknown terrors of a change in life, is now unbearable. The emotional scales have become unbalanced for the first time in thirty years. The fear of the future in the known situation has become greater than the fear of the unknown changes that may result from taking responsibility for her life. It became more threatening for Rivka to stay as she was than to try and do something about it, once and for all. She forced herself to approach her Rabbi and ask for help. And help must begin with understanding. Rivka must first learn to understand herself and the world around her.

The Critical Question: Where Is Happiness?

Rivka, like all of us, is searching for happiness. If complete happiness is unattainable, we hope for at least a small measure. Our goal can be expressed as aiming for the state of minimal suffering (which is the opposite side of the same coin). It seems that all living beings, animals as well as humans, are motivated by the instinct to live and the desire to experience minimal suffering and maximum pleasure. For humans, who have *daas*, the more appropriate word is happiness (*osher*).

As a child, Rivka sought happiness by obeying her parents' will, as is the general case in children. The option of rebellion would have caused her less happiness, even in her teenage

---

self a tiny bit do we come to taste the elixir of His grace.

148. *Devarim* 4:30.

years. Otherwise, she would have rebelled like many teenagers in similar conditions. But the pain of denial from sweets and snacks was constant and unbearable. Therefore, Rivka developed compensatory behavior, such as excellence in school, sports and music. The happiness of achievement in these areas neutralized (compensated) the pain of food denial. Nevertheless, the hunger for sweets was her gnawing companion every hour of her life. Rivka also accumulated excruciating feelings of guilt just for **thinking** about these foods.

Thus Rivka felt torn between crime and punishment, even before she actually surrendered to her weakness. She had tragically built a life-script in which her search for happiness is thwarted at every turn by the evil called "desire for food." Despite her academic successes, despite a nice marriage, despite wonderful children, Rivka was further from happiness and in greater pain than she had ever been before.

Rivka had tried to compensate and find happiness in all possible directions except one. She had refrained from coping with the painful **guilt feelings** that had become ingrained in her. As she grew up, she was dimly aware of this emotional "minefield," and she invested much effort to keep it as far back from her consciousness as possible. Now, at age thirty, life has become unbearable, and Rivka had to take the giant step to turn for help. She made use of her free will for the first time in this new direction. Although she could have done it before, she preferred not to change her life, because her pain then was less than her fears of the uncertain future.

The Power of Choice (Freedom of Will)

During her many years of compulsive eating, Rivka had chosen not to choose. She stuck grimly to her difficult life-script. Her ability to weigh the options and choose between them had deteriorated, much like a muscle that atrophies from disuse.

Therefore, although Rivka accepted the fact that she was still free to choose as rational, she nevertheless denied it in the depths of her heart. In the area of compulsive eating, she "knew," better than anyone else, that there was no hope for change.

In other areas of her life, such as dress, religion and social ties, Rivka made full use of her freedom to choose. Freedom of will is a God-given power that may control many "muscles." Those that are used remain flexible, and those that are unused — like eating habits — slowly atrophy. Rivka felt that she chose freely in areas such as the daily menu for supper, or when and where to buy clothes for her children. That made her all the more frustrated and angry at herself when, in the sphere of her eating habits, she felt completely subjugated to the dictations of her parents.

What is the nature of this subjugation? Rav Dessler writes that the will is neutralized by the imagination.[149] When reason points one way, and man does the opposite, it is because his imagination is preoccupied with other matters, **deflecting attention** from the reasonable goal. In Rivka's case, reason and rationality pointed at the necessity to take control over her eating habits. She was aware that, while exercising her free will in many areas of her life, here, in her compulsive eating habits, she **disregarded** this basic freedom of choice.

Therefore, Rivka's problem is deflecting attention from her free will, or disregarding her inherent power to choose what is good for her. To solve her problem, she must bring attention to bear, as often as possible, on her freedom to choose. By dealing directly with her problems at their basic level, and by constantly using techniques to occupy her mind with the "right" thoughts, Rivka can gradually bring herself to **believe** that she

---

149. *Michtav MeEliyahu*, vol. 1, p. 112.

can choose in this area as well. Then she will choose whether to eat without feeling guilty, or to control her desire for food in accordance with some reasonable rule.

Repentance — Teshuvah

This is the basic process that every *baal teshuvah* (he who repents) undergoes. Tremendous effort is exerted, calling up a lot of emotional energy, to **believe** that we can change and improve the quality of our service of God. What is true in everyday life, such as eating and smoking (an example brought by Rav Dessler), holds no less for the more spiritual changes of our lives. In essence, it is a matter of the imagination distracting us from believing in ourselves as the owners of free will.

This idea may perhaps shed light on the social phenomenon called the *teshuvah* movement. So many people have seen the light of Torah and changed their lives that this may be termed a social (and not just spiritual) revolution. Yet, there are many others that are distant and growing ever more so. Many people, especially those who are termed *baalei teshuvah*, ask the obvious question: why? Why do two close friends split up because one attaches himself to Torah and its observance, while the other remains estranged and often antagonistic? Is it a matter of one's lineage (*zechus avos*), or perhaps the cycles of the soul (*gilgulei neshamos*), or simply aid from Heaven (*siyata dishmaya*)?

Of course, the answers to these questions are significant in one's journey back towards his Father. However, the above explanation might deepen our understanding of the basic process of *teshuvah*; for one thing is certainly common to **all** *baalei teshuvah*: **They decided to take charge of their lives and actually change them!** Well-worn patterns of dress, language, behavior and thought were completely set aside to make way for new modes of living. As we saw above, this personal revolution stemmed from the new imbalance of the "internal scales." This was caused by weighing the present troubles in life against the fear of change. Herein is to be found the difference between one man and another.

There are so many components that make up the present existential pain or the fear of future change, that there are infinite possibilities. No two people are exactly alike. As discussed previously, just as no two faces are identical, so too no one has exactly the same *daas* as another. Only the Creator, who delves into our depths and knows all about us, can truly know why Reuven became a *baal teshuvah*, whereas his close friend Shimon remained where he was.

However, we must be wary and not make the mistake of analyzing repentance as a mechanical process. One may assume after the above explanation, that *teshuvah* is an automatic reshifting of internal balances between existential pain and fear of the unknown. It sounds like a mathematical equation in which one side increases above the threshold of suffering, causing the other side to compensate by adding more weight and realigning the equation. As a result, life is changed, and what do we have? A *baal teshuvah*. In that case, we are nothing more than robots! Where in all this is our freedom of choice?

Choosing Pain

The formula offered is accepted. It is correct. The internal shift is expressed in an external shift. But the mechanical approach, so blatantly contradicting our freedom of will, is based on a false assumption. Suffering and pain, we assumed, are not under our control. We tend to see them as fated, as part of "everything is in the hands of Heaven except for fear of Heaven." Pain and suffering seem to be part of the "external world" into which we tumbled on day one. That is the illusion, yet it is a false one.

Then again, it is partially true. Suffering caused to us in childhood was indeed parceled out to us by Heaven. Out innate hunger to find happiness is also not of our choice. But there is another type of pain that is not preordained, which is dependant on *daas*. This is the pain of seeing the truth against the background of falseness, seeing light against dark and realizing the extent of the abyss between them. This is referred to by King Shlomo, in his words: "He who gains *daas* gains pain."[150]

This is existential pain, and it is under our control. We are at liberty to increase it, as we use our *daas* to delve more deeply into the existential truths of our lives. This way we attain more knowledge while simultaneously suffering the pain of our ignorance and misguided ways. Or we can choose to disregard our "point of truth" and continue plodding on according to our well-worn life-script. In this case, suffering is truly brought upon us by God, so that we should finally live truthfully. The road of passivity and meekness might be less painful existentially, but it is also less meaningful and, therefore, of greater suffering in the long run.

The Choice of the Baal Teshuvah

We see then that freedom of will is fundamental to the process of *teshuvah*. Furthermore, it is applicable to all people at whatever spiritual stage they find themselves. We are always faced with the option of remaining where we are, secure in the familiar ways of our lives, or striving to change and improve. Deep in our hearts, we know that we are not yet living in complete accordance with life's truths, with God and His Torah and *mitzvos*. It hurts us to admit our shortcomings, and it is hard to change our actions to suit our fundamental beliefs. When, nev-

---

150. *Koheles* 1:18.

ertheless, the option of continued blindness becomes unbearable in our hearts, we repent. We become *baalei teshuvah*. We **freely choose** the pain of giving up certain "pleasures" and dealing instead with painful memories. The fruits are sweet enough to justify the toil. The sacrifice is actually an investment.

We should take note that the pain which causes change of direction is not necessarily physical. It is usually emotional and, even deeper, existential. Therefore, this point may be reached by a person who **rationally** attempts to comprehend his world and existence, and discovers God and Torah. The result is regret for many wasted years, and the desire to finally live meaningfully and truthfully. What had until now been a necessary way of life is now seen as insufferable, for the light of truth is too painful to disregard.

Torah Therapy and Teshuvah

At this point we return to Torah Therapy. A fundamental part of this therapy is that each and every one of us is obliged to "come back" (*chozer*) in repentence (*teshuvah*) every day. It is now clear that the need to reassess our lives and improve them is imperative for all of us, whether "healthy" or not, whether secular or religious, reform or orthodox. This is referred to by Rav Dessler in his treatise on *bechirah*, freedom of will, as the constant struggle to raise our personal "point of choice."[151] Furthermore, we shall be chastised for **not** exercising our free will to improve our lives.

During therapy, a conscious effort is made to positively reframe the painful process that brought the patient to ask for help. He is encouraged to view his efforts to allay his suffering as a courageous step towards dealing truthfully with his life,

---

151. *Michtav MeEliyahu*, vol. 1, p. 114.

despite the pain involved. This freedom to change his life is a God-given grace. By taking repsonsiblity for choosing our personal road, we are meaningfully involved as "partners" of creation.

But are we not overly involved with **ourselves**? Should our hurt and suffering be so central to our choices? This sounds rather egocentric. Should we not be more socially oriented, more involved with helping others overcome their pain? Why should our personal suffering be more important than that of countless others?

These questions arise from an assumption that our egoistic tendencies are frowned upon by Torah. The next chapter will discuss egoism and egocentrism and the Torah's viewpoint.

Chapter 12
Chesed to Oneself

Sensitivity to Egoism

We are egoistic, yet we are taught that we should not be so. Therefore, when we try to assess ourselves from a moral point of view, we can become quite confused. Just how much are we supposed to fulfill our personal needs? Where is the thin line that divides between justified self-investment and anti-social egocentrism?[152]

These questions are especially troublesome to those who strive to live in accordance with God's will, i.e. *halachah*. On the one hand, we are commanded to maintain a healthy mind in a healthy body. On the other hand, we are constantly reminded of our obligations towards our fellow man, especially those around us: spouse, children, parents, neighbors, poor people, etc. We wish to do *chesed*, but it is often misdirected (or so it feels when we are awash with guilt feelings).

The truth is that there is no clear answer. Most people find their personal formula for living between these two poles out of

---

152. Egoism is not the same as egocentrism. The former is the natural state of man in which he is involved with satisfying his needs. In contrast, egocentrism is a facet of the *yetzer ha-ra* in which these needs precede those of all others. An egocentric person feels that he is the center of the world (ego-centric), rather than one among many and parallel worlds.

habits carried over from childhood and adolescence. Even when they suffer, they usually do not stop to think if this habit is justified. A typical example is the sad fact that many women invest all their energies in their households, while neglecting to care for themselves. They often feel that it would be immoral to ease up on themselves when it is usually at the expense of others. The tragic result of this attitude is that they often collapse at some point, either physically or emotionally or both.

Another example, of the opposite nature, is more often present in men. It occurs when people misinterpret the dictum of our Sages, "If I am not for myself, who [will be] for me?"[153] Some people are so preoccupied with their needs and pleasures that they have no time and energy to consider the needs of others, even though they love them. In the first example, the woman feels that she has no right to take care of her own needs, an attitude which she "inherited" from childhood. In the second example, the man feels — and has always felt — that no one has the right to demand of him to be sensitive to others. He is certain that his suffering is greater than that of others, and therefore justifies his selfishness.

Here, too, the result is tragic. Although the man in this example does not collapse as an individual, his social framework — family, friends and associates — slowly disintegrates around him, leaving him alone and isolated, lacking the love and support which he needs so much.

Investment or Sacrifice

Another way we can express the issue of *chesed* is by asking the following question: Am I **investing** in others, or am I **sacrificing** myself for them? There is a tremendous difference between the emotions accompanying an investment in others and those that

---

153. *Pirkei Avos* 1:14.

accompany a sacrifice for others. When investing, we generally feel satisfaction and positive expectations for the future, which make the present hardship worthwhile. However, when we sacrifice, we tend to resent the time and effort that we must expend. We are often angry and frustrated because we feel coerced into taking care of others' needs while neglecting our own. We feel exploited, and the *chesed* we accomplished leaves a bitter taste in our mouth.

It is incredible that most people are ignorant of the vast difference between these two attitudes. Too many of us feel that we are sacrificing for the sake of our loved ones, and have no idea that this is a bad investment. Some of us **believe** that we are wisely investing, but we are unaware that we **feel** that we are sacrificing. Ignorance, self-contradiction, subconscious motives and confusion run rampant in this area of life. Yet this is understandable.

The reason we are so unaware of our true selves is rooted in the personal life-script that each person unconsciously writes for himself. We have already discussed how the innocent child's life revolves around this axis, and why he stubbornly holds on to it throughout his life. Parental and social values that were absorbed uncritically in a person's early childhood thus become unquestioned axioms of "eternal truths" in his adulthood.

It is therefore the Torah Therapist's task to help the patient reexamine his basic beliefs in respect to egoism and *chesed*. What does Torah have to say on this matter? Is there a specific formula that we can follow? Is there a definitive path that differentiates between invested *chesed* and sacrificed *chesed*?

Giving and Taking

Rav Dessler defines two basic and opposing forces within us: the power of giving and the power of taking.[154] The power of giving is rooted in the divinity within us, our soul, which, like its infinite Creator, desires to give of its own to others. Our Sages express this similarity in the following words: "As He is merciful, so shall you be. As He is charitable (*gomel chasadim*), so shall you be, etc."[155] The power of taking is rooted in man's *yetzer*, which God created ex nihilo. The purpose is to allow God's goodness to be received. By having a *yetzer*, man is like an "empty vessel" (*kli kibul*) which may be filled. This is a prerequisite for accepting — there must be a receptacle if we wish to receive blessing.

Rav Dessler explains that both powers, although of contradictory nature, are rooted in the essence of man and are God-given. They must both be used wisely, for their purpose is to enable man to become a "partner" with God. He must **give** to others as God gives. But he must also **accept** what is bestowed upon him by God, so that he may be full enough to give others, in turn.

It is wrong to say that man should only give. It is equally wrong to say that he should only take. Man must use both powers, of giving and of taking, while maintaining balance between them.

The Balance of "Give and Take"

How can we define this balance? Let us imagine that man were a hollow tube, with a conical opening at its top and a narrow spout opening from its bottom. In order to enter into his Divine "partnership," he must accept blessings from God through the

---

154. *Michtav MeEliyahu*, vol. 1, p. 32.
155. See Rabbeinu Bachye on *Shemos* 15:3.

upper opening. Then he runs it through his system and brings it out through the bottom "faucet," from whence he gives it to others. The more he empties himself by giving to others, the more he receives from God and replenishes himself. In conclusion, we see from this analogy that true balance is achieved when giving is done in full force, thus allowing man to receive in full force in return.

But if we hold on to what we receive, then the process is slowed down, or may even be stopped to a large extent. We might be afraid to give lest we remain empty. Or perhaps we are so enamoured of what we received that we prefer not to share it with anyone else. In such cases, giving is seen as a sacrifice rather than an investment. As long as we hold ourselves full with God's blessings, we have no room for further gifts. We are full of ourselves!

The result is spiritual stagnation. As we know, life is movement. Death is the absence of life. Even water loses its freshness when it stops flowing. Anything stationary over a period of time begins to rot, decay, dehydrate or stagnate. Likewise, when man is stuck existentially "between heaven and earth," holding stubbornly to what he receives without passing it on to someone else, he gradually dies a spiritual death.

As the pain increases, he may realize that there is still a chance. This is because, unlike physical death, spiritual death is gradual and therefore not terminal. By opening himself to others, he is resuscitated. This is one of the meanings of the blessing with which we praise God: "Blessed are You...for giving life to the dead."

A Fly within the Heart

There is an amazing analogy that explains the subject of giving and taking and the workings of the *yetzer ha-ra* (the evil inclination). The Talmud[156] says as follows: "The *yetzer ha-ra* is like a fly in the openings of the heart." At first, this analogy seems quite strange. Why a fly? After all, a fly is not dangerous, nor is it poisonous. It doesn't sting, or even hurt. A fly is merely a nuisance. Is that all the *yetzer ha-ra* is? Just a nuisance? Shouldn't it rather be compared to a snake or a scorpion? Furthermore, what are these "openings" of the heart, and what is a fly doing there? It would be more likely to presume that the openings in the head, such as eyes, ears or mouth, are more appropriate for the traps laid for us by our *yetzer ha-ra*.

Let us explain the "openings of the heart" first. What are these openings, and what is their purpose? Every biology student today knows, as did our Sages thousands of years ago, that the heart has four chambers. They are linked by "openings" or valves, which allow blood to stream in one direction and not the reverse. As blood flows into the top chambers, it continues into the two bottom chambers, where it is compressed and pushed out of the heart. From the left chamber it is pushed out and dispersed through the many arteries that convey its life-giving oxygen to all cells of the body. The same pressure pushes the now-depleted blood into the veins that carry it back into the right side of the heart. From the right lower chamber it is once again pushed out into the lungs so that they can be enriched with newly inhaled oxygen. It then returns to the heart for yet another cycle. And so on and so forth....

Basically, the heart synchronizes two interlinked cycles. In one, the blood is replenished with oxygen. In the other, the blood gives the oxygen to the millions of cells that comprise the

---

156. *Berachos* 60a.

body. The blood volume must be constant in both cycles because they are intimately linked one to the other, and what
goes in must also come out. One cycle "gives" while the other
"takes," and this goes on endlessly and smoothly, thus maintaining the health of the body. Health is maintained as long as
the blood is replenished with oxygen, which it transfers to the
body's cells (as well as taking their wastes and dropping them
off in the lungs). To give is to receive, and to receive is to give.

Blood and Man

The Torah identifies blood as the physical counterpart of our
spirit, our *nefesh*. *"Ki ha-dam hu ha-nefesh"*[157] (for the blood is the
nefesh). In other words, our Creator teaches us that our spiritual
essence is linked to the physical body through the blood. Furthermore, the blood's behavior is the spiritual counterpart of
the behavior of man's spiritual being. The logical conclusion
must be that just as the heart gives and takes equally, so must
the spirit give and take in equal measures.

This idea is given credence by the Hebrew words for
"blood" — *dam* — and "man" — *adam*. In other words, man is
described as *dam* with the addition of the letter *alef*, which signifies his uniqueness as the spiritual "champion" (*aluf*) of this
physical world. His Divine essence is expressed in his physical
existence through the medium of his blood.

Let us return to the analogy of the fly within the chambers
of the heart. It is obvious that by simply lodging itself within
one of the valves leading from chamber to chamber, a harmless
fly can cause a person's death. The disruption of the continuous
flow of blood through one or both of the cycles would cause
heart failure, which leads to certain death. Oxygen would no
longer be absorbed through the lungs, nor transferred through-

---

157. *Devarim* 12:23.

out the body.

In the physical body death is sudden and final. Fortunately, this is not the case in the spiritual body. Spiritual heart failure is gradual and therefore reversible. As long as the physical body is alive, man can remove the blockage in his spiritual circulation, and thus return to life. He must learn to give and receive in one continuous flow exactly as the blood itself must give and receive in a smooth flow.

The goal of the *yetzer ha-ra* is no more than the disruption of the even, continuous flow of giving and receiving. That which is natural and "built in" within us — to give and to receive - is constantly threatened and easily disrupted. There is no need for a venomous "bite" by the *yetzer ha-ra*. A small disruption of the circulation in our spiritual circuit is sufficient to choke us. This invisible process, however gradual, tends to escalate unless it is stopped. The result is our inability to be God's dynamic partners in bettering the world which He created for us. This is exactly what the *yetzer ha-ra* wants.

The Torment of Doubts

How does this "fly" announce its presence? How can we be aware of it so that we can take precautionary measures? The answer is simple: we suddenly feel that we can no longer give or receive to the extent that we have been giving or receiving until now.

If we have been giving selflessly, it dawns upon us that we must start taking care of ourselves rather than others. It is high time, we feel, that we gather in those many "pipelines" of support that we have extended to parents, partners and children. We must self-righteously give our strengths to **ourselves**! We have been drained physically and emotionally.

The opposite case, in which we receive "too much" out of consideration towards others (which feels like voluntary self-strangulation), also attests to the threat of the hidden "fly." We may feel that the giving is insincere, or, even if not, that we don't deserve it. In the latter case, feelings of guilt at being falsely appreciated serve to close us off from the giver. We feel that we need to stop being so selfish and first take care of our spouse, siblings, and those numerous duties that are "naturally" more important than our own needs. "I can't afford to cater to my needs as long as I haven't taken care of my responsibilities towards those who depend on me."

On the other hand, the need to give and receive is instinctive. Therefore, we are often confused — if not torn apart — by these contradictory forces. We are tormented by doubts whether to allow ourselves to give or receive, or whether we should close the valve of our pipeline with others and escape to our "personal island" of the mind. We tend to vascillate between these two extremes, constantly switching from connection to isolation, over and over again. The reason is that neither of these options is truly satisfying, and after a while, we must escape to the other extreme. In any case, we do not maintain that life-giving balance of continuous flow between accepting and offering. We "die" far too often.

Not only is this unstable behavior confusing, it is also painful. We hurt our children, our spouse and our friends when we suddenly back off and close ourselves from them. They are hurt because they cannot understand. Often we ourselves do not understand either. Our confusion makes our behavior contradictory and therefore incomprehensible to ourselves. We may reach that painful point at which we question our own sanity. We may become so unpredictable even to ourselves that our self confidence slowly disintegrates. Life seems like one big, inscrutable mess!

Do Yourself a Favor

We finally realize (sometimes with a little help from our friendly Torah Therapist) that the solution to our problems is that we must not only learn to give more, but also to receive more. We should strive to open ourselves in both directions so as to achieve a healthy balance. But how do we begin? Do we increase our capacity for giving to others first, or should we initially try to "open up" and receive more than we thought we should or could? The answer, in most cases, is that we must first improve our capacity to receive. After all, it is **we** who asked for help for ourselves! Sometimes we come for help because we find it hard to give to others as much as we wish.

In any case, the starting point is that we need to help ourselves first. Only by learning to be sensitive to our own needs, both physical and emotional, can we truly satisfy them. And only then will we be content and fulfilled enough to sincerely and satisfactorily give to others.

As simple as this sounds, it is not so easy for a *ben-Torah* (disciple of Torah) to apply to himself. For all his life he has been taught that one must be altruistic and take care of others' needs before his own. Self-sacrifice in doing acts of *chesed* is one of the foremost characteristics of the observant Jew. This trait of disregarding one's needs for the welfare of others was modeled by our holy forefather Avraham, who was the archetype of true *chesed*. Even when suffering from the pain of circumcision at the age of 99, Avraham ran towards three traveling "Arabs," and begged them to allow him to serve them. He offered food, drink, and rest in his tent, and then hastened to fulfill his promises. He even gave up the exquisite pleasure of speaking with God in order to attend to his guests. Truly altruism at its highest!

It seems incongruent to claim that Torah demands that we must first look after ourselves. This desire seems to be no more than the familiar temptation of the *yetzer ha-ra*. A person who espouses this popular approach is actually completely unaware that he has been cunningly persuaded by his **own** *yetzer ha-ra* to maintain this destructive position. Instead of learning to balance his powers of giving and accepting, he is convinced that he must give of himself until he is left weak and empty, if not destroyed. But what about Avraham and altruism? We shall see that Avraham was the model of *chesed* **because** he achieved that delicate balance between giving and accepting.

Chesed shel Emes (True Chesed)

This balanced approach to *chesed* is discussed by our Sages. For example, when dealing with the burial of the deceased, we are described as performing *chesed shel emes*. What does *emes* (truth) have to do with the *mitzvah* of burial? The obvious answer is that there is no payment made by the deceased for the favors bestowed upon him. Therefore, whatever efforts are expended on his behalf are completely altruistic, perfect *chesed* in which one gives without receiving at all.

But are we not enjoying less tangible rewards, such as the appreciation of the deceased's relatives? In fact, when payment is sometimes appropriate, they willingly come forth with whatever is due. And what about our belief that the deceased will pray for us as well, for having given him the respect and honor of those significant last hours on earth? What about our personal reward in this life and the next? After all, we are constantly reminded that for every *mitzvah*, however small, we are rewarded so generously that we have no idea what awaits us in the next world! Is perfect *chesed* a meaningless term, an unapproachable ideal?

Yet our Sages call this *chesed* with the deceased *chesed shel emes*. We must therefore conclude that when the *chesed* is done without expecting reward from the beneficiary, then its primary goal was altruistic. Even though we receive secondary rewards, the **primary** goal is simply to give and to serve others. With this definition of true *chesed* in mind, we may now resolve a difficult question concerning Avraham *Avinu*.

Did Avraham not receive pleasure from giving to others? When he preferred to leave the Divine presence, and despite the noon sun and the pain of his circumcision, ran to offer hospitality to three perfect strangers, was he not happy in doing *chesed*? Isn't this happiness and pleasure a worthy reward for Avraham? The answers seem to be positive. Did Avraham suffer more from his sacrifices than the satisfaction and fulfillment that he must have felt when providing hospitality? We may assume — despite the tremendous spiritual gulf between ourselves and Avraham — that the answer is negative: the pleasure was greater than the pain. So it seems, at first glance, that Avraham's motives were self-centered, rather than altruistic. How can this be?

The answer is obvious. Avraham enjoyed the exquisite pleasure of pure *chesed*, giving for the sake of benefiting others. His was true *chesed shel emes*. **When giving is its own reward, then it is as pure as is possible.** If, on the other hand, one feels **sacrifice** in the act of *chesed*, then it is not as pure, for there are other rewards that make it worthwhile. The greater the pleasure in giving, the more truthful it becomes, for there are no ulterior motives. In other words, the primary goal of Avraham was to give to others. The pleasure involved was secondary, a by-product. Of course, this deep pleasure of the spirit serves to reinforce the desire to continue giving. The wonderful feeling that accompanies acts of true *chesed* is intuited as proof of its worth and value in the eyes of God and man. With this understanding, let us turn back to Avraham.

Our forefather Avraham was rich both materially and spiritually. He was loved by God, who returned his love (*"Avraham ohavi"*[158]). He was highly esteemed by all, as the Torah testifies (*"Nesi Elokim atah b'socheinu"*[159] — you are the Lord's leader among us.) His greatest pleasure was serving God by obeying His will. This he expressed by performing deeds of *chesed* unceasingly and with all his heart. He is justly referred to as "the pillar of *chesed*." He is our model for giving **because** there is a very definite immediate reward in Avraham's *chesed*: the pleasure and satisfaction of giving!

"Gomel Nafsho Ish Chesed"[160]
(He Who Gives to Himself Is a Man of Chesed)

It is becoming clear that in order to give, we must also learn to receive, as pure as the giving is. This idea is further explained by Rabbi Nosson Tzvi Finkel, z"l, the "Alter of Slobodka," in his *sefer Or Ha-tzafun*.[161] He too discusses Avraham, the pillar of *chesed*, in reference to a *midrash* at the beginning of *Chayei Sarah* which states the following:

"And after this Avraham buried his wife Sarah." As it says: "He who chases after charity and *chesed* will find life, charity and respect."[162] He who chases charity is Avraham...and *chesed* [refers to] when he did *chesed* with his wife Sarah [burial and eulogy — E.L.]...God said to him: "My craft is doing *chesed*. You have taken my craft, then come and take my clothes."[163]

The Alter of Slobodka asks: why do our Sages portray Avraham as being chosen **at this point**, late in his life, as God's earthly partner in the craft of *chesed*? Besides, what is so special

---

158. *Yeshayah* 41:8.
159. *Bereishis* 23:6.
160. *Mishlei* 11:17.
161. *Or Ha-zafun*, vol. 1, *"B'netivos ha-chesed"*.
162. *Mishlei* 21:21.
163. *Midrash Rabbah, Chayei Sarah, parashah* 58:9.

about the simple routine — however sad — of burying one's spouse and eulogizing her? This act is accepted and natural among all people. In contrast, Avraham's amazing hospitality mentioned above, or his desperate attempts to save the wicked people of Sodom and Gemorah, are definitely acts of unparalleled *chesed*. Why didn't Avraham receive God's accolade at these unique high points of his life?

The Alter answers as follows. True and pure *chesed* includes the minimizing of **humiliation**, which is often felt by the receiver. As noble as charity may be for the giver, it can nevertheless be quite humiliating for the receiver. It is only when *chesed* is **expected as natural** that it is received without shame. This is the situation between people who are intimate enough to give and take without a second thought. Therefore, *chesed* is more pure when it is offered to members of one's own family, since they are unashamed to accept it. For this reason, our Sages state the *halachah* that when a person gives charity, he must do so in an order of priorities. First on the list are members of one's family — "*bnei beischa kodmim*" (your household members come first).

So it turns out that a criterion for true *chesed* is the relationship between the giver and the receiver. If the giver disregards the needs of those dependent upon him, and he prefers to bestow his grace upon those who are less intimate with him, then he displays *chesed* which is "impure." Obviously, he seeks the rewards or thanks from those who make much ado about his charity, unlike those who expect it on a daily basis. This imperfection of *chesed* is quite familiar to most people, for we are all far from perfect.

Avraham, however, is another story. His *chesed* was truly perfect. The Alter of Slobodka explains the *midrash* as follows. Our Sages stressed the point made above — that *chesed* begins at home — by choosing the burial and eulogizing of Sarah as the point at which to anoint Avraham with the crown of *chesed*. His final act of giving towards his wife is the testimony to a lifetime of pure *chesed* that **started at home and spread out to include all of humanity**. Avraham had no ulterior motives other than the simple pleasure of giving for the sake of giving. No wonder he is the pillar of *chesed* for all mankind.

Hillel the Elder

The Alter then quotes the *midrash* about Hillel *Ha-zaken* (the elder), who would daily end his lessons abruptly. He would explain to his students that he had to leave off studying Torah with them because he had to take care of the needy guest at his home. One day his students asked him if he always had some guest awaiting him at the end of the day. Hillel answered: "And is not this poor *nefesh* of mine a needy guest in my house [body], that today is here and tomorrow is there?"[164] Our Sages saw Hillel the Elder as the embodiment of the verse: "*Gomel nafsho ish chesed*"[165], (He who gives to his own *nefesh* is a man of *chesed*).

Hillel was teaching his students that no less important than **learning** Torah is **applying** it. We are commanded to do *chesed* to our close relatives first, and who is closer than his own *nefesh*? Since his *nefesh* is the lower part of his spiritual self (the part which connects his spirit to the physical aspects of his existence) and it is transitory in this world, he must satisfy its basic needs as long as he is responsible for it. If the *nefesh* is required to move the physical body within this world, it must be supplied with energy, such as food, drink and sleep. These are the basic needs of every person's *nefesh*, and are **first in line** for receiving *chesed* from its master.

---

164. *Midrash Rabbah, Vayechi.*
165. *Mishlei* 11:17.

This priority — we have seen — is based on the lack of shame (*nahama d'kisufa*, in the words of the Zohar) by the receiver. For this reason, *chesed* is considered purer when it is offered to one's family rather than to strangers. After all, it is universally accepted that a parent gives to his children and married couples give to each other. Because it is natural, it is expected, and therefore the thanks are minimal.

Even more natural and axiomatic is the attitude of the *nefesh* towards its own master, the *ruach* (spirit) or the *neshamah* (soul). This is the ultimate in *chesed*, strange as it may sound. What we learn from Hillel is that when the time comes to satisfy the **basic** requirements of the *nefesh*, mundane and physical as they are, they take precedence over all other forms of *chesed*, including teaching Torah. (This is akin to the principle of *pikuach nefesh docheh es ha-Shabbos*, that saving one's life takes precedence over Shabbos.)

Priority Levels of Chesed

In summarizing this approach to *chesed*, Rav Dessler points out that there is a natural evolvement of giving that forms different levels of *chesed*, each with a different value of priority. He brings the *midrash* about Elkanah, the *shofet* (judge) of his generation, who was the husband of Chana and father of Shmuel. The Torah describes Elkanah with the words: "*v'alah ha-ish ha-hu*"[166] (and that man ascended). Our Sages added to these words the following: "He ascended within his household, he ascended within his courtyard, he ascended within his city, he ascended within all Israel, and all these ascents were from within his own self."[167] In other words, explains Rav Dessler, the process of giving others from God's blessings begins within

---

166. *Shmuel I*, 1:3.
167. *Midrash Yalkut Shimoni, Shmuel I, remez* 77.

oneself. When these blessings begin within one's being, then they overflow to others, starting from those closest to him and spreading out.

A simple analogy brings the point across. If we fill a wine goblet completely and continue pouring, it will overflow. Naturally, the wine spreads out around the goblet, gradually encompassing more and more area. So too, *chesed*, God's blessings, overflow from within the righteous person and encompass those around him, his wife and children. It comes to include his students, friends, neighbors, etc. Finally, the whole world is blessed from this Divine "wine," stemming from Heaven, and passing through the righteous person.

This may be likened to the results of throwing a stone into a pond. As it hits the water, it creates a small concentric wave, which spreads out quickly and smoothly. Its circumference increases until it reaches the banks of the pond, whereupon (according to physical laws of nature) it returns to its point of origin. Because of friction and other forces, this goes unnoticed, but nevertheless that is the nature of things.

Similarly, the *chesed*, when performed from pure motives of the pleasure of giving, starts from oneself and spreads out to all directions. At some point it comes back to the giver, endowing him with greater pleasure and reinforcing his desire to continue the spread of God's blessings **to him**. The light shining out from his heart is reflected back, making the true *baal chesed* shine ever more strongly in his own reflection.

"Olam Chesed Yibaneh"
(The World Is Created by Chesed)

This is the message that is brought across to the majority of people who come for help and advice. "Start taking care of yourself!" is not a message to disregard one's family or friends. It might seem that way at the beginning, since we have been brainwashed that we are **bad** when we are egoistic. But the truth eventually wins over. We discover that as we learn to fulfill our true needs in the light of Torah, we naturally tend to give of ourselves to others. First, those who are most intimate with us testify to this change. And then the ripples become felt and **returned** even by those further away. The change is remarkable. If, in the past, *chesed* was given grudgingly, if not bitterly, as a wearisome burden of sacrifice, now it is a natural outpouring of love and care.

The strange part of this amazing process is that *chesed* towards others is not a goal. It is merely a natural extension of *"gomel nafsho ish chesed,"* of learning to accept from God all that He offers us. Because man cannot contain all of God's *chesed* within his being, it simply overflows. Avraham did not tell himself that he must give *chesed* to the three passing strangers. He simply did it, because it was the natural thing to do. It was natural because he was overflowing with God's blessings. Likewise, when a mother feeds and takes care of her baby, she is not "doing *chesed*" with the baby. She is simply giving, for that is the natural thing to do when overflowing with love.

This natural *chesed* comes back to the giver, increasing his pleasure and the desire to continue giving. As much as he gives to others, so does he give to himself. We see then a deeper meaning in the words of our Sages *"olam chesed yibaneh,"* the world is created by *chesed*. Not only do we create the world as God's earthly partners when we truly give to others; we also **create our own world**. Every giving becomes, eventually, a receiving, even though that was not the goal. And as our world receives and becomes lit up through the blessings of God and of those who received from us, we rekindle the world around us. Finally, we come to discover that there is no definite boundary between our personal world and that which surrounds us. *Olam Chesed Yibaneh!*

Chapter 13
Withdrawal and Aggression

The Reaction to Being Hurt

Why is it that we often disregard our own needs, while tending to those of others? Why do we feel that *chesed* is giving to others, but giving to oneself is egoistic and therefore frowned upon? Why do we need the wisdom of Hillel the Elder to point out that *chesed* starts at home? It seems reasonable to suggest that this is due, at least in part, to a familiar childhood experience. As children, we naturally sought personal satisfaction, without self-limitations. These were gradually imposed on us by our elders, for our benefit. Not always was our education easily achieved. We often got hurt along the way. This seemed to be the natural order of things. Even a happy childhood contains its moments of pain.

Whatever the case, we were often told to stop being selfish, to think about others as well. We may have developed the belief that any self-care is immoral. Similarly, whenever we demonstrated negative behavior, we would feel the pain of being put down by our elders. This sequence of events became familiar, like any habit.

We developed many distorted conclusions regarding this phenomenon: that we are vain, egoistic, lazy, despised, unloved, unworthy, etc. Our reactions to being hurt became ingrained through habit into our systems, as part and parcel of our life-scripts. Therefore, we are normally unaware that we have the freedom to change these reactions. In the chapter on free will, we saw that we cannot successfully use this freedom of will **before** we accept the fact that we had unconsciously enslaved ourselves to childhood habits of thought and action.

Once we realize how this reaction rules us through habit, we have the chance to change it if we wish. Why should we want to? Because, due to negative habits (reaction-formations), our connections with those we love are twisted. These same negative habits also disconnect us from God. We feel alone and afraid when our "hotline" with God suddenly becomes "cold."

Yes, we suffer when we let our habitual reactions rule our lives, even though this seems to be the natural course of life. This is inevitable, and we are blameless to a certain degree. We are not at fault for developing these habits, for they were formed when we were children and, as such, had no other options. Now, however, as adults, we are responsible for making ourselves happier by improving the quality of our lives. To do so, we must understand the root of our problems. How did these negative reactions begin?

When Children Get Hurt

Children are usually much weaker than adults. They therefore have fewer behavioral options when they get hurt. They can either withdraw or strike back. Being weaker, they tend to withdraw. An adult, on the other hand, may choose to confront the aggressor directly or indirectly, with others' aid, or perhaps later when he is alone but stronger. He may wish to plan a reaction, or he may insist on immediate confrontation.

These, as well as various other options, are unavailable for the average child. Most children learn early in life that if they express their negative emotions, such as anger, sadness or frustration, they often do not receive compassion and support. Instead they may be reprimanded or ignored, and sometimes even criticized or hit.

The child initially reacts by crying, getting angry or refusing to eat. His rebellion is, however, usually short-lived. After all, he is the weaker half of this natural struggle. It is preferrable to surrender rather than be humiliated. That means cutting himself off to some degree from those with whom he has struggled. This is the price he must pay when he correctly concludes that it is best to keep his feelings inside, even though he would much prefer to share them with others.

This process becomes a habit over the years, and is so automatic that by the time he has grown up, it is almost entirely subconscious. However, the suppression of emotions creates internal emotional pressure. The steam builds up, like that of a volcano, until it forces its way out in a sudden explosion. The tremendous energy of suppressed pain and frustration must somehow be expressed.

Therefore, over the years, the child might explode in anger for seemingly insignificant reasons. He might become aggressive towards his peers, or he might develop learning problems. Then again, he may become so subdued that he withdraws into his personal shell, preferring the loneliness of his private world, to the dangers of social contact. If crying was frowned upon, he might even "forget" how to let tears wet his eyes. His suppressed energy is effectively used in building a thick wall of defense against the threatening world outside.

By the time he has reached adulthood, he seems, at times, heartless. When we need compassion, he offers scorn. When we offer love, he may disdainfully question our motives. When we seek communication, he cuts us off. When we criticize, he explodes in anger, or clams up and disappears. We may give up on him. As for him, **he has long ago given up on himself**. The tragedy of this situation is undeniable.

Where Does the Anger Go?

As we saw, a child may develop low self-esteem as a result of having been denied the right to express negative emotions. This is because the denial, always authoritative and often painful, carries an existential message in the eyes of the child. The message is: you are unworthy, we don't love you, you are bad, naughty, fresh, disappointing, lazy, good-for-nothing, tiresome, and so on.

This negative evaluation of the child contradicts the inherent goodness of his being. God has imbued within every human being an instinctive positive value of his existence. Deep inside, we all feel that we are worthwhile beings. Being told otherwise creates within us an awareness of injustice. We are good! How unfair it is to be accused as bad! Our basic worth is being trampled upon. We must deny this injustice, we must fight it. We are angry and justifiably so.

But we quickly learn that it is dangerous to express this anger, so we learn to suppress it. As children, we fight our battles for justice within our silent worlds, in our minds and our hearts. However, we can gradually turn on ourselves. We may criticize ourselves for being afraid to stand up for our rights against those who belittle us. Or we may join them in being angry at ourselves for being lazy, stupid and worthless. Unwittingly, we become our own victims! Our anger at this injustice builds up more than ever. It must somehow be let out or we will explode.

One solution for letting out this anger is aggression. The child is "an angel" at home, but "a devil" at school. Another solution is to suppress it under a thick wall of indifference and apathy. The child refuses to learn or partake in any social activity, such as sports or art. The former may become a cruel bully.

The latter may become a cowardly good-for-nothing. The common denominator between them is the pain of injustice for being devalued, and the anger that justifiably arose. Neither is aware of this anger. The former blames others for whatever conflict arises, while the latter simply feels nothing. When people hurt him, he is not aware of the pain. He is unaware of the anger which this pain creates. He is anaesthetized. If someone is to blame, it is himself.

These reaction-formations are also blessings. God allows these mechanisms of the heart to develop so as to permit the child to survive from day to day. He is unaware of the extent of pain suppressed within his heart, and that is as it should be, for he is incapable of dealing with it. But, when mature enough, when *daas* is present, he **is** empowered to deal with painful communication. We are not supposed to live life with the emotional weaknesses of the child we once were. How sad it is to see mature adults reacting to negative words much as they did decades ago, at the age of five!

Volcanic Explosions

Levi used to fight quite a lot with his brothers and sisters. He was also aggressive at school. His was a rebellious spirit. No punishment could keep him docile for a long time. When Levi married and had children, he was lovable and affectionate...as long as he wasn't opposed. But if someone happened to hint at some negative quality of his, Levi would explode with anger, verging on a tantrum. Everybody around Levi, parents, wife and children would tread carefully when he was around, for everyone knew: Levi has a very short fuse. We can liken Levi to a chronically active volcano.

Rochel seems quite different. As a child, she opted to "swallow" her humiliation. She managed quite effectively to suppress her anger and frustration. She was considered a very good and well-behaved girl. She always did as she was told, and accepted all criticism (which was rare) as justified. Even in her teenage years, Rochel showed no perceptible tendency to rebel...until she got married.

Rochel's anger started coming out once she was outside her parents' home. At first, the outbursts were mild and occasional, but gradually they grew louder and more regular. The suppressed anger of many years finally came out, at the expense of Rochel's husband and children. She wasn't an angry person, but she could easily be provoked by seemingly insignificant remarks that she felt were derogatory. Rochel can be compared to a volcano which erupts surprisingly from time to time, even though it seems otherwise inactive.

Then there is Avi; always cool, calm, and collected. His mildness is very apparent and quite amazing. Nothing seems to faze him. Is Avi a *tzaddik* (righteous person)? Not necessarily. More likely he was a child who managed to suppress his anger and frustration so effectively that even as an adult he manages to cope with life without dealing with hurt and anger. He is truly mild — on the surface. He is quiet and introspective, and even sociable. But he never really makes deep emotional contact. It is too dangerous for him. His life-script dictates that he maintain light acquaintances only, those that allow him to retreat whenever he is threatened with intimacy or other deep emotions. His life is rather stagnant in that sense, and that is no small price to pay, especially when it comes to marriage and having children.

Avi is challenged by life to step out of his shell. His emotions are needed by his wife and children. Avi's gut reaction to these justified demands would be to feel that he is being strangled. He would prefer to cop out, to retreat to his private corner, at home or at work. If the pressure is unbearable, Avi might pack up and disappear. Another option Avi has, but rarely uses, is to explode in tears of frustration or in extreme anger. Avi is like a gentle hill that could someday erupt as a volcano, though much to everyone's astonishment. Avi has been harboring resentment towards all those who hurt him, without letting anyone know...including himself!

Freedom of Choice — In the Present

How can we teach people like Levi, Rochel and Avi (and ourselves) how to change their accustomed reactions to being hurt? After all, they have convinced themselves that for them, no other option is available. They can and do offer very convincing rationalizations for their behavior. Whether they are angry or aggressive, withdrawing or clamming up, there always seems to be a perfect explanation.

Obviously, we **cannot** teach them that they are usually mistaken until they are willing to learn and find out for themselves. They have been suffering for so long that finally the day comes when they can't hold out any longer. The demands of family members, along with the daily treadmill of life, no longer allow them to escape from the pain of their life-scripts.

It is only now that they are prepared to hear that their lives are not predetermined. Their behavior, their *middos*, their attributes are all changeable. They may have tendencies that are inherited, but they also have the choice to change habits of behavior, emotions and beliefs. "Everything is in the hands of Heaven, except for fear of Heaven." Our behavior, emotions and beliefs are all contained within this concept of "fear of Heaven."

But teaching the concept of freedom of choice is not enough. Although it is necessary to understand it first, the real test is its application, *halachah l'maaseh*. To learn the "applied art" of freedom of choice, we must become aware **in the present**, in real-time. We reassess ourselves from a new viewpoint:

how do we react and to whom? Why do we do certain things or
say certain words and phrases? We must learn to be aware of
ourselves as close to the present as possible. This is contrary to
our habitual way of taking the present for granted, and losing
ourselves in past memories or dreams of the future.

We already learned above that true reality is a constantly
unfolding series of present moments. The future and past are
merely imaginative scenes that take place in our minds for our
pleasure or pain. Our life-script is built from these imaginings.
They reinforce it as long as we continue to lose ourselves in
these familiar pictures of the mind, both past and future. Our
freedom of choice, however, is anchored in the present. To use
this freedom, we must escape the clutches of past and future,
and grasp firmly onto the present. This is called awareness,
which is the activity of *daas*. It is firmly entrenched in the **here
and now**.

Working on Awareness

At this point, the Torah Therapist must show the way. Otherwise, the idea remains purely theoretical. Torah needs to be not
only learned, but also practiced. This is the rationale behind
"aseh lecha rav"[168] (make for yourself a rabbi). A wise person can
serve as an external source that will enable us to see ourselves a
bit from the "outside." The job of the therapist, therefore, is to
make us aware of the tremendous difference between our
imagined relationships with people and the resulting reactions
so familiar to us, and the true messages that are being sent and
received in the present.

For example, let us suppose that we had been criticized
once too often by a friend. Now we meet him again, but in contrast to previous encounters, we resist the temptation to "open

---

168. *Pirkei Avos* 1:6.

up." We remain aloof and nonchalant, and we simply say: "Hello, how are you?" After getting the usual answer "Fine, thanks," we walk away. Anything more from us would make us feel instinctively threatened, because we had been criticized more than once by that person.

The therapist might ask us to look into the person's face the next time we encounter him. They may be expressing genuine personal interest. If so, we might wish to prolong the conversation. We are encouraged to risk reopening old friendships that have gone sour. People change. Maybe we misjudged others or were misjudged by them. Isn't the renewed friendship worth the effort? Besides, are we not by now more mature and capable of dealing with criticism than we were in the past?

The Torah Therapist may offer several statements to direct our thoughts to the present. They may be:

1. What are you feeling at this moment?
2. Did you notice your voice at this point, when talking about your brother's death?
3. What are you doing with your hands now?
4. Is this emotion, which you are feeling now, familiar to you from some other time and place?

The result of redirecting our thoughts to the present is the realization of how disconnected we usually are from it. We discover that we have been enslaved to our imaginations, to past memories and future dreams. Now we are regaining much of the vitality and exuberance of experiencing life which, as children, was so natural to us.

The Torah Therapist — Torah-Seeker Relationship

Another method of redirecting one's consciousness to the present is to draw his attention to the feelings exchanged with the therapist, here and now. There is no mention of past or future because the relationship is usually short-term. That makes it a bit easier to refer to the ongoing present. Nevertheless, this is still difficult for those who are accustomed to rocky personal relationships, which normally clutter up their minds with past and future images.

There are some people whose relationships with others are so threatening that they cannot look anyone in the eye. Even when coming for help to the Torah Therapist they do not look at him directly. If invited to look up and stare into our faces, they can become anxious and agitated. They have grown accustomed to the defense mechanism of **not** facing any person in the here and now. It is too threatening and overwhelming.

However, when gently prodded to look someone in the eye, they gradually lose their fears. They discover the wonder and freshness of direct personal encounter in the present. The sudden freedom emphasizes their previous imprisonment within the confines of their minds. They gradually realize the sweetness of the fresh air of freedom, after years of lonely stagnation. This amazing emergence "from the cold" is often heady and overpowering.

Over a period of time, the relationship with the therapist becomes a living lesson, a model for other new — or renewed — relationships. The emphasis is to live in the present moment, and to be conscious of what is transpiring between the people in the relationship, emotionally, mentally and physically. The Torah Therapist does not criticize or judge. He accepts every person as he is, thus teaching him to accept himself. Only on the basis of this acceptance — by others and, especially, by himself — may he eventually change and improve the quality of his life.

"Ba-asher Hu Sham" ("Where He Is At")

This approach by the therapist towards his fellow man is

learned, as always, from the Torah. The Torah describes the attributes of God towards man, and we must strive to learn from His ways. "As he is merciful, so must you be; as He offers *chesed*, so must you offer *chesed*, etc."[169] Likewise, we learn to accept a person as he is at the present from the way God related to Yishmael.

Avraham sent away Hagar and their son, Yishmael, as Sarah demanded and after God told him to accede. However, they soon lost their way in the desert and ran out of water. Yishmael was dying. Hagar left him lying under a bush and went off to cry at a distance. Suddenly, an angel appeared and said to her: "Do not fear, for the Lord has heard the voice of the child, **where he is at.**"[170]

Our Sages explain these last three words with the following *midrash*. The angels were astonished at God's intention to spare Yishmael, in light of the fact that in the future he would wage war against God's children. The Lord answered: "Right now, what is he, righteous or evil?" And they answered: "Righteous." "Then he is worthy of being saved!" In other words, man is judged for what he is **now**, not for what he was or what he will be. The important consideration is "where he is at."

God uses this approach to judge us as well, both individually and as a nation, on Rosh HaShanah. On this sacred day, He sits in judgement and decides our fate for the coming year. Our present status is what matters. The past merely serves as a backdrop for our present evaluation. The future is an infinite array of options from which we may choose, when we get there. What we deserve to receive in the forthcoming year is what we are **now,** in the fleeting non-graspable present!

We must learn from God. When we evaluate someone, it

---

169. *Shabbos* 133b.
170. *Bereishis* 21:17.

must be done in terms of his present status. Whatever his past was, or his future, we must — in all fairness — see him as he is now. This is only possible if we learn to judge **ourselves** in similar fashion.

The Difficulty of Seeing Others "Where They Are At"

It is quite difficult to be non-judgemental. This is especially so for those of us who developed spontaneous reactions of self-defense, i.e. criticizing or belittling others, when we were disparaged for so many years. We simply emulated those who judged us unfavorably in the past. We didn't know there was any other choice. What we inherited, we very naturally passed on. And just as we misjudge ourselves (for that is what we learned from our peers), so we misjudge others.

It is paradoxical that this negative attitude may become reinforced by Torah observance. In this context, the laws and prohibitions are used to criticize and humiliate, rather than to enhance and support. How tragic! A person who was misjudged in the past uses Torah as ammunition to belittle others. It is instances like these that demonstrate the power of Torah as a potent poison, a potion of death (*sam ha-maves*), rather than a potion of life (*sam ha-chayim*.) This abuse of Torah is obvious to others but not to the person himself. It is his blind spot. He feels that he is doing God's will, but he is actually poisoning himself, as well as others.

One could call such a person compulsive. He feels that he must judge others as he was judged in his childhood. He internalized the message that he must pay dearly and now projects this negative feeling onto others. They must pay dearly for **their** sins, as he has been doing all his life. More often than not, he is totally ignorant of this process. It is so habitual that it has become unconscious.

In such a case, no *mitzvah* or learning Torah can "purify" either him or others. He remains lacking, impure, unworthy. All he sees is his imperfections and those of others. He finds proof for his pessimism in phrases like "I am a worm, not a man."[171] Or: "Do not believe in yourself until the day of your death."[172] (We discussed this complex of guilt feelings in the chapter about *teshuvah*.)[173]

This man judges himself as he had been judged as a child, and finds himself guilty. Rav Dessler points out that this judgement is passed in the continuous present. "Every man is like a judge in the Court of Heaven as regards himself and his dependants [family members — E.L.], and not after his death, but **actually during his life**."[174] It is so unfortunate when a person who, as a child suffered from humiliating and painful criticism, continues as an adult to judge himself and those he loves in the same way. He is never free from torment and sees no way out.

As common and "natural" as this state of affairs is, we are prohibited by Torah to accept it. God demands of us to rid ourselves of the negative judgementalism we internalized in childhood. We must learn from Him how to love our brother — and ourselves — "where he is at."

The Tools for Limud Zechus (Giving Credit)

When the Torah Therapist begins to teach his fellow Jew that

---

171. *Tehillim* 22:7.

172. *Pirkei Avos* 2:5.

173. Rabbi Shlomo Wolbe in *Alei Shur* vol. 2 gives warning to all who begin to work at becoming better *ovdei Hashem* in *middos*. They should first recognize their noble and elevated side before beginning to criticize themselves. Otherwise they will become despondent and fall into depression. For man is paradoxically noble and elevated in his likeness to God, and low and of small stature in terms of his ego. Many fall into this trap of self-criticism with which they also judge their fellow man.

174. *Michtav MeEliyahu*, vol. 1, p. 125.

he has many good points to his credit of which he is unaware, mere words are not enough. He must convey this message by means of the personal bond that evolves between the two as they interrelate. His manner, speech, body language and eyes — all these and more — should help to bring across the idea that the patient is a worthy and unique person, made in the likeness of God, innately pure and beautiful.

The ability to convey respect and admiration for the unique and Divine "humanness" of the patient is not so easy to acquire. The therapist must obtain these ethical values, expressed by God Himself, through constant practice and daily exercise. He must learn to **reflect** man's Divine nature to his "blind" self. This can be achieved using the following four steps.

1. Recognition
2. Comprehension
3. Attentiveness
4. Desire to connect

In short, the Torah Therapist must learn to **"recoad"** (an invented word made up of the first letters of the above four tools, and hinting at the words "re-coding" and "recording"). As our Sages teach us, we must learn to be *dan l'chaf zechus*, to evaluate (judge) favorably.

True recoading requires that one must be humble enough in his own eyes that he may leave his own world of thought, emotions, values and judgements, and enter the world of his fellow man. In the final analysis, my world is no better — or worse — than yours. We are all basically equal as human beings rooted in the Divine. To leave my world and enter yours is to rediscover my roots through you, without leaving your world.

To Recognize — Not Fantasize

Recoading begins by **recognizing** the uniqueness of the other person. This recognition is — as we learn from God — in the present. The pitfall here is that we tend to fantasize and project our own world on to that of the other person. This was discussed in chapter five, when we dealt with the structure of man. We learned that man unconsciously tends to assume that his worldview is shared equally by others. This habit was picked up naturally during childhood.

The child is convinced that everyone around him thinks, feels and understands the world the same way he does. After all, we all seem to live in the same world. The concept of individuality is not a simple one to grasp. True maturity is the gradual realization that every person is a unique world unto himself, and therefore he is different "inside" as well as "outside." This truth is absent from so many people. This immaturity underlies the problems that make us suffer. It is the tendency to think that "everyone thinks like me" that causes us to misunderstand the words which are spoken to us. This results in frustrating and painful relationships for which we eventually seek help.

Therefore, it is incumbent upon the Torah Therapist to expose the fallacy of this naïve approach. The question that he must pose to himself is: what is going on in his patient's private world? He does this by reflecting the patient's world as perfectly as possible, without "contaminating" it with the therapist's own personal world. (When the time is right, the therapist will reveal **his own** world, without projecting it forcefully on the patient.) The message that must come from his heart is: "You are you, and I am I. You have your problems, and I have mine. You have your solutions, and mine might be different. We are, paradoxically, equal, yet totally different. I respect your world, and I expect you to respect mine. We are brothers in a fascinating journey together, yet we are distant stars shining upon each other. I have my needs, and you have yours. How wonderful is this creation of God called 'my self'! How fortunate we are to be alive!"

This positive and optimistic message — when coming from the heart — serves to awaken the patient to the sad fact that he has only ever seen the negative side of life, both his own and those of others. He now discovers that there is another option. For the first time in many years he is being addressed as a person in and of himself, someone created in God's likeness, like all human beings. He is truly respected. Perhaps he even feels loved for what he is, and not for what he can give in return. He feels himself transforming. His despair gives way to hope in the new vitality of positive living. He is finally being recognized for what he is! This optimism needs to be reinforced, of course. But this beginning is definitely a turning point, a true revolution that signifies a more mature way of thinking.

To Comprehend without Trying to Mend

The next tool that must be used is that of **comprehension**. To comprehend is to answer the question: **why** is his world the way it is? It is understanding on both a rational and emotional level, the activitiy of *daas*, and it must be completely non-judgemental. We cannot allow our values and ideals to intervene when we attempt to truly understand our fellow man. We must be, at this point, one-hundred percent neutral. Only then can we discover the logic of his subjective world. All components are interlocked in a cause-and-effect relationship or in analogous relationships. It all makes perfect sense...from **his** point of view. We must not try to **mend** before we **comprehend**.

This self-neutralization is referred to by our Sages in their words: "Do not judge your fellow man until **you have reached** his place."[175] We must feel as he feels, think as he thinks, and connect past and present as he connects them. We must be with him as one, in his place. This requires a large amount of mental and emotional energy. Therefore, it is quite rare to find someone who can truly enter another's world. It is especially difficult when we are dealing with transgressions and negative behavior. Yet there is another facet of comprehension that is even more difficult.

Comprehension is just that: understanding how everything fits together. In addition to feeling that we are one with our fellow man, we have to "out-think" him. While identifying with him, we must continue his thoughts and feelings for him to those areas which he was unable to reach on his own. We must work with his mind, and connect the important parts of his life into one unified whole.

This is an awesome experience. It is characterized by the sudden insight that makes so much sense, also known as the "Eureka!" or "Ahah!" moment. The thought process ends with the comprehension that a person's life is complete in its own logic.

This two-phase comprehension (identification and thinking through to unification) is not easy. It is impossible, if the therapist lets his personal values and thoughts intervene. But when it happens, it is enlightening both for the listener and the speaker.

For example, consider a yeshiva student who left his studies behind, and is presently roaming the streets aimlessly, doing whatever comes to mind, including various transgressions. His behavior may be so abhorrent in the eyes of his rabbi that when he interviews him, there is no chance to really listen and comprehend this young man's world. His rabbi, despite his love for

---

175. *Pirkei Avos* 2:4.

him — or perhaps **because** of it — can barely hold himself in
check from chastising him, or at least demonstrating his deep
disappointment in his student.

In this case it would be more beneficial for the young man if
no attempt is made to help him. There is only one way to
"mend" him: don't! First he must be comprehended in depth.
Then, when we have gained his trust by actually "being in his
place," the change evolves almost naturally.

To Listen without Missin': Attentiveness

The third tool needed is that of listening attentively. This form
of listening is much more than just using one's ears to hear
words. It includes the concentration needed to hear the nu-
ances of the tone used by the patient, the phrases he uses, the
dialect, the pronunciation, the timbre of his voice as it changes
from subject to subject. Every small tremor of voice, any change
in volume, small hesitations, the speed of speech — these and
many more are part and parcel of attentive listening.

This attentiveness demands that the listener completely put
aside his own thoughts. Even when an answer or comment is
expected, it should not be offered immediately. The listener
must wait attentively, allowing the patient to answer his own
questions eventually, as much as possible. The focus is completely on the patient: his thoughts, mannerisms, voice, body-
language, and so on. The goal, at this point, is to experience the
unique individual who is a world of his own.

This total concentration and attentiveness is a powerful
drug for the patient. For him, it is an unprecedented experience
of being interesting and of value to someone. This attentiveness
is unnatural and to be found only within the therapeutic relationship. It is one of the greatest compliments that a person can
receive. Its pleasure is enhanced tenfold since he is allowed to
air his thoughts and feelings with complete freedom. He has no

fear of being criticized, interrupted, scorned or belittled. Because of this personal safety, the patient may reveal himself truthfully for the first time. Thus he allows his therapist to truly see his problems, from whence he may eventually grow and receive the support he needs to solve them.

To Desire That Which Is Higher

The last "tool" needed to "reach the other's place" is the desire to make contact with the real person inside, the "higher self" that lodges within this specific body. This is not as simple or as natural as it may sound. We normally tend to be choosy when it comes to making true spiritual contact with someone else. We are not easily enamored of the other, for his personality includes an outer layer which is often discouraging, if not distasteful. The Torah Therapist must overcome his natural inclination to back off. He must consciously overcome the initial distaste by actually desiring to recognize the *tzelem Elokim*, the Divine-like human being who is facing him.

However, to desire that which is higher in the other is not enough. Even when the therapist himself is capable of overcoming his own personal shortcomings, he must pierce the personal armor of the patient. Sometimes he must endure the unpleasant task of dealing with an offensive person. He must "see through" the mask that the patient has been wearing for years as his defense. There are times when all efforts at making real contact are stumped. Both sides are at an impasse.

At that point, it would be quite natural to surrender and tell the patient to go home. But it is at this exact stage that the therapist must exert himself to remember that there truly is a higher self behind this exterior. He and patient are two souls rooted in the Divine, both beautiful human beings. It is precisely this truth, which is so difficult to find, that brought the patient to seek help. He had been suffering from hurtful rela-

tionships which were based on his thorny exterior, rather than
his attractive higher self. Therefore, he desperately needs closeness. Even though he cannot put it into words, he wishes and
expects that the therapist be able to withstand his negative exterior, and allow him the pleasure of true personal connection.

The ability of the therapist to meet this urgent need for true
connection is, to a large degree, a God-given gift. Nevertheless,
we can gradually attain this wonderful quality by consciously
working at loving our fellow man. With effort, we will slowly
come to feel that the higher self within us and within our fellow man becomes something alive and real, not just a nice theory. We learn to look beyond the unattractive exterior of human masquerades in our desire to connect with the souls that
peer out at us with hope and fear. Every person is worthy of
this effort, not only those who seek our help. Actually, it is this
common bond of deep human relationship which is our primary goal. Solving people's problems is secondary. This calls
for explanation.

The Solution: From the Ayin (Void)

A person comes for help. He has a problem, and he needs our
help to solve it. If he lacks information, then we may offer to fill
him in, and the problem is solved. But more often than not, his
problem is of a deeper nature. His personal life is stuck, usually
because of bad habits of action and thought. It is not so simple
to solve his problem.

In truth, although he had come for help, what he really
seeks is much deeper. He usually does not know it, but what he
wants is to love and be loved. We have already learned that
there is really only one doctor for us all — God. The Torah
Therapist is merely a messenger. Now we can add that, as a
messenger, he really doesn't offer solutions. What he does offer, however, is love!

By offering the patient love, he fulfills the patient's deepest need, rather than addressing his external problems. The latter are mere symptoms of the lack of love in his life, whether towards God, towards his fellow man, or both. Whatever his problems, he is basically lacking in true self-esteem. He does not feel his spirituality, his Divine origin, his capacity to love and be loved. As a result, his relationships with others suffer.

His negative self-image gave rise to greater and greater defense mechanisms, making his personal interrelationships ever more difficult and unpleasant. These conscious and unconscious blocks also denied him the spiritual wealth that God bestows unceasingly upon man. His cup is so full with wine gone sour that it cannot be filled with the Divine elixir God constantly offers to His children.

Therefore, the goal of the Torah Therapist is to enable the patient to break down his "blocks." He will then reach the solutions to the problems that now frustrate him. Or — better yet — they will dissolve of their own accord, as the reason for their existence, the self-image, gradually improves. What he will discover is that beneath his ego lies a true "I-ness" which is connected with God. The true Divine nature of the *ani* (אני) is *ayin* (אין). This discovery is accompanied by pleasure and overwhelming happiness. This is where we find our true strength, the source of our security and love for ourselves and for others.

This is rather paradoxical. The more we invest in our ego, the more blocks are constructed. These defenses increase our weakness, for they isolate us even more from maintaining a deep connection with our *neshamah*. But as we learn to surrender our personal defenses, we become more powerful. When we realize that the ego is really an insignificant construction of childish imagination and fears, we begin to **let go**. As these false constructions start to dissolve, we discover our true inner worth in the "nothingness" which is at our core.

Gradually, and with the therapist's help, this truth becomes apparent. The process includes the amazing discovery that the problems that initially seemed insurmountable (and for which the patient came for help in the first place) were actually illusions. They were provoked by outside intervention, but really existed only within the mind of the patient. The ego built them. As the ego becomes more humble, these constructs dissolve. Life looks much brighter. With the love, attentiveness, and encouragement offered by the therapist, the patient rediscovers his true self. He realizes that beneath the stormy waves of his imagination, there exists a truly beautiful and Divine soul. This vitality, this feeling of self in union with God and the whole world, is the goal of Torah Therapy.

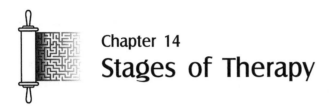

Chapter 14
Stages of Therapy

"Erech Apayim" —
Patience and Tolerance

One of the qualities that is probably lacking in the person who has come for help is that of *erech apayim*, patient tolerance. If he had patience in the past, it has most likely faded. Whatever the case, he is now greatly lacking in patience, tolerance and open-mindedness. The reason for this is that the problem which forced him to come for help also reduced his level of tolerance. He is therefore either overly talkative, nervous and anxious, or silent and withdrawn. In both situations, it is difficult for him to listen to others. His attention span is minimal because he is so completely involved with his problem. It is quite a chore for him to listen, let alone comprehend new ideas.

He must therefore be calmed down and gently prodded to leave his turbulent thoughts and be rather in the present. We can look out for this switch of modes, for it is readily apparent, especially in his eyes. If he is "here" or "there," we can easily discern by the focus of his eyes, or its absence. This loss of presence can be understood as a desire to escape from the problems of the moment. He is either drowning in his troubles or distracting his mind by being far away on some utopian island where everything is good. In any case, he is not here! How can we bring him back in order to deal with his problems?

The Wonders of Breathing

The answer, as usual, is forthcoming in the Torah. There too we find a situation in which the troubles and tribulations of everyday living resulted in nervousness and lack of patience and concentration. We are referring to Bnei Yisrael in Egypt, about whom the Torah says: "... and they did not listen to Moshe for shortness of wind (*"kotzer ruach"*) and from arduous work."[176] A definite connection is made here between shortness of breath and the inablility to listen and pay attention. This is brought out by Rashi when he explains: "Whoever is troubled, his spirit and his breath are short, and he cannot lengthen his breath."

Why is short breath symptomatic of stress? The Ramban explains: "They did not give ear to his words because of *kotzer ruach* (shortness of spirit), as a man is short of spirit in arduous work, and he does not want to live the present moment for it is painful, and rather [he looks to the next moment] when he shall feel peaceful." In other words, the stress and anxiety of the present moment create a feeling of urgency to reach the next moment, which will hopefully be easier and calmer. This urgency is translated as a quickening of the breathing tempo. He feels that by accelerating his breathing, he can more quickly escape the present and find haven in the future. This process is both unconscious and natural.

To summarize, we learn from the Torah's description of the state of mind of the Jews in Egypt that lack of concentration is typical in a person who is anxious or stressed. One of the symptoms characteristic of this emotional state is shortness of breath, or "hollow" breathing. Therefore, the opposite — deep breathing — obviously characterizes the stable and calm emotional state, in which concentration is fixed and controlled. It seems that deep breathing serves to reorganize and reunite our spiri-

---

176. *Shemos* 6:9.

tual, mental and emotional energies by refocusing them within ourselves, rather than dealing with the myriad problems that besiege us from the outside. That means that attentive listening is enabled by deep breaths.

We learn from the Torah how to calm down a person who comes for help. His agitation denies him the concentration needed to listen, comprehend and internalize. He is therefore encouraged to take several deep breaths before doing anything else. The results are obvious. Besides allowing him to calm down, we have also given him a simple "aspirin" to take home with him. It is effective, the results are immediate, and it is priceless.

It is odd that this effective short-term pacifier is ignored or forgotten by most people. It is recommended to close one's eyes while breathing deeply, in order to enhance the calming effects and the internal orientation of the spirit. By breathing in through the nose, we sift out the dirt particles in the air. We let out the breath through the mouth, thus creating a closed loop that begins with the nostrils, passes through the lungs and ends at the mouth.

In addition, we may deepen and intensify the process by imagining our breath traveling in and out, enriching our bodies with oxygen and carrying out the wastes of our lungs. This method is also very effective when there is pain somewhere in the body. By directing our concentration to the painful area, we use our imagination to decrease the pain. We can actually feel the soothing effects of the incoming oxygen as it gradually de-sensitizes that area.

Homework and Torah Therapy

Daily repetition of these easy techniques is necessary. Only then will we become accustomed to use deep breathing whenever we are agitated, nervous or anxious. In therapy, this is the first lesson given as "homework." This is also the opportunity to explain that the patient's improvement is proportional to the effort he invests in the periods **between** therapy sessions. *Avodas Hashem* is the private, moment by moment, day by day striving to be a better servant of God, a more complete Jew. When the patient actively participates in his therapy by "doing his homework," he is opening the gateway through which God has blessed him: "Open for me an opening as small as the tip of a needle, and I shall open for you an opening as big as an auditorium."[177]

Internal Order and Organization

Most people do not have very organized thoughts and emotions. Those who come for therapy are usually at a loss to make sense of the mental and emotional turbulence that causes them to feel so small and powerless. This serves to increase their confusion and suffering, obscuring whatever solutions might be available. Therefore, the therapist must first help the patient organize the many details of his internal world. By putting things into order, he can begin to regain control of his life.

The stages of this process are as follows:

1. First, the patient must give vent to his emotions. He is encouraged to talk about his problems and suffering. Thus he unburdens himself (ventilation) to the attentive therapist: "[When there is] a worry in a man's heart, he shall converse [about it]."[178]

2. The next step is to separate the actions from the thoughts and the emotions that lie behind them. This is the stage in which order must be made among the many emo-

---

177. *Shir HaShirim Rabbah* 5:3.
178. *Mishlei* 12:25.

tions, which, more often than not, conflict with each other. This means assigning importance and priorities to those emotions which are directly connected to the problem that must be solved. Secondary emotions and those of associative connections must be put aside for now. Perhaps later it would be wise to consider these as well. (Many patients find this stage extremely difficult, for one of two reasons: either they are unaware of their feelings, or they are incapable of giving them expression.)

3. The last stage of organization deals with the hierarchies of the emotions connected with the problem at hand. Their respective significance is brought out by careful analysis. In this crucial stage the therapist must skillfully aid the patient in discovering which emotion is deeply rooted in the problem, and what thoughts and feelings are involved in its development over time. "For man is like the tree in the field."[179] Both have roots that lead to a trunk, which branches off to smaller and smaller appendages, which finally end with leaves and fruits. This human "tree of life" is rooted in the *tzelem Elokim* that unites him with God through the *neshamah*. But the "trunk" is the need for human love, esteem and security, as the child grows unaware of his connection with God. From these basic needs stem the branches of emotions and thoughts that include fears, anger, disappointment, frustrations, as well as happiness, ambitions, trust, etc. These in turn bring forth leaves and fruits in varying degrees of success. Every person is a unique tree, a life story that is his alone, that may be drawn in a few simple lines.

---

179. *Devarim* 20:19.

Daas Torah

This "mapping" of the heart is the work of the *daas*, that uniquely human faculty that synthesizes rationality and intuition, mind and heart, and fuses them into knowledge-in-depth. (This was explained in detail in the first section of the book.) Torah teaches us to use this delicate and deeply probing tool as a means of reordering our lives, thereby improving our relationships with God, man and ourselves. This is *daas Torah*. It is gained by painstaking learning and application of Torah, especially the Talmud.

Learning Talmud requires — among other things — a constant effort at systematically comprehending many details as they pertain to one or several problems. Mental versatility develops as rigorous analysis is coupled with intuition in this process called "learning Gemara." Details are sifted through, categorized and catalogued. Gradually, sense begins to arise out of what seemed like a big confusion of facts and stories. Slowly and systematically, and with evident *siyata dishmaya* (help from Heaven), the learner reveals the underlying structure of the *sugya*, the section being learned.

The experience is exhilarating. The roots appear, followed by the trunk, then its branches, the leaves and the fruits. This is the tree of life that every Torah learner creates for himself and, eventually, for others. The myriad details that were originally total confusion formed and coalesced to create a beautiful picture of Torah in one of its many aspects, including a practical guide for action: *halachah*.

A siginificant part of this rigorous learning is the need to identify the source of each comment or idea. *Daas Torah* requires that the individual separate his own ideas and thoughts from those of others. He must ascribe what he learns to the written Torah, or to *Tanaim, Amoraim, Rishonim, Acharonim*, or even to his rabbis and friends. This is not only for the sake of honesty or authenticity; it also carries a *halachic* significance in terms of authority and wisdom. Therefore, he must neutralize his natural tendency to judge and approve or disapprove, until he has rigorously learned all the sides involved. Every detail and opinion must be carefully examined and weighed against the others. It must be evaluated in various angles and against many backgrounds of other *sugyas*, before he allows his own opinions to intervene and sway him towards one side or another.

No wonder, therefore, that this ability to judge carefully and create a tree of life out of sheer chaos can be applied to life itself. Using *daas Torah* to solve everyday problems means applying this same rigorous honesty and concentrated effort at sifting out the underlying causes and results. *Daas Torah* enables the Torah Therapist to quickly discern which detail is significant and which is not, what should be considered primary and what is secondary, what is important now and what can be deferred to a later date. Disorder is removed as the picture becomes evident for the patient. It is an event that can be compared, on a very small scale, to creation *ex nihilo*.

This idea is more than a simple analogy. Just as God created the world by "looking at the Torah" ("*histakel b'oraysa u-vara alma*"[180]), so does the therapist apply his *daas Torah* to create a tree of life for the confused and broken spirit. Out of the chaos (*tohu va-vohu*) of the patient's inner world emerges a structured and sensible portrait (life-script) that delineates his heaven and earth, day and night, etc. The goal is to reach "the seventh day" so that the patient may experience "and on the seventh day He ceased work and rested."[181] The Torah Therapist thus becomes a faithful partner of God. *Olam chesed yibaneh* — the world is

---

180. *Zohar, Shemos* 161b.
181. *Shemos* 21:17.

created by *chesed*.

The Revelation Begins...

After creating a well-defined portrait of the patient's present situation, the therapist leads him to discover the personal axis around which his life has evolved. This is the focal point of his life-script, from which he judged and evaluated all his life experiences. This personal existential viewpoint usually stands out starkly after the life-script is revealed. It is generally based on feelings of low self-esteem and inferiority which, tragically, are logical and natural...from the child's point of view. His mind is not yet developed enough to conclude otherwise.

We instinctively build our self-evaluation on the basis of our undeveloped childhood mind. **Our ego is our primitive understanding of the reactions that we produce in the people around us, especially our parents.** Without the faculty of critical evaluation, we are at the mercy of our emotions. Therefore a simple statement, such as "Can't you eat like a normal human being?" is taken at face value; "I am not a normal human being, and therefore Mom is angry with me." After several repetitions by Mom, the child adds "... and she doesn't love me." And, after several more repetitions, the child deduces: "... and I do not deserve to be loved." (All this is intuited, of course, and therefore subconscious.)

The child is unaware that Mom was upset for many reasons that are not connected with him. His child's mind cannot evaluate the feelings and the words that were aimed at him other than as Mom's attitude towards her child. He is the center of his own little world, and everything he sees and knows revolves around him, as far as he is concerned.

Now, however, as a grown person who is mentally able to recognize that there are other personal worlds, the patient is urged to take a different look at himself and at others around him. As simple as it sounds to us, for him this is a totally new and amazing discovery. He discovers that he had unwittingly stuck to his childish appraisal of his self and his parents, relatives and friends. Despite his mental and emotional development, he remained a child vis-à-vis the most significant people in his life, including himself. This is understandably, a bit of a shock, and it takes time to assimilate. But this new understanding and evaluation becomes the focal point for the ensuing sessions and the new axis for a rewritten life-script.

Tikun Ha-Adam ("Completion" of Man)

When the patient changes his view of himself and the world around him with the aid of *daas*, he has completed the first stage of *tikun ha-adam*. This term refers to the goal of every man as an individual, as well as mankind as a whole. Since Adam's fall, we — his descendants — strive to "fix" (*tikun*) the blemished perfection of man. Through Torah, we gradually achieve that wholesomeness, as perfect servants of God. Thus, mankind returns to its previous exalted stature, as God intended.

As grand as this universal ideal is, it imbues our personal lives as Jews with meaning and significance. We have a very important part to play in the "stage" of this world, starting from our small personal worlds, going through our roles as members of the Jewish nation, and, finally, contributing to the overall welfare of mankind. Thus, the discovery that our lives can be reevaluated and viewed from a mature point of view becomes a crucial first step in this personal journey. By contributing to ourselves spiritually, we are also contributing to all of mankind.

What are the next stages? Is there practical guidance to be found in the Torah? Is there a step-by-step process by which we can achieve wholeness in spirit and body? Are there practical suggestions that Torah gives that are appropriate to us today?

The answer, of course, is yes. The Torah does indeed offer

specific directions that must be carried out, resulting in mental, spiritual and physical health. Generally speaking, when a person obeys all the laws codified in the *Shulchan Aruch*, he is, in practice, gradually achieving this goal, whether he is conscious of it or not. But in truth, since we do not always fully observe all the laws we are meant to; we must resort sometimes to specific rules and regulations. (This was explained in the introduction.)

One of these, needed for the first stage of rehabilitation, is that *daas* must be employed in order to reach a new understanding of ourselves. We also begin to understand others from this new viewpoint, and our life script is open for change. This process is described in the words of *Chazal* as an escape to freedom from the subjugation of the *sitra achra* ("the other side"). By gaining a new and more mature outlook, we break away from many problems which had plagued us endlessly. In a sense, we have left the world in which our spirit is oppressed, and connected our world with a higher world, which is much more gentle, understanding, logical and happy. (Of course, this is not a one-time affair. It is a never-ending process which works "in percentages" over the years.)

This is the beginning of what is termed "ascending through the worlds." The world of action (*maaseh*) is connected with the world of emotion, and these two together are connected with the world of thought.Then the total is connected with the deepest and highest world, within us. This process underlies the morning prayer of *Shacharis*, until the point of *Amidah*. There, too, must we disconnect first our actions from this world, and then our emotions and thoughts as well. We thus "ascend" from the mundane to the sanctified "holy-of-holies" by refocusing our whole being on the innermost spirituality within us. Through it we connect with God. This process of *tikun ha-adam* is made possible only by disconnecting from the impurities of the world outside. That is the requisite first stage in becoming healthy. The next stages in Torah Therapy parallel those underlying our ascent to and during the *Amidah*.

What is the logical basis for applying this process to the psychological health of an individual? There are three truths that, when taken together, lead to this conclusion:

1. The Ramchal writes: "The world of 'maleness' (*alma d'dchura*) and the world of 'femaleness' (*alma d'nukva*)...are the general [basis for] the laws of **giving** and the laws of **accepting**."[182]

2. The Maharil Bloch writes: "Man's soul includes within it the whole of creation... and man is a small world, and all that is found in the world is to be found within man." Later on (p. 38) he writes: "All things, in essence, that are found in this world are present in the higher worlds and in the highest of worlds; and they are all of one reality in all the worlds, but this reality itself assumes a different form, in accordance with the world within which it is viewed."[183]

3. Rav Dessler writes: "When God created man, He made him a giver and a receiver."[184]

The Giver and the Receiver

The combination of these three basic ideas allows us to understand man's strengths and weaknesses. Using them, we may reach a diagnosis and then a prognosis, in general terms.

The Ramchal is teaching us that the world is built on the ba-

---

182. Rabbi Moshe Chaim Luzatto (Ramchal), *Sefer Ha-klalim* (Book of General Rules), rule 20.
183. Moreinu Harav Yehuda Leib Bloch (Maharil Bloch), *Shiurei Daas*, p. 12.
184. *Michtav MeEliyahu*, vol. 1, p. 32.

sis of complementation between the "male" and the "female."
(He is not referring necessarily to a man or a woman, but to the
basic essence of giving or accepting.) This fact — we learn from
the Maharil Bloch — is present everywhere, throughout the
worlds, and within man's individual "small world." In other
words, the basic male/female nature of creation is found analogously in the individual nature of man. This fact is expressed,
in Rav Dessler's words, as the ability to give, *nesinah*, and the
ability to accept, *kabbalah*.

We can see that lack of giving or accepting goes against the
nature of creation. It must therefore lead to some form of "sickness." The *tikun* (correction) of this malady, whether on the
world-scale or the human individual scale, is to **give and accept
in fullness**. In other words, we can achieve our personal *tikun*
by realizing, in actual, practical, every-day life, the full potential
of our nature to give and accept.

As an example, we find Rav Dessler offering the following
advice to a newlywed couple, while standing under the *chupah*:
"One must strive to fulfill the needs of the other." (Thus, your
own needs will be met in the same measure.) More explicitly,
your giving should not be dependent on your receiving. Each
of these two basic natures is a powerful force of its own and
must be expressed in its entirety.

Blood Circulation: The Physical Counterpart

As we are taught by Maharil Bloch, this must be true for all
worlds, at every level. Therefore, it comes as no surprise that
these two complementary forces exist in man's physical
makeup as well. We have already discussed the fact (in chapter
12) that the circulation of blood around the body involves two
cycles. One is the cycle of **giving** blood to all the body's cells.
The other is the cycle of **accepting** oxygen from the lungs.
These two cycles are interconnected to such a degree that if a

tiny fly (the *yetzer ha-ra*) were to lodge in one of the heart's valves, it would cause an imbalance that could result in a heart attack. (On closer examination, we can find this same give-and-take between the blood and the cells themselves, because the cells excrete waste to the blood which accepts it, even as it deposits its oxygen within the cells. The same holds true in the interchange between lungs and blood, where the opposite is the case: the blood deposits its wastes even as it is replenished by the lungs.)

Many heart attacks are initiated by the partial or temporary blockage of the blood's circulation. Some, as in the case of thrombosis, occur by blockage of the arteries (in the giving cycle) or the veins (in the accepting cycle). Others occur within the crossroads, the heart itself, and are therefore much more dangerous. The body's health is dependent on the smooth, uninterrupted flow of blood from one cycle to the other, in a never-ending closed-circuit pattern.

The Dangerous "Fly"

It follows that this harmonious and symmetrical flow is present in our spiritual body as well. We learned that *chesed* towards others must be balanced by *chesed* towards ourselves. This idea is included in the *mitzvah* of "Love your friend as yourself."[185] Rabbi Akiva emphasized that besides being a *mitzvah*, it is a *klal gadol baTorah*[186] (great rule of the Torah). He points out that this commandment is basic to our lives, which the Torah sustains. The love we show and feel to others must be balanced by our love for ourselves. The flow of *chesed* must be strong and continuous **in both directions**.

The job of the *yetzer ha-ra*, as discussed previously, is to dis-

---

185. *Vayikra* 19:18.
186. *Sifra, Kedoshim*, chap. 2.

rupt this delicate mechanism. It is sufficient for him to merely sit — like a fly — within the heart. The process of two-directional *chesed* is effectively halted. In other words, the moment we decide that we must give less than is actually within our abilities, or request less than we need to receive, we cause damage to ourselves. Whenever we feel that we have given more than we should, or whenever we are incapable of accepting from others (or requesting what should be given), we are weakened by our *yetzer ha-ra*. Whenever one or both of our basic strengths — to give and to receive — is blocked, even partially, we are spiritually, mentally and physically threatened.

The *yetzer ha-ra* uses a simple strategy to achieve its end. We are persuaded to believe that our giving must **equal** our accepting. Now this is perfectly true when we are speaking of maximum giving and maximum accepting. However, when one of these powers is employed at less than maximum level, the *yetzer ha-ra* tells us that we must **reduce** the other to an equal level.

This is the catch! Instead of maintaining maximum efficiency in giving or accepting (when there are no external deterrants, such as poor health), so as to encourage the opposite power to come to full force, we limit our total efficiency to the **lowest** level of the two forces. Instead of temporarily maintaining the imbalance caused by the *yetzer ha-ra* so as to negate its influence and reassert our full potential, we succumb to the fear of this imbalance and accept a partial immobilization of our lives.

Here are a few examples showing how the fly in our heart buzzes away our freedom to be fully alive:

"Don't give more until you begin to get something in return."

"Don't ask. You won't get it anyway."

"Stop being so naïve and helpful. Stand up for your rights!"

"Why are you always thinking about yourself? Your duty is towards others, not yourself. You're an egomaniac!"

"You're incapable of loving because you weren't loved. So forget it!"

"If you give, then you shall receive."

"If you don't ask, maybe there's a chance that you'll receive. So shut your mouth and wait patiently."

These are just some of the many comments that our personal fly throws at us from within our heart, day by day, hour by hour, minute by minute. No wonder we are so far from living our full potential in both crucial areas of giving and accepting. This is a slow and gradual "death." Its expression, or symptoms, include: problematic communication, aggressive behavior or speech, idiosyncrasies, social isolation, erratic behavior and much pain. The pain is partially conscious, but for the most part unconscious. We repress a lot in order to survive. But it is all the more powerful for being concealed. The fly is dangerous because it is so effective in secretly killing us slowly but steadily.

The Goal of Torah Therapy

By diagnosing our sickness at its roots, our Sages — through Torah — could demonstrate its cure. They pointed out that if the two basic forces of giving and accepting "short-circuit" each other (as described above), then they must be separated. To extend this analogy, we can say that each "wire" must be isolated completely except through the point where the circuit should close. Thus, the current flows at maximum efficiency from the live wire into the neutral wire, allowing it to be used constructively.

In similar fashion, the two opposing forces of the patient

must be isolated at first. The therapist encourages the patient to bring each force to its fullest potential. This is done by concentrating on one of them at a time. At a later stage, they are bound together in a mutually reinforcing position, and health is gradually achieved.

More specifically, the therapist urges those patients who feel weak in their giving capacity to do *chesed*, regardless of the fact that they do not receive anything in return. The therapist also encourages those patients who are weak in accepting to receive with gratitude, or, when necessary, to request that which they need. (This entails becoming conscious of one's needs — a task in itself.)

The Stages of Torah Therapy

Stage One: Construction

We learned in chapter two that man was initially created in a "dual mode," male and female. Our Sages described this double creation as "standing back to back." At this stage of our comprehension, this idea can be understood as describing every person's inner world. This world was created for him, and added to by him, from the moment he is born. It is composed of two basic forces: the ability to give and the ability to receive. These abilities, we now discover, are "back-to-back," meaning that there is no **conscious** connection between them. Each develops on its own, without drawing on the other until *daas* is gained. The baby is only aware of his need to receive warmth, milk, hugs and lots of love. He is completely unaware that he is capable of giving as well.

Over the years, the child learns that he has the ability to actively give to others. He is encouraged to do *chesed* as he matures, and he is expected to be more and more helpful at home and in society, and less and less dependent on his elders. Therefore, his needs are gradually less emphasized. Most parents naturally feel that it is acceptable to pay less attention to their children's needs as they mature, for they suppose that their children have grown up. Now they can take care of themselves. Instead of seeking to fulfill their needs, most parents increasingly draw on them for help and support. The assumption here is that whatever needs the children have and cannot meet on their own will be asked for.

As natural as this assumption is, it is nevertheless a mistake. Most children are either unaware of their emotional needs, or they are incapable of expressing them. The reason is simple: most parents do not discuss these issues. They are more or less taken for granted, for better or for worse. So, for example, when words such as "love," "support" or "encouragement" are not mentioned in the household, children do not develop the ability of expressing to themselves — let alone to others — that they need love, support or encouragement. Parents generally do not discuss these basic needs because they themselves grew up with this same "handicap." Their parents were similarly lacking, through no fault of their own.

The result of this lack of awareness, which gets passed on through the generations, is the tendency to externalize our emotional hunger to the physical world surrounding us. We assume that money, power, wealth or material goods will satisfy our emotional hunger. Being that something material will never fill an emotional lack, this naturally leads to bitter disappointments, hurt, pain, depression and frustration. Through this all, our hunger for emotional support and love grows stronger and stronger. Thus we fall into a vicious cycle, the end of which is often tragic, unless we pull ourselves out and rebuild our lives.

In Torah Therapy we begin this by reversing our dependencies from the external to the internal. Instead of obsessively clutching whatever is valued **outside** of us, we are taught to relinquish our hold and search for meaning from **within**. We learn to quench our emotional thirst from the waters of the Eden inside us, with Torah as our guide. The instrument we employ is *daas*.

Using *daas*, we learn to connect our actions to our emotions. These, in turn, are connected to our thoughts and beliefs. Our Sages teach us that each of these human expressions of existence is a world of its own. There is a world of action, a world of emotion, and a world of thought. They are each rooted in one human soul, but all too often they are disconnected or even contradictory. Torah teaches us to use our *daas* in order to exist on these three levels in harmony. This is a process whereby we gradually achieve internal unity.

This first phase, the construction-of-man phase, is realizing that our world is not made of separate components, but is actually a unified whole. We come to understand that as long as our search for peace involved gratification from the world around us, then each event and detail was viewed as a disconnected part of our existence. But as we looked inside ourselves for the real values within us, these external events and details became relevant expressions of our internal values and beliefs. The separated parts of the past converged into one big pattern. They now fit each other and interlock, like a puzzle, forming one picture. This picture may not be pleasant, but at least it is unified and clear.

Another very significant result of this personal unification is the realization that we ourselves give meaning to our lives. Previously we attributed our successes and failures, our moods and thoughts, our actions and decisions, to external influences. Now we realize that it is our internal mode of existence that determines how we react to external phenomena. In other words, instead of seeing the outside world as responsible for our lives, **we have taken that responsibility on ourselves.**

Having achieved this stage of development, we are prepared to deal with the second phase of Torah Therapy. In it we learn about the two basic powers within us, those of giving and accepting.

Stage Two: Splitting

By this time, we have already taken responsibility for our lives. Rather than accuse others for our suffering, we realize that it is the private world within us that is the ultimate criterion for our happiness. **From the weakness of dependency we have graduated to the strength of independence.** With this new-found power within us, we are prepared to undergo spiritual surgery. We will discover that our powers of giving and accepting are two distinct and separate entities within our being. This idea must be explained, for it is not easily grasped.

We are quite familiar with giving and accepting, but it is usually only on a superficial level. For example, we easily discern our need for accepting food. We feel hungry. We are then able to satisfy this natural need. But we are usually unaware that we are in constant need of being loved and appreciated. Therefore, we often go hungry emotionally, even as we claim to be happy.

We are likewise unaware that we are capable of giving ten times more than what we are at present accustomed to give. For example, we are usually proud of our ability to give of our time and money to our children. We exert great efforts to make them happy. Nevertheless, they may often surpise us when, as mature young adults, they complain that we did not **show** our love. We learn — albeit in retrospect — that we were unaware that our love for our children was not obvious to them. Had we known that we were holding back overt expressions of our love, we would have strived to display our affection towards them more openly and to express it freely. We held back what was ours to give. Why is this holding back so natural? Why do we not recognize our deeper emotional needs to give and to accept?

The Torah offers the answer. God created Adam and Chava as two separate beings.[187] After putting Adam into deep sleep, He took a rib from him from which to create Chava. As we saw earlier, the Sages teach us that every person has both a feminine nature, the power of accepting, and a masculine nature, the power of giving. Therefore, the Torah's description of the division of Chava from Adam is analogous to the creation of man himself on an internal level. In other words, just as woman was separated from man and made into a self-contained entity, so can the power of accepting be separated from the power of giving and made an autonomous unit.

The first creation of man, as male and female in a back-to-back position, leads to the natural — but mistaken — feeling that we are one unified being in our giving and accepting capacities. This predetermined human error causes us to "hold back" in giving and accepting, as was demonstrated in the examples of the "fly." It whispers phrases that make us rein in our legitimate needs to accept or to give. The yetzer ha-ra begins to work on us when we are still young and do not have the tools to fight it, leading us to form thought-habits that take a lifetime to unlearn.

We must learn to separate our accepting entity from our giving entity, so as to let each of them come to full bloom. They must work together harmoniously without tying each other up or causing conflict. This split occurs only when the "male" side is asleep (much as Adam was put to sleep in order to create Chava as a separate entity, detached from his body). In other words, the patient can discover his deeper needs only when he

---

187. *Bereishis* 2:21-22.

surrenders his compulsion to be active, giving, powerful and wise. As fine as these qualities are, they also have a negative side. They allowed him to disregard his deeper needs for affection and support from others. These needs had been hidden behind a fa(ade of strength as a defense mechanism. Now he must allow this dominant part of his personality to retreat temporarily (sleep) in order to honestly face those legitimate needs, which have usually been repressed since childhood. This is neither easy nor is it always welcome.

Stage Three: Pain

We learned from Hillel the Elder (in the previous chapter on *chesed*) that the *nefesh* within us may be described as a *nefesh aluvah*, meaning "poor" or "made humble." The *nefesh* is the lower part of our being, our ego, that connects our *ruach* (spirit) and our body. It gives life to the physical body, and as such, is constantly aware of its needs for food, drink, warmth, exercise, etc. The *nefesh* is humble because it does not possess the power to satisfy these needs. It must draw on the power of the *ruach* (spirit), rooted in the *neshamah* (soul). We saw that Hillel employed his free will, his spirit, when he decided to cease that day's learning and to begin to attend to the needs of the *nefesh ha-aluvah*. He pitied his ego, not his body. It was time to leave matters of the spirit — even the teaching of the Torah — and attend to the needs of that poor *nefesh*, residing as a **"guest inside his house"** [Hillel's words].

In this light we may better understand another maxim of our Sages: "If I am not for myself, who is?"[188] Of course, our parents have always been there for us, as much as they could. They certainly deserve our thanks and respect, the basis of *mitzvas kibbud av v'eim* (the fifth of the Ten Commandments).

---

188. *Pirkei Avos* 1:14.

But there was still much left for us to try to deal with on our own. After all, our parents were not infallible. Nobody else can do this job. Although we can help and encourage each other, we are mostly on our own. That is because our deepest needs are known and felt only by our very private and unique *nefesh*.

Characteristic of this personal quest for truth is **pain**. This pain is at the core of our emotions when, instead of feeling loved and encouraged, we felt rejected, scorned or criticized. As we saw above, this pain was repressed time and again, whenever it became too much to bear. We repressed the pain by repressing the need that had not been met. We thus became unaware of those needs of our *nefesh*, and they remained unsatisfied over the years. Usually these include the need for love, appreciation, encouragement and being close to others. As we rediscover those neglected and forgotten parts of our *nefesh*, we are confronted once again with the pain associated with our past and present longing for love and support.

However, if we truly wish to learn how to fulfill the needs of the *nefesh*, this pain is unavoidable. Cleaning out a wound is the first necessary step to its healing. We cry out with pain, but we do it willingly if we understand that we are only benefitting from it. Our repressed needs and the accompanying negative emotions have accumulated to such a degree that the festering wound has become unbearable. So we undergo a quick minor operation to reduce the painful pressure by freeing the accumulated pus (the body's defense against dangerous foreign intruders), thus allowing healing to begin.

The first thing we discover is that the pain or hurt that we experienced was "shared" by both entities that comprise our "self," the power of accepting (*nefesh*) and the power of giving (*ruach*). As our need to receive was rejected, so was our capacity to actively give and create discouraged or criticized. Just as we learned not to ask or even expect to assuage our thirst for love and appreciation, for example, so too we also learned to curtail our natural desire to give, express, create, smile, laugh, talk, etc. Over the years we learned to become dumb to our inner voice as it called for help. We grew accustomed to partial self-paralysis when invited to move, help or converse.

At this point, the Torah Therapist encourages the patient to **transfer** the pain of immobility and helplessness to the *nefesh*. That is where the hurt is actually felt, not in his active, "male," powerful *ruach*. By assuming that we were powerless to act, we "emasculated" ourselves; **both** entities within us became feminine. Even if we partially realized our potential to give to others, we felt disabled when it came to ourselves. We became frustratingly dependent on others to satisfy our own needs, for we felt powerless to do so on our own.

When we learn to relegate our weakness to our receiving entity, our "femaleness," we free our creative and active "male" entity. The therapist encourages the patient to attempt to do new things, create, converse, offer help, etc. He is prodded to reuse the stagnant "muscles" of his *ruach*, through which he will develop the ability to give more to others, and ultimately to himself. When he allows himself to face his pain, he can finally address it. He discovers that his giving capacity can be directed towards his *nefesh* as much as it can towards anyone else. The pain gives way to insight and to *chesed*.

An example may help to facilitate our understanding of this profound and difficult process. Leah was invited to a family wedding. Ordinarily, she would have been happy to accept the invitation, because she enjoyed spending time with her relatives and was well-liked by them. However, this time she decided to decline because the oldest son of the family had hurt her feelings. He was supposed to call her up to discuss a certain possible candidate for marriage, and he did not. Leah waited in vain for the call. She was bitterly disappointed and hurt. Therefore, she deemed it undignified for her to attend this wedding.

Unwittingly, Leah was about to hurt herself a second time. Instead of letting herself have a good time at a wedding which she was sure to enjoy, Leah felt that this was wrong. Despite the fact that she would have smiled at her relatives and they would have flooded her with attention and compliments, she could not bring herself to accept the perceived rejection at the hands of her cousin and continue her life as if nothing happened.

Leah sought counsel in the spirit of Torah Therapy. She was shocked to realize that she was "neutralizing" herself masochistically because of her pain at being rejected. Instead of easing herself out of her bitterness by having fun, she had planned to **increase** her pain by denying herself the enjoyment of socialization. She learned how her humbled *nefesh* clung tenaciously to her active *ruach*, and made it equally miserable and powerless. Leah was encouraged to use her freedom of will to disengage this active part of her being. She had all the right in this world to grant herself and those whom she loved the joy and fun of an important social event. She should disregard her hurt feelings when it came to enjoying life. Leah went to the wedding. She came back proud of herself and happy. The night was wonderful, as she had expected.

Leah succeeded in splitting her "self" into a humbled and disappointed *nefesh*, who remained hungry for love, and an active, positive, enriching *ruach*, who did something to satisfy this very basic need. Her active personality was freed from her passive and hurt personality, and thus was empowered to put her back on her feet and have a good time. Rather than spreading the pain of rejection between both facets of her personality, Leah had the courage to **intensify** the pain by relegating it in toto to the *nefesh*. Thus, she could feel pleasure as her *ruach* offered her *nefesh* compensation for her bitter disappointment.

Stage Four: Sweetening (Mituk)

Leah still had a problem. True, she managed to transfer her pain to her *nefesh*, freeing her *ruach* to help herself. But the hurt was still there. It pained her to recall the cutting disappointment of rejection. Leah felt deeply humiliated, and she could not forget it. Now she must learn to "sweeten" this bitter pill by discovering the *chesed* that underlies this traumatic episode.

Leah advanced to the next stage. She learned to reconstruct the past in a positive light, and the bitter memory became an important stepping-stone towards growth and understanding. This is *mituk ha-dinim*, which was discussed at length in chapter 3.

Leah learned that *dinim* are not arbitrary arrows of some cruel fate. Since God is their source, they have meaning and purpose. One possible goal could be to teach Leah that she must trust Him, even when she is disappointed. This trust, when achieved, is a joyous escape from dependence on others. Another lesson that may sweeten the past is the fact that her cousin may have had reasons of his own when he did not phone Leah. She is not necessarily the main reason. She is now free to realize that the world does not revolve solely around her. Her egocentric, childish view of the world has changed to a mature acceptance of the many autonomous worlds of those around her. Another realization is that because of her pained reaction to cut further ties with the family, she learned to free her *ruach* from the paralysis of the humiliation. She learned to help herself. It was painful, but worth it.

With her new-found knowledge and maturity, Leah rediscovered the joys of relationships with family and friends. There is a new vibrancy in her conversation that is lost on no one. She is super-alive and her happiness spills out, energizing those around her. Leah's connection with God is likewise strong and fulfilling. This new Leah is the result of *mituk ha-dinim*.

Stage Five: Acceptance (Hashlamah)

This is the last stage of the cycle. (The process is cyclical because it is a continuously recurring "creation of man" by himself.) Being the last stage, it also serves as preparation for the next cycle, which — built on this one — is higher, deeper, and broader. In this fifth stage, acceptance, the "female" entity is fully accepted by the "male" entity. The split personality thus becomes one unified whole. The "giver" satisfies — as much as possible — the needs of the "receiver."

In Leah's case, that means that she turns her powerful giving capacity towards her own *nefesh*, building her confidence and satisfying — to some degree — her need for love. Having learned that her happiness is not dependent solely on others, she learns to give herself positive self-reinforcement. She can give herself a loving hug as one of many techniques of self-nurturance. In return, her *nefesh* enlivens her total being, allowing her to feel great joy. There is more enthusiasm and spontaneity, as the pain that paralyzed the *nefesh* is gradually replaced by words of comfort and self-support, offered by Leah's *ruach*.

There is now greater harmony within her total personality, as she learns to make peace with **both** aspects of her being. To make peace means **to accept the strengths and weaknesses of both aspects as a basis for mutual support.** This is Leah's personal *shalom bayis* (marital peace).

This blissful state of being is symbolized by the two *keruvim* (angel-like figures) who stood on the holy ark in the Mishkan and the *Beis HaMikdash*. The ark was in the *Kodesh Kodashim*, the Holy of Holies, and between these two figures the *Shechinah*, the voice of God, would issue forth. According to the Ari z"l,[189] they represent the two basic forces, the "male" and the "female." They therefore face each other, one to give and the other

---

189. *Shaar HaPesukim, parashas Terumah.*

to accept, in mutual complementation. As such, they also represent the strong connection between God and His people. When the connection was weakened, the *keruvim* were to be found "*pneihem el ha-bayis*,"[190] facing the wall rather than towards one another.

Similarly, when Leah's two entities united in mutual support, "face-to-face," she could partake of the voice of the *Shechinah*, to some degree, as if allowing God to speak through her being. In the past, when these two powers were in disharmony, she was accustomed to self-criticism that came out as self-negating sentences and phrases which were partially conscious.

This internal dialogue reinforced itself over the years until Leah only heard the vocalized expletives which would sometimes burst out of her mouth in anger or frustration. Most of it was unconscious.

When Leah began listening to her two entities, she was startled to hear sentences such as:

"You are worthless, Leah! Nobody wants you!"

"You're going to be an old maid, Leah. So face it, you're a loser!"

"Stop hoping, you dimwit! Give up already..."

These and similar derogatory sentences are the basic weapons of the *yetzer ha-ra*, the "fly" sitting in our hearts. It effectively used the "male" power of authority to control and subdue the "female" power of acceptance and life-giving. Leah gradually became paralyzed. Her two entities were "back-to-back." Her situation was similar to the pain of chronic marital strife.

But as these entities slowly began to turn towards each

---

190. *Midrash Yalkut Shimoni, Melachim I*, 6:181.

other, Leah was taught to replace the negative internal dialogue with positive reinforcement. Now she began saying sentences like:

"Don't worry, Leah. You do your thing, and God will do
His, when the right time comes."

"You're really okay. You deserve someone special... and
he'll come. It just takes a while to find someone special
enough for you."

"Smile, Leah. Life is a present from God. Enjoy! It's beautiful!"

This is the work of the *yetzer ha-tov*, the good attribute. It
utilizes Leah's strong "male" entity to build up her "female"
half. It replaces words of scorn and retribution with those of admiration and encouragement. The effect is gradual but definite.
Leah becomes less frustrated, stronger and happier. Her belief
in herself and in God's help gains strength and momentum as
this positive reinforcement becomes more natural from day to
day. It is internalized bit by bit until, after a length of time, it becomes unconscious.

On the operational level, Leah discovers that *shidduchim* can
be fun. If in the past she felt threatened and fearful, today she
feels free to enjoy and let God lead the way. Whereas at one
point she had unconsciously transferred her lack of confidence
and negative emotions, thus sabotaging her efforts, now things
have changed dramatically. She gives off an air of happy confidence and easy-going cordiality, making her immediately like-
able and appealing. Her face radiates that positive feeling that
comes from being secure within herself, rather than dependent
on others. Therefore, it came as no great surprise when, a
month after finishing treatment, Leah was engaged to be married.

Summary of Five-Stage Torah Therapy

We have discussed and explained the five stages of Torah Therapy, the building blocks of *tikkun ha-adam*. We learned from man's creation by God how to "fix" (*tikkun*) ourselves and our lives, and "recreate" our egos around the Divine and good within us. This process, we saw, is cyclical and therefore never-ending. Each level that is reached serves as the basis for further work and betterment at a higher, more refined level. We probe deeper into ourselves, discerning more and more areas that need "fixing." There is no end to this process, because there is no limit to our beings, as there is no limit to the Divine within us. This is true *avodas Hashem*, the service of God. Every step of the way is a holy *mitzvah*. Each of the five stages is an end and a beginning of doing God's will. These stages are:

1. Construction (*binyan* — בניין)
2. Splitting (*chalukah* — חלוקה)
3. Pain (*ke'ev* — כאב)
4. Sweetening (*mituk* — מיתוק)
5. Acceptance (*hashlamah* — השלמה)

The first letters of each of the Hebrew terms form the word *b'chochmah* (בחכמה) meaning "in wisdom." This brings to mind the *pasuk* in *Mishlei*: "ה' בחכמה יסד ארץ"[191] (God in wisdom founded the world). Using this association may help us remember these five basic steps.

When a person lives "in wisdom," in accordance to Torah, he achieves internal and external harmony. Rather than suffer chronically from the opposing characteristics of the two entities within his being, he merges them into a unified and complementary whole, and slowly becomes filled with love and happiness.

---

191. *Mishlei* 3:7.

This is a lifetime job, and it has its ups and downs. But just as a married couple can achieve blissful harmony after years of trials and tribulations, so can we improve our quality of life by making peace within ourselves. Just as the *Shechinah* may be felt within a peaceful home, so can it rest within a loving, wholesome *oved Hashem*, servant of God. In either case the road is never-ending, and that is what gives meaning to our lives. Those who live such a life are truly healthy. This is the goal towards which the Torah Therapist leads each and every patient, including himself.

Rambam's Method

In addition to the *"b'chochmah"* 5-stage method, we can also use Rambam's method to change one's attributes.[192] As was mentioned in the introduction of the book, this is a behavioral method to change an accustomed mannerism or attribute. However, it is almost impossible to apply outside of the therapeutic framework (at least, in our day and age) because of its rigorous and exacting nature. Within therapy, however, this method can be put to work in practice, demonstrating its powerful curative powers.

The Rambam's method is based on habit-formation. By temporarily assuming a stance in direct opposition to that which we wish to change, we come to reform our habits of thought, feeling and action; they will eventually fall within the "middle road," which is our goal. This process aims to achieve the right balance of traits which exists between the opposing poles.

---

192. Rambam, *Hilchos Deos*, chap. 1–7. There are other important details in these guidelines which are implemented by the Torah Therapist. For example, the final synthesis lies somewhat to one side of the center in accordance with the attributes of the patient. But this need not concern him, so these details were not enumerated within this book.

For example, a miserly person who wishes to learn to become generous must become — for a period of time — wasteful and reckless in spending his money. This will break his habit of miserliness, allowing him to choose the "middle road" of generosity. Thus, he ultimately combines wise thriftiness with loving *chesed*.

As simple as the formula is, it is exceedingly difficult for us, when alone and left to rely on our own strengths, to actually behave in a fashion that is diametrically opposed to our entrenched habits. Even when the desire and need for change are truly great, we usually lack the inner strength and discipline necessary to carry out this ambitious plan. We normally find ourselves unable to hold on to this plan long enough to really undergo the internal change that we seek. We surrender in frustration, sometimes even before we begin.

It is only when we are gently prodded and encouraged by the therapist that we find the strength to successfully apply Rambam's method to our lives. We need that weekly shot of Torah-adrenalin from "outside" to keep us going. After a while we are strong enough to go it alone.

Furthermore, who can judge how long we must be active in the opposite extreme? When can we allow ourselves to fall back to the "middle of the road"? We are often too involved and biased to answer these questions. The Torah Therapist, however, is in the very position — external but close, uninvolved but extremely familiar — that allows him to answer these questions accurately.

His position allows him to suggest not only the length of time needed for each phase, but also the content or area of change that is needed. For example, a person might come in order to learn to be less lazy and more diligent in his work. The therapist may suggest that he change his workplace altogether, or perhaps even his profession. Bad habits must be replaced by good, but we are often unaware of what we need to change.

We are normally encouraged to delve within ourselves in order to discover which way of life is suitable for our unique being. After years of attempting to find the right answers and living accordingly, we may be shocked to realize that we had erred. Our self-evaluation is so weighted by emotions and thought-habits that we need to turn for outside help. To really change matters, within and without, we must find our "Rav." "*Aseh lecha rav*"[193] (make for yourself a rabbi) is a requirement for any Jew who sincerely wishes to improve his life within the context of *avodas Hashem* (service of God). This is where the Torah Therapist comes in.

First, this skilled individual assists the patient in revealing his most flawed attribute. This often entails uncovering a basic existential misconception, which, through habit, was the axis of the patient's life-script. This in itself is already a giant leap forward in *avodas Hashem*. Second, he may help the patient choose a secondary attribute or behavior pattern which should be changed, prior to working directly on the basic problem. In addition, the process is dynamic and therefore open for change over time. The Torah Therapist may advise him to develop another facet of life, internal or external, for a certain period of time. Whenever possible, the therapist will point out that this is *avodas Hashem*, and not merely self-realization. We are all servants of God even as we attend to our personal needs.

The "Good Friend": The Diary

Throughout the process of Torah Therapy, the patient is encouraged to work on his own every day. The counseling sessions serve as guide-posts. The actual work is within the rigorous everyday existence. A constant companion is needed, and that is where a personal emotional diary comes in. The patient

---

193. *Pirkei Avos* 1:6.

is encouraged to write daily reports on his emotional ups and downs of the day. He should try to enhance his awareness of the different moods that he experiences. What brings them on? What causes them to disappear? Which events, people, words and actions serve as triggers to these emotions? Why is that so?

This is not simple. The mind must exert great effort to understand the heart. This is *daas* at work, **outside** of the therapy session. Usually there is great satisfaction in discovering ourselves and all sorts of truisms that make up our lives. This is made possible by focusing all mental and emotional energy, which is a prerequisite for writing an emotional diary. These insights were previously out of reach, flowing vaguely within the turbulence of the internal lives that are the background of normal, everyday living.

Now, the need to express our experiences with words and sentences forces us to delve within ourselves and try to comprehend that which had previously been unknown. We discover the deep connections between events, emotions and activities in the past and present. We learn to differentiate between cause and result, between the significant and the unimportant, and between the "root" and its "branches."

This technique of writing as a means of understanding and ordering our thoughts is a common tool in the world of Torah. Specifically, when learning Talmud, students are encouraged to write down what they learn, whether summarizing the *shiur* or explaining to themselves the tractate they are presently learning. Memorizing comes through understanding, and both are achieved through writing or talking about the *sugya*. The learning of *mussar* also employs the diary as a means for daily *cheshbon ha-nefesh* (self-reflection).

After years of writing, summarizing and reordering our thoughts, the initial notebook becomes a *kuntres*, an exposition, and ultimately a book of *chidushei Torah*. What began as a simple summation of whatever was learned may end as a truly original and inspired work of Torah, worthy of publishing. We are called *am ha-sefer*, the nation of the book.

On the personal side, the diary becomes more than just a means for introspection. Its uniqueness, as a reflection of our being, transforms it into a sort of friend, a close and intimate pal. Even though its nature does not allow for publication, nevertheless its significance for us — the writers — is no less than that of a famous book. It is our most private "confidante." Its pages are the thrilling unfolding of the greatest adventure that could be found: our lives. It is a loyal mirror of the dramatic changes which made us what we are today.

Who Is the Torah Therapist?

It is appropriate, at this point, to add a few words about the Torah Therapist himself. Who is he? What are his qualifications? What characterizes him? Being responsible for therapy in the spirit of Torah, must he be a certified psychologist, or an ordained Rabbi, or both, or neither? Can the Torah Therapist be of either gender? What is required to qualify as a Torah Therapist?

The answer is simple yet complex: an *oved Hashem*, a servant of God. This is not merely a title. It is inaccessible by any means other than years of living as an *oved Hashem*, to the best of one's abilities. Being a Torah Therapist is more a process than an achievement. Who decides whether someone is qualified to be a Torah Therapist? No one...or perhaps every one decides for himself. It is an elusive distinction. The most we can do is to characterize, rather than define.

A Torah Therapist must be well versed in Torah of course, including its various expressions. These include *halachah*, (knowledge of laws), *mussar* (ethics), and *hashkafah* (Jewish philosophy). This knowledge must be internalized through practical application, *halachah l'maaseh*. Only after years of living a To-rah-life can we develop the sensitivity and wisdom to love and counsel others, **as well as ourselves**. We must honestly be humble and simple in our own eyes, but not self-deprecating. We must first and foremost be our own patients, constantly striving to be better servants of God.

As our Sages put it: *"na'eh doresh v'na'eh mekayem,"*[194] meaning, basically, practice what you preach. (This is a foreign concept within the non-Jewish world of therapy and counsel.) A person who offers advice which he himself is incapable of following is essentially dishonest, unless he admits it straightforwardly. Words are only as powerful as the person behind them. Therefore, to be effective they must be truthful.

In summary, the process needed to be a Torah Therapist is years of personal ups and downs in *avodas Hashem*. The road is characterized by victories and failures, success and disappointment, joy and sadness, pleasure and pain. The *oved Hashem* comes to feel that life is purposeful, even as our egos are — in truth — fleeting shadows of nothingness. We make peace with this paradox without ever truly understanding it.

At some point along this path, we feel capable enough to answer the call for help. Actually, every Jew must be a Torah Therapist to some extent, for we are all responsible one for another. ("A man shall aid his friend and say to him 'Be strong!'"[195]) Every observant Jew has this potential. It is simply a matter of naturally extending the influence of Torah-living, by caring and loving in an ever-expanding circle. His occupation as a Torah Therapist is therefore a sacred and personal mission, a natural offshoot of his self and the way he lives his life. He feels led by *hashgachah*, the hand of God. He himself is no

---

194. *Chagigah* 14b.
195. *Yeshayahu* 41:6.

less a patient, turning for help to **his** rabbi, whenever necessary. This is a far cry from the average professional psychologist. In short, Torah Therapy is not a profession. It is an enhancement of Torah-living.

Therefore, the Torah Therapist does not take credit for his success, even when rejoicing in the fruits of his labor. Nor does he succumb to frustration when things do not work out, even as he bereaves the growing pain of his patient. And he constantly checks himself to see if he has erred, or if he is blemished to the degree that he is not fit to be a beneficial messenger of God's will.

Summary

The processes described above truly bring positive changes, with the help of God. But it takes time: weeks, months, sometimes years. As the patient confronts his life, using his mind and his heart, he undergoes both painful and joyous experiences. These dynamics are obvious in the changes within himself and with those around him. Much of this drama remains hidden both from the patient as well as his therapist. Deep and unconscious emotions and beliefs undergo dramatic movement, as life changes within and without. Only God knows the intricate maneuverings in the depths of man, as he seriously applies Torah to improve his life.

As for us, despite our limitations and short-sightedness, we can appreciate results. And we get results. These are not always dramatic or obvious. They are often gradual and — at the beginning — barely perceptible. But change does occur; we start becoming calmer; our speech becomes more expressive; our hearts are less heavy, more hopeful; there are more moments of pleasure or happiness than we had assumed possible. In adherence to Torah, we can justly be called *bnei aliyah*, (those who ascend).[196] Even though we may fall from time to time, we are actually ascending, because these falls are *yeridah l'tzorech aliyah*, descent for the purpose of ascent.

Therefore, Torah Therapy is not necessarily a weekly session of private therapy. Rather, it is living life in the service of Hashem, with emphasis on offering help and counsel to whomever seeks it. This means that the student of Torah in the *yeshivah*, the husband in *kollel*, or at home, or at work, or their spouses...they are all dealing with Torah Therapy in one way or another. The purpose of their Torah is to learn in order to practice. And practicing means giving to themselves and to others. When a woman becomes a wife and a mother, whether she is a homemaker or helps with the income, she is practicing Torah Therapy when she expresses Torah in her daily routine.

All these people, and many others, are striving to become better servants of God, as well as to improve their quality of living. They seek positive change by learning and practicing Torah, the Divine cure-all for all maladies. If the *bnei aliyah* are still very few — as Rabbi Shimon bar Yochai claimed[197] — we may find consolation in the words of our prophets. They promise that the day shall come — (and it seems close) — when all of mankind will be thirsty to learn and practice Torah.

The End...and the Beginning

It seems appropriate to end this book with the profound words of Rav Dessler. In his typically succinct manner, he captures much of the essence of Torah Therapy, encouraging us to express Torah in action.

---

196. Rabbi Wolbe, in *Alei Shur*, vol. 1, p. 141, proves that the first and foremost characteristic of a *ben aliyah* is self-awareness, without which he cannot change and ascend.

197. *Sukkah* 45b: "I have seen *bnei aliyah* and they are few."

The evil within the heart denies the good. Therefore, he whose heart contains evil does not accept criticism, as the evil component kicks at it [in rejection]. This is the reason why this generation does not accept reproof. For the sin within the heart (negative values [such as "I am worthless" — E.L.]) denies man the ability to perceive the true goodness within him. It is therefore impossible to counsel him on the right path by reproof. There is only one way to teach the sinner-of-the-heart. That is by demonstrating the wholeness of spiritual unity, such as the unity of the giver and the receiver — the unity of man and wife and his household in service of God, or the Rabbi and his students within the *yeshivah*...for even the sinner-of-the-heart can recognize the truth in others, and from this he discerns the evil in his heart [destructive misconceptions — E.L.], and he may cure it.[198]

Every book is only theory until it is applied in everyday life. Therefore, although this is the end, may it really serve as a beginning.

---

198. *Michtav MeEliyahu*, vol. 1, p. 128.

The Torah Therapist's Prayer

May it be Your will, my Lord and Lord of my fathers,
To make me Your faithful messenger,
And make me a conduit of blessing
To every person who comes to me for help;
Enable me to reconnect him to You, O Lord,
So that he shall no more be alone and in pain,
So that he shall be united and joyful.
Give me strength to erase the bad aspect of my yetzer,
And to offer chesed to Your children with humility —
Not conceit,
With love and compassion, as Your faithful servant,
With no self-serving motives.
May my thoughts and words serve to strengthen the needy,
And may these efforts be accepted by You
As if they are a pure offering from my heart
Of my love
To you.
Amen, may it be Your will!

תפילה לפני מתן ייעוץ

יהי רצון מלפניך ה׳ אלוקי ואלוקי אבותי
שתזכני להיות שליח נאמן לפניך,
ותשלח דרכי מזור וברכה
לכל אדם הפונה אלי לעזרה,
ותסייע בידי לקשר אותו אליך, יתברך,
ולא יהיה עוד בודד וכואב אלא מאוחד ומאושר.
ותן לי כוח לבטל את הצד הרע שביצרי
ולעשות חסד עם בריותיך מתוך ענווה ולא מתוך גאווה,
מתוך אהבה תמימה של עבד ה׳,
ללא פניות אישיות.
ויהיו מחשבותי ודברי לסיוע ולחיזוק של כל נצרך,
ויעלו לפניך לרצון כאלו כוונתי בהם
בכל לבי
לאהבתך....
אמן, כן יהי רצון!